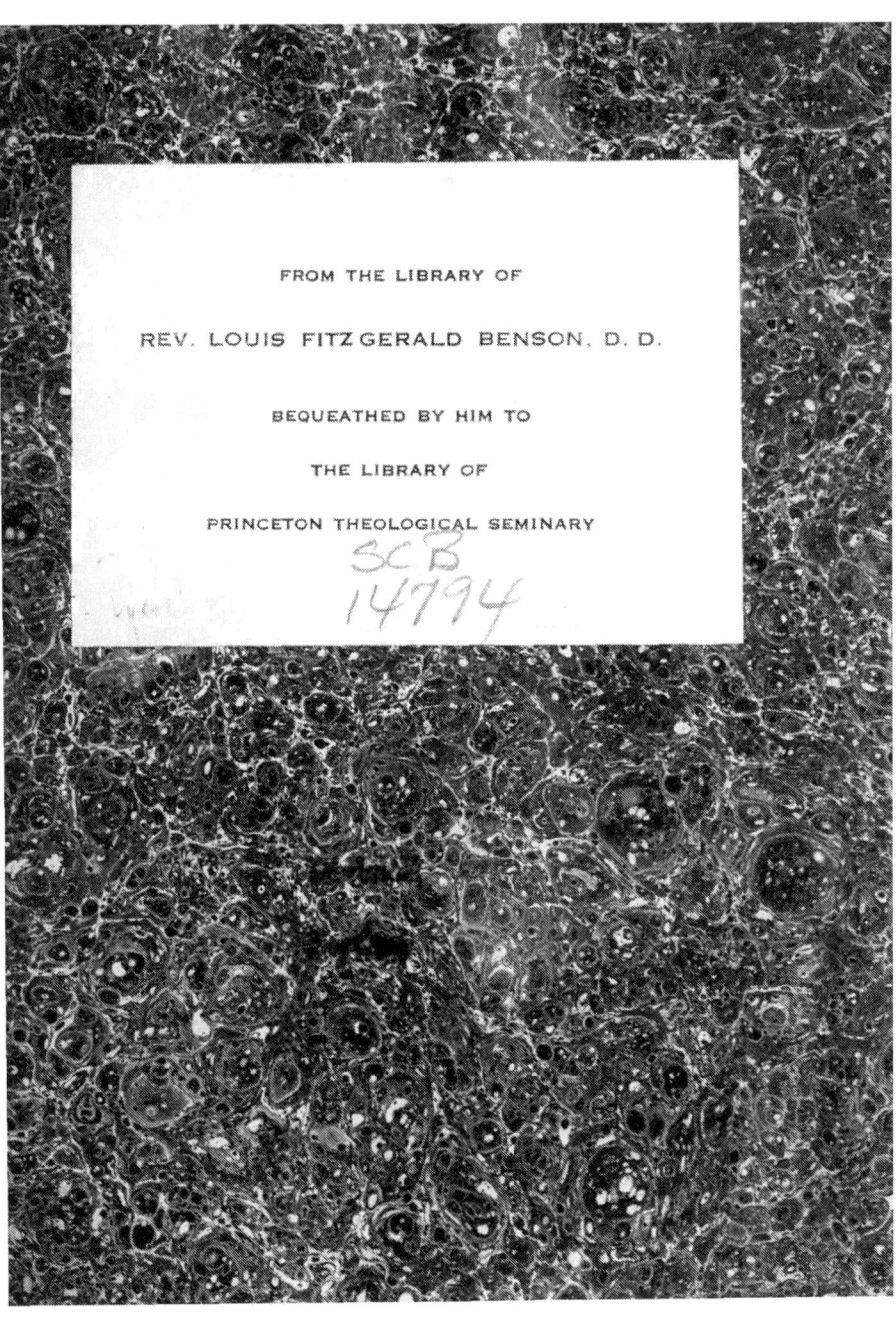

Bound by
H. FAULKNER
George Court,
ADELPHI.

A Brief discours

off the troubles begonne at Franck
ford in Germany Anno Domini 1554. Abowte
the Booke off off common prayer and Ceremonies/and continued by the Englishe men theyre/to thende off Q. Maries
Raigne/in the which discours/the gentle reader shall see
the very originall and beginninge off all the
contention that hathe byn/and what was
the cause off the same.

William Whittingham

Marc. 4.

For there is nothinge hid that shall not be o-
pened neither is there a secreat but that it shall come to light/yff anie man haue eares to heare/let
him heare.

M. D. LXXV.

The Preface.

To the Christian readers / grate mercy / and peace in Christe Jesu our Lorde.

Vche as doo well obserue the varietie of mēnes Judgementes abowte these matters off cōtrouersie / and the supposed causes of the same / shall finde it a thinge more thē wōderfull to beholde / and passinge strange to heare. But who so shall well waye and cōsider / what extreame calamities and miseries this broile hathe broughte with it to manie godly persons whiche vnfainedly feare god: the same muste off force / as I think (iff he haue but one drop off humanitie within him) drawe forthe deepe and sorowfull sighes from the harte / and teares from the eyes. To passe ouer sundrie I will note but this one. where as in tymes paste (bothe at Paules crosse and other places) the soundes whiche were wont to be so sweete as might iustely haue moned the godly hearers to crye owte with the Prophet Esay O howe beutifull are the feete off them which bring glad tydinges off peace / &c. are nowe become (commonly so soure and vnsauery / that in steede off sweetnes / is founde litle or nothinge but wormewood and bitter gall. And

A ij yet

II.

yet I speak not off suche/ whose cruell scoffinge / and vnbridled natures / are to well knowen so farr to exceede/ as fewe/(discreete and wise in dede)can be muche moued with anie thinge almoste they eyther speak or write: but euen off those I meane / whose wisedomes grauitie/ and lerninge / as the same claimeth by good right / dew reuerence to the persons / bycause off those good giftes whiche God hath bestowed vpon them so shuld it also put them in minde (especially in such places)to vse (me semes) some other veine. And for so muche as some impute the cause off all these troubles to the ambitious heades off certeine speciall persons / who shoulde (as hathe bene at Paules crosse bothe publickly and very furiously declared)stirr vpp this strisse in the churche for that they could not attaine to Bisshopprikes when as other enioned them: Some also imputinge it to the strange churches aswell beionds the seas as here amonge vs remayninge/ therby to prouoke the displeasures of the Magistrates against them:

By D. Yonge in Nouember. Anno, 1573.

And some supposinge / yea roaringe owte) that this hath happened by such fantasticall headesas cã abyde no platforme but off their owne deuisinge: I haue for theis and suche like considerations thought good by a shorte and brieff discours to let your se the verye originall and beginninge off all this miserable contention/leauinge nee

Such as D. Elbowrome.

ge neuertheles to your discreet iudgmentes/ who
(in theis matters) are to be thought innocente/
and who most to blame.

And as one bothe off credit/ learned/ and off au‑   *M. Mullins*
thoritie/ thought is not onely meete and expedi‑   *in October.*
ent openly at paules crosse (in presence off the ho‑   *An. 1573.*
norable and worshipfull there) to signifie vnto
them that such a hotte contention (abowte theis
matters had bin/ but also/ noted the place where
and the time whan: So J in this discours/ thou‑   *Franckford*
ght it needefull/ least happelie that honorable au‑   *the place,*
dience might mistake the matter) to set fourthe by   *in Q. Ma‑*
writinge the verie order/ maner/ and proceadin‑   *ryes tyme.*
ge off the same: followinge herein the steppes off
such/ whom god off his goodnes hath raised vp   *Platina, Pau‑*
at all tymes and amonge all nations / to com‑   *lus Iouius.*
mit thinges to memorye / whiche hath passed   *Sledcin, Fox*
in commonweales/ who haue with great fredom   *with many*
and libertie byn suffred to make manifest to the   *other.*
whole worlde the ill dealinges euen off Popes/
Cardinalls/ Emperours/ Kinges and Princes/
where as (in this discours) the highest that J tou‑
che (and that with great grieff off hart) are
(to my knowledge) but certeine Bishopps/ and
therfore J hope the more to be borne withall/ be‑
sechinge allmightie god that as by theis my poo‑
re simple trauailes/ my meaninge was not (either
in contempt or sekinge reuenge) to prouoke the
farther displeasures off the meanest: that so iff
              A iij   it be

IIII.

it be his blessed will/the same maie finde fauor in in the eies off oure soueraigne L. the queenes most excellēt maiestie/ and the right honorable/ whom it hathe pleased him to place in high au- thoritie/ for whose prosperitie and welfare it be- commeth all true and faithfull subiectes (as they are dutifully bounde) moste earnestly to praie.

The

V.

The historie.

After that yt had pleased the lorde God to take awaie for our synnes that noble prince off famous memorie/ kinge Edwarde the sixthe/ and had placed/ Queene Marie in his roume: Sundrie godly men aswell strangers/ as off the Englishe nation/ fledd/ for the libertie off their consciences/ ouer the seas/ some into France/ some into Flanders/ and some in to the high countries off the Empire/ and in the yere of oure lorde. 1554. and the 27. off June came Edmonde Sutton/ William Williams/ William Whittingham/ and Thomas wood/ with their companies/ to the citie off Franckford in Germany the firste Englishe men/ that there arriued to remaine and abide. The same night came one Maister Valaren pullan Minister/ vnto their lodginge/ ãd declared howe he had obtained a churche there/ in the name of all suche as shuld come owte off Englande for the Gospell/ but Especially from Glassenbury whiche were all french men. Answere was made him/ that as god was to be praised/ who had moued the Magistrats hartes to shewe the frenche suche fauour: Euenso/ for so muche as fewe off them vnderstoode the frenche tonge/ it woulde be small commoditie to them/ or to suche as shulde come afterwarde to ioyne themselues to that churche.

The nexte daye they communed with Maister Morellio another Minister of the frenche churche/ and also with maister Castalio a Senior off the same/ (bothe off them godly and lerned mẽ) By their aduise and connsaile it was determined/ that a Supplication shulde be drawẽ owt/ and offred to the Magistrats/ to knowe/ firste whither they woulde be contented/ that not onely the parties before named/ but also all other Englishe men that woulde repaire thither for the like cause/ might through their fauour be suffred saffely to remaine within

their

V.I.

their city. This supplication was subscribed aswell by the sayed Sutton / Whittingam /, and the reste off the Englishe men /, as also by Morellio / Castallio / and one Adrian a Citezē there / with whom they lodged. And within three daies after the offringe vp off their Supplication / they obtained their requestes.

The 5. off July followinge / labor was made (by the counsaile and aduice off Morellio and Castalio (who duringe their lyues shewed them selues fathers to all Englishe men.) to Maister John Glawberge one off the chiefest Senators / for a place or churche / wherin they and all their country men might haue gods worde truly preached / and the Sacraments sincerely ministred in their naturall tonge / who ientlie promised his furtherance / and that he also woulde moue the whole Senate theroff / the whiche he did accordingly. And the 14. daie off the same monethe yt was graunted that they shulde haue libertie to preache and minister the Sacraments / in that churche which the freche men had / the freche one daie and the Englishe an other daie and vpō the Sundaie / to chuse also the houres as they coulde agree amonge them selues / but yt was with this commandement / that the Englishe shulde not discent from the frenchmen in doctrine / or ceremonyes / leaft they shulde thereby minister occasion off offence / and willed farther / that before they entred their churche / they shulde approue and subscribe the same confession off faith / that the frenche men had then presented / and abowte to put in printe / to the whiche all the afore named (and others whiche were by this time come thither) did subscribe.

When the churche was in this sorte graunted / they consulted amonge themselues / what order off seruice they shulde vse (for they were not so stricly bownde / as was tolde them / to the ceremonies off the frenche / by the Magistrats / but that iff the one allowed off the other it was sufficient.) At lenght / the englishe order was perused / and this by generall consente was concluded that the answeringe alowde after the Minister shulde not be vsed / the letanye / surplice / and many other thinges also omittted / for that in those reformed churches / suche thin-the thinges woulde seeme more then strange. It was farther agreed vppon/ that the Minister (in place off the Englishe Confession shulde vse an other / bothe off more effecte / and also framed accordinge to the state and time. And the same ended/ the people to singe a psalme in meetre in a plaine tune as was / and is accustomed in the frenche / dutche / Italian / Spanishe / and Skottishe churches/ that don/ the minister to praye for thassistance off gods holie spirite and so to proceade to the sermon. After the sermon/ a generall praier for all estates and for oure countrie of Englande was also deuised/ at thende off whiche praier / was ioined the lords praier and a reherfall off tharticles off oure belieff/ whiche ended the people to singe an other psalme as afore. Then the minister pronouncinge this blessinge. The peace off god/ &c. or some other off like effecte/ the people to departe.

And as touchinge the ministration off the Sacraments sundrie things were also by common consente omitted/ as superstitious and superfluous. After that the congregation had thus concluded and agreed/ and had chosen their minister and Deacons to serue for a time: they entred their churche the 27. off the same monethe. Then was it thought good amonge themselues/ that forthwith they shulde adnertise their countrie men and betheren dispersed off this singuler benefit/ the like whereoff coulde nowhere else as yet be obtained/ and to perswade them (all worldly respectes put aparte) to repaier thither/ that they might altogather with one mouthe and one harte bothe lamēte their foremer wickednes and also be thankfull to their mercifull father that had geuen them suche a churche in a strange lande wherein they might heare gods worde truly preached/ the Sacraments rightly ministred/ and Discipline vsed/ which in their owne countrie coulde neuer be obtained. And to this effecte were letters directed to Strausburgh/ Zurick/ Densbrugh/ and Emden in the 2. off Auguste. And for that it was thought the churche coulde not longe contynewe in good order withowte discipline/ there was also a brieff forme deuised/ declaringe the necessitie/ the causes/

B and

VIII.

and the order theroff/wherunto all those that were present subscribed/shewinge therby that they were ready and willinge to submitt themselues to the same/accordinge to the rule prescribed in gods holie word/ at whiche time it was determined by the congregation that all suche as shulde come after/shulde doo the like/before they were admitted as members off that churche.

Here followethe the generall letter sente from the congregation off Franckforde/to Strausbourge/Zurick/Wezeil/Emden/&c.

Grace mercy and peace in Christ our Lord:&c.

We dowte not (dearely beloued) but yow haue harde/ aswell by letter/as by reporte/off the excellent graces and mercy whiche oure good god and heauenly father hathe shewed vnto oure litle congregation in this citie off Franckford/ for that he hathe not onely made the Magistrats and commons very fauorable towards vs and louinge/ but also/ has the geuen them hartes/ with muche compassion to tender vs/in so muche that euerie man helpethe vs/no man is againste vs/muche loue/ no grudge/ glad to please/loth to annoie vs/ yea/ and to declare this good will not to be off the meane sorte/ nor so small as oure brethern haue felte others were/they haue graunted that thinge/ whiche amonge others and in other cities/ we coulde not obtaine nor durste allmoste hope for. For what greater treasure or sweeter comforte can a Christian man desier/then to haue a churche wherin he maie serue god in puritie off faithe/ and integritie off lyfe/whiche thinge yff we wishe for/ let vs not refuse it/seinge where we woulde/we coulde not there obtaine it. And here yet it is graunted in so ample wise/ that beinge subiecte to no blemishe/no/nor so muche as the euell off suspition (fro the whiche fewe churches are free) we maie preache/minister/ and vse Discipline/to the true settinge forthe off gods glorie
and

IX.

and good ensample to others. And for our partes/we haue not bene negligente as touchinge the execution off the sayed benefit graunted. For the 19. of July/we had (god be thanked) 2. sermons to oure singuler comforte/ and great ioye off all godly men heere. Wherfore brethern/ seinge your haue indured the paine off persecution with vs/ we thought it likewise oure dewties to make your partakers off oure consolation/ that altogether we maie geue thankes to oure louinge father/ who is more tender ouer vs/ then the mother ouer hir childe/nether suffreth vs to be temped aboue that we maie beare/ but euen to the issue off the tentation/ geueth prosperous successe/trustinge by gods grace/ that he whiche hathe geuen yow that gifte/not onely to beleue in Christe/but also to suffer for his sake: will so directe your hartes/ that no respecte off commoditie there/nor yet feare of burthen here maie once moue yow to shrink from your vocatiō/ whiche is/in one faithe/ one ministration/one tonge and one consente/ to serue god in his churche. *Cor. 10. Phil. 1.*

What more manifeste signe/ what plainer declaration/what worde more expresse and lyuely can we haue off dewtie and vocation/ then when god speaketh in oure hartes by faithe/ guideth vs owte off perills throughe his grace / and nowe laste of all offreth vs a restinge place of his exceading mercy. Now remēber that before/ we haue reasoned together in hope to obtaine a churche / and shall we nowe drawe backe as vnmindfull off gods prouidence/ whiche hathe procured vs one free from all dreggs off superstitious ceremonies? What/thinke yow/ yf the Prophet Dauid had had this offre who desired to be porter in the house of God/and more estemed one daie so spente/ then a thousande otherwaies. *Psal. 42.*

Either what mente he when he saied: one requeste I demaunde off the Lorde/ Whiche I will secke after/ that is/ that I maie dwell in the howse off the lorde all the daies off my lyfe. Had Dauid no experience? or felte he not what grieff yt was to wante the congregation? And surely we muste graunt that he was farre more perfect then we be: For he beinge conuersant in this worlde / sett his delight *Psal. 27.*

B ij wholie

wholie in heauenly things. And many off vs/(we speake it to
our shame) as if we had already forgotte the ende of our crea
tion/are plunged in earthlye affectiōs/and worldly respectes/
so that throughe oure infirmities/this excellente benefit is li
ke to be frustrate. For/some dowte who shalbe preferred: o
thers seeke increase off lerninge: Many followe the commodi
tie off lyuinge: certein/looke for a newe vocation/so that it is
a wonder to se the deformitie off mans affections: God gran
te/we maye lerne at their ensamples whiche beinge called to

Matth. 22.

the mariage came not/what it is to esteeme in time the worh
thenes off gods benefits/leaste/by the losse off the same we af
terfall vnto vnprofitable repentance/seekinge againe oure
losse withe teares as the reprobate Esau and yet neuer the ne
ere. We charge no one man (brethren) nor yet meane all/and

Mich. 3.
Heb. 11.

on what considerations theis excuses were pretended/we su
spende oure Judgmentes/referringe the same to our imper
fection and infirmitie:/wherby the aduersary ceasethe not to
batter daikle the walles off Gods temple.

As touchinge the pointe off preferremente/we are perswa
ded throughly that it hathe this meaninge/that euery mā tho
ught of himself modestlie/humblie submittinge himself to all
mē vnablinge no man/for so muche as your knowe that he wh
iche seketh ambition/glory/aduantage or suche like/is not mo
ued withe gods spirite as witnesse the instructions that Chri
ste our Maister gaue to his disciples/who laboring of like di
sease were admonished that he whiche did excell amonge thē/
shoulde abase himself to his inferior: whiche malady S. Paul
perceauinge to infecte like a canker/moste diligently frame the
his style/that he might not seeme to preferr hi selffe to others
in the course of his ministery. And as for lerninge/as we wishe

Philip. 1.
Col. 1.

to all men moste abūdantly: so we moste ernestly require/ that
compāringe the congregations necessitie with your owne priua
te cōmoditie/your woulde rather for Christs sake chose the bet
ter. yea/and we assure your one good aduertisemente/that tho
rowe/gods grace/when we shalbe assembled together/suche or
der wilbe taken/that/besides those thinges whiche oure natiō
shalbe

shalbe able to furnishe/ we haue the citie moste forwarde to procure others. Yff anye woulde pretende the hardnes off the countrie and charges/ oure experience maie sufficiently satisfie them/ who hauinge traueiled throwgh moste places/ where the gospell is preached/ haue not founde so manie commodites nor lesse charges.

Resteth the tyme off callinge/ whiche we referre to your consciences / besechinge yow for Christes sake to descende into your selues withowt all parcialitie / wayinge the grauitie off the matter whiche is goddes / and the selfe excuse whiche the flesh be ministreth. Consider what god woulde saie/ I haue prepared a plentifull and ripe harueste whiche standeth in a redines and waiteth for the mower and I haue appointed the thy taxe. I haue geuen instrumentes/ and all thinges fit for the labor / yff thow forslowe it/ the croppe is in daunger yff thow loke for oft warning thow declarest great negligence.

This speache (Dearly beloued) or very like / god vsed to Noah. Abraham/ Jeremiah/ &c. and they thought their vocation stronge. But yow through Goddes benefit / do not onely heare god thus perswadinge in your hartes / but also haue bene by externe callinge confirmed/ and accordinge therunto haue walked to the great glorie off God and profit off the congregation. We truste therfore (brethern) and in Jesus Christe require it/ that your woulde hyde your talent no longer but hauinge newe occasion to imploye it/ your woulde put it forthe for your Maister his aduantage and your owne discharge. For iff your feele in your hartes comforte as wee doo whiche are here assembled to heare the worde of god preached and the Sacramentes ministred/ we assure yow/ yow should sensiblie perceaue that which the Prophet speaketh in the eistermes: as the harte chased panteth for gredines off waters : euen so/ (o lorde) my soule seeketh after thee. My soule burneth for thirste in seekinge the Lorde and saithe: Alas when shall I be able to appeere before the face off the lyuinge god? what: thinge then ought we to haue in greater recommendation/ then the order and policie whiche god hathe established *Psal. 42.*

B iij in his

in his churches that we maie be taught by his worde, that we maie worshippe him and call vpon his name with one accorde, that we maie haue the true vse off his Sacramentes to helpe vs to the same. For theis be the means wherby we muste be confirmed in the faithe, in the feare off God, in holynes off conuersation, in the contempte of the worlde, and in the loue off life euerlastinge. And for this consideration

Ephes. 4. S. Paule saithe not that this order whiche the Lorde hathe set in his churche shulde onely be for the rude and symple, but maketh it common to all, exceptinge no man. For he hathe ordeined (saithe he) some to be Apostles, some prophetes, some Euangelistes, others, to be teachers and instructors, to confirme the godly and to labor to finishe the buildinge off Christes body till we be all brought to one consente in faithe to the knowledge off the sonne off god, to a perfect man, and finally, to the iuste measure off a ripe Christian age. Let vs all marke, that he saithe not, that god hathe left the scriptures onely, that euery one shulde reade it, but also, that he hathe erected a policie and order, that their shulde be some to teache, and not for one daye, but all the time off our lyffe euen to the deathe for that is the tyme off our perfection. Wherfore brethren, let vs submit our selues, and leaue off farther to tempte God, seinge, that yff we wilbe off the body off Christ, we must obeie to this generall rule. Let no respecte off worldly policie staie vs. Let no perswasion blinde vs. But let vs fulfyll in oure selues that whiche Esaias forwarneth that goddes children shalbe as pigions, whiche flee by flocks in to their douehouse, whiche is the place where the worde of god is preached, the sacramentes ministred, and praier vsed.

To conclude therfore (dearely beloued) let euery man call his conscience to counsaile, and besides these sweete allurements, let vs learne to preuent our aduersaries, who sekinge euer to obscure goddes glorie, maye easelie couell at this dissipation. And woulde to god the slaunder were not allready to our great grieff in sundry places scattered in so muche, that in Englande, manie take occasion to remaine in their filthe.

And

XIII.

And some thinke they maye dissemble, vntill a churche be confirmed, perceauinge that this our scatteringe, augmentethe the griefe of persecution, and so throughe our negligēce we lee se them for whom Christe died. Consider brethren, it is gods cause, he requirethe yow, it is your dewtie, necessitie vrgethe, time wilkethe, your father speakethe, children muste obeie, oure enemies are diligente and the aduersary is at hande.

Almightie god graunt for his sonnes sake that we maie rightly ponder the maiter, followe oure callinge, serue the turne, heare the speaker, walke in obedience and resist oure enemies. We desier yow all take this in good parte, seinge we haue written nothinge but what charitie did indite and that whiche we truste, and wishe yow woulde haue don to vs in case like. From Franckford this 2. off August. 1554.

Your louynge brethern.

Iohn Stanton.	William Williams.	William Hammon.
Iohn Makebray	William Wittingham.	Thomas Wood.
		Mighell Gill.

Shortlye after, the lerned men off Strausbrough answered to this generall letter before mentioned in this sorte: That they had considered the contentes theroff and perceiued that the effecte was no other but to haue one or two take the chieff charge and gouernaunce off the congregation. And that in case they might get. D. poinet. Maister Scory. D. Bale or D. Cox, or two off them, they shulde be well furnished, yff not, they woulde appointe one at Strausbrough and an other shuld come from Zurick to serue the turne at whiche tyme master Grindall wrote to master Scory at Emden perswadinge him to be Superintendent off this churche off Frankf. who (in 2. senerall letters to his priuate frinds, offred his seruise to the congregation, but before the receipte theroff the congregation had writtē their letters to maister Knox at Geneua to master Haddon at Strausb. and master Leuer at Zurick, whom they had elected for their ministers and aduertised master Scory by a generall letter off the same.

Now

XIIII.

Nowe/when the answere that came from Strausbrough was read / and compared withe the letter written vnto them/it did not in anie pointe answere it. For the congregation wrote not particulerly for anie certeine nomber/ but generally wishinge all mens presence / nether did they require to haue anye superintendent to take the chieff charge and gouernement/ for the choise and election theroff (yff suche a one had bene necessary) ought to haue byn reserued to the congregation / whiche fully determined at that tyme to haue the churche gouerned by 2 or 3. graue/godly and lerned Ministers off like authoritie / as is accustomed in the beste reformed churches.

The 1. off October the Students off Zurick wrote also an answere to the generall letters afore saied in this wise.

The grace and peace off God the Father and off our Lorde Iesus Christe be vvith your all Amen.

AS God by his singuler prouidence hathe wonderfully blessed vs aswell in mouinge the hartes off the Senators and ministers here/ to lament oure state / fauor and aid vs in oure requestes: as also in geuinge happie successe for all kinde off prouision to oure vse and behoufe: So he well knowethe/ that we no other wise esteeme the same then maie stande withe his glory/oure professiõ/and the comforte off his afflicted churche/ but dailie labor in the knowledge off his worde to thintent that when god oure mercifull father shall so think good/ we maie be bothe faithfull and skilfull dispensers theroff.

And as runninge in the sweete race off oure vocation/ye haue ernestly written vnto vs for to repaier thyther / burtheninge vs so sore with your necessitie/ that ye think our shrinking back in this behalff shulde argue want off charitie/ keepe manie in Englande still whiche else wou'd willingly come foorth/ and shewe oure selues careles off that congregation whose

XV.

whose edefyinge and winninge to Chriſte we onely pretend to ſeeke. Theſe are great cauſes/ but touchinge vs nether ſo truly obiected/ ſo firmely grounded/ nor yet ſo aptlie applied/ but that as ſounde reaſons on our partes might fully anſwere the ſame. Yet notwithſtanding/ in as muche as yow appeale to our conſciences whiche in the daie off the Lorde ſhall accuſe or excuſe vs in this thinge and all other/ we will not vtterlie deny your requeſts/ but ſhewe oure ſelues as ready to ſeeke gods glorie and the increaſe off his kingdome other there or elſe where to the vttermoſte off oure powers/ as euer we did pretende to do/ requiringe yow all in the name and feare off god/ that as we/ all reſpects ſet aporte and vnfainedly trauelinge in the neceſſary knowledge off Chriſte to the profit off his churche here after/ refuſe not for your nedie comforte to accompliſhe your deſyres: So ye will not interrupte oure ſtudies/ vrge oure remouinge/ and bringe vs thither/ feelinge here allreadie the exceadinge goodneſſe off god towardes vs/ vnleſſe ye thinke/ and that before god/ that oure abſence on thone parte ſhulde greatly hinder/ and oure preſence one the other ſide verie muche further your godly attemps alreadye begonne for the furniſhinge off that churche ſo happely obtained to all oure comfortes/ for the whiche in oure dailie prayers we geue god moſte hartie and humble thankes. Yff by this doinge ye geue occaſion to breake oure godlie felofhippe/ to hurte our ſtudies/ to diſſolue oure exerciſes/ and vtterly to euerte our godly purpoſes/ ye haue to anſwere euen vnto him which is a faithfull and a iuſte Iudge/ and will geue to euerie man accordinge to his dedes. Wherfore/ deare brethern/ in conſideration that we be all not onely off one nation/ but alſo members off one miſticall body in Ieſus Chriſte our head/ and ought therfore eſpecially in this time off exile and moſte worthely deſerued croſſe by all means poſſible/ one to aide and comforte an other/ beſechinge god for his mercies ſake to aſſwage his wrathe/ to geue vs repentinge hartes and patient continuance to our brethern at home with pity to beholde his vineiarde there miſerablie ſpoiled and trod

C   den

XVJ.

den vnder foote/ and to call vs home after his fatherly chastisemente eftsones frutefully to worke in the same: we briefly make this answere. Jff vppon the receipte hereoff/ ye shall withowte cloke or forged pretence/ But onely to seke Christe aduertise vs by your letters/ that our beinge there is so nedefull as ye haue alreadie signified/ and that we maie altogether serue and praise god as freely and as vprightly/(wheroff pryuate letters receiued lately from Franckf. make vs muche to dowte) as the order laste taken in the churche of England permittethe and perscribethe (for we are fully determined to admitt and vse no other) then/ abowt easter nexte (for afore we cannot) god prosperinge vs/ and no iuste cause or occasion to the contrary growinge in the meane time wherby our intente maie be defeated with one consente we agree to ioine oure selues vnto yow and moste willinglie to doo suche seruise there/ as oure poore condition and callinge dothe permit. In the meane space/ we shall moste intirely beseche almightie God so to assiste yow withe his holy spirit/ that your doings maie helpe to confounde papistrie/ set forthe gods glorie/ and shewe suche light in the face off the worlde/ that bothe the wicked maie be ashamed/ hauinge no iuste cause off reproche/ and also oure weake brethern confirmed and woone to the truthe. From Zurick this 13. off Ortober, 1554.

Your louing frinds.

Robart Horne.	Iohn Mullings.	Iohn Parkhuste.
Richard Chambers.	Thomas Spencer.	Roger Kelke.
Thomas Leuer.	Thomas Bentham.	Robart Beamont.
Nicholas Karuile.	VVilliam Cole.	Laurence Humphry.
		Henry Cockrafft.
		Iohn Pretio.

Abowte this tyme Letters were receyued from maister Haddon Wherin he desired for diuers consideratious to be excused/ for comminge to take the charge vppon him at Franckford.

The

XVII.

The 24. off October came maister Whithead to Franckford/ and at the requeste off the congregation/ he tooke the charge for a time/ and preached vppon the Epistle to the Romains.

Abowte the 4. off Nouember came Maister Chambres to Franckford with letters from Zurick wh che were partlie an answere to an other letter written vnto them from Franckforde the 16. off September/ whiche was as followithe.

Grace mercy and peace, &c.

After/ longe hope off your answere to our letter/ we thought it good to put you once againe in remembraunc. And as we in our former/ so nowe in theis also in gods behalff moste ernestly require yow deeplie to waie this matter off gods callinge/ and the necessitie off this congregation. We haue throughly lerned your estate and also made yow priuie to oures/ and eftsonnes/ wisshe we might be together to bewaile our synnes paste/ to praie together for oure poore brethern that are vnder Antechristes captiuitie/ to comforte/ instructe/ and profit one an other. And finally to bestowe the time off oure persecution together and redeeme theis daies whiche are so euell. And iff anye desier off knowledge staye yow/ certenly/ it woulde not be so litle increased here that yow shul de iustly repent. For as touchinge the companie off lerned men (as yow cannot here be withowte) so/ that thinge whiche chiefly your can require of lerned mens Judgmets and knowledge owte off their workes/ your maie suck moste plentifully wherof with vs yow can lake no store We nede not/ brethern/ to make lõge discouse in reasoninge. for we partlie knowe that gods spirit/ whiche worketh in your hartes shall preuaile wi͞t he yow more/ th͞e disputinge/ not dowinge/ but the same holie spirit knecketh at the dore off your cõscieces not only to moue yow of oure behalffs/ but to admonishe yow/ to auoide the incõueniences of talkes/ and the offences of oure poore brethern

XVIII.

of Englande/ whose marueilinge cannot otherwise be satisfied. Remember therfore (dearly beloued) that we wryte as bretheren/ to oure deare brethern/ who altogether seeke oure fathers honor/ oure owne discharge and the comforte off oure afflicted countrie men.

The same sweete father graunt for his Christe sake that we maie assemble together/ to the buildinge off this his Temple/ to let the false workemen/ and vnderminers/ and diligently in our vocation to helpe to the furnishinge off the same till it rise to perfection. Fare ye well in Christe. From Franckford this 16. off Septemb. 1554.

Your louinge frinds: as in the letter afore so vnder this subscribed.

The Answere to them off Franckford was/ as foloweth.

WE beinge placed here in quietnes/ withe many and great commodities for oure studies tendinge all to edification off Christes churche/ haue/ vnto the earneste requeste off your letters vnto vs / answered in our letters vnto yow/ that to discharge all dewtie in conscience / and to increase and instructe your congregation at Franckford withe oure presence and diligence will not deny to remoue from hence vnto yow/ so that yow charged off conscience do constantly affirme/ that ye haue so great neede off vs as by letters was signified/ and certeinly assure vs that we with yow maie and shall vse the same order off seruice concerninge religion whiche was in Englande laste set forthe by kinge Edward. And nowe also for the better vnderstadinge off suche requestes and charitable performance of dewtie/ vpon bothe partes desired and procured Maister Richard Chambers our beste frinde/ a man moste charitable and carefull for the Christian congregation/ to take pains to trauell vnto yow and withe yow for vs : so that this matter as it is begon and moued in writinge maie be fully

XIX.

be fully debated and concluded by his faithfull meanes and diligence. For we be all agreed and do purpose to allowe and performe what so euer he shall saie and promes in oure names vnto yow. Wherfore/ we besechinge yow in Goddes name conscionably to consider the estate and condition bothe off yow and vs/and iff there vppon yow conclude withe the saied master Chambers off oure comminge vnto yow/then let him not lack your charitable helpe in necessary prouision for our continuance withe yow. And thus besechinge god that your doings maie tende to his glorie/ and the spedy comforte off his afflicted churche we wishe yow all helthe and increase off true knowledge in Christe our lord and sauiour. From Zurick this 17. off October. Anno 1554.

Your lovinge frinds as in
the letters before

When Maister Chambers had conferred with the congregation and sawe that they coulde not assure him the full vse off the Englishe booke withowte the hazardinge off their churche/ he prepared to departe from whens he came/and by this time was Maister Knox come from Geneua/(and chosen minister) vppon the receipte off a letter sent him from the congregation/ whiche letter was as folowithe.

WE haue receiued letters from oure brethern off Strausbrough/but not in suche sorte and ample wise as we loked for/wheruppon we assembled together in the H. Goaste we hope/and haue with one voice and consent chosen yow so particulerly to be one off the Ministers off our congregation here/to preache vnto vs the moste liuely worde off God / according to the gift that God hathe geuen yow for as muche as we haue here throughe the mercifall goodnes off God a churche to be congregated together in the name off Christe/ and be all of one body/and also beinge of one natiō/tonge/and countrie, And at this presente / hauinge neede off suche a one

as yow/

XX.

Mark the calling off Knox to the pastor-shipp.

as yow, we do desier yow and also require yow in the name off God not to deny vs, nor to refuse theis oure requestes, but that yow will aide, helpe and assiste vs with your presence in this our Good and godlie entreprise, whiche we haue take in hand to the glorie off god and the profit off his congregation and the poore sheepe off Christ dispersed abroad, who withe your and like presences, woulde come hither and be of one folde where as nowe they wander abroad as losse sheepe withe owte anie gide. we mistruste not but that yow will ioifully acepte this callinge. fare ye well from Franckford this 26. off September.

Your louinge brethern.
Iohn Bale
Edmond Sutton.
Iohn Makebraie.

William Whitingham   Thomas wood.   Michell Gill.
Thomas Cole   Iohn Stanton   Iohn Samford
William Williams   William Walton   Iohn Wood.
George Chidley   Iasper swyft   Thomas Sorby
William Hammon.   Iohn Geofrie.   Anthony Cariar
Thomas Steward   Iohn Graie   Hugh Alforde.

Nowe to ruturne to the tenor of the letter which the congregation off Franckford wrate by Maister Chambers to the students off Zurick.

WE haue receyued your 2. seuerall letters the one dated the 13. off October sent vs from Strausbrough and the other the 17. off the same by the hands off your deare frinde Maister Chambers and haue conferred with him at large, touching the contents theroff. And when as after diuers assemblyes and longe debatinge the saied Maister Chambers perceyued that we coulde not in all points warrant the full vse off the booke off seruice (whiche semethe to be your full sco-
pe and

ye and marke) and also waying in conscience the great benefit that God hathe in this citie offred to our whole nation/ be not only reioised at the same/ but also promised to trauell in perswadinge yow to the sutheraunce therof. As touchinge the effecte off the booke/ we desire the execution theroff as muche as yow/(so fair as Gods worde dothe commende it) but as for the vnprofitable ceremonies/ aswell by his consent as by ours/ are not to be vsed. And althoughe they were tollerable (as some are not) yet beinge in a strange commō wealthe/ we coulde not be suffred to put them in vre/ and better it were they shulde neuer be practised/ then they shulde be the subuersion off oure churche/ whiche shulde fall in great hassard by vsinge them.

The matter is not oures more then yours/ (excepte anie excell others in godly zeele) but bothe wishe gods honor.

Iff a larger gate be opened there/ to the same then to vs/ vppon your perswations/ ye shall not finde vs to drawe back for this is that necessitie/ brethern/ that maie not be neglected/ yff we wishe the comforte and gatheringe together off oure dispersed brethern. Yff anie think that the not vsinge off the booke in all pointes shoulde increase our godly fathers/ and bretherns bandes/ or els anye thinge deface the worthie ordinances and lawes off our Soueraigne Lorde off moste famous memory. K. Edward the 6. he semethe ether litle to waie the mater/ or ells leied through ignorance knowethe not that euen they themselues haue vppon consideratione off circunstances/ altered heretofore many thinges as touchinge the same. And iff god had not in theis wicked daies otherwise determined/ woulde here after haue chaunged more/ yea and in oure case we dowte not but that they woulde haue don the like. Theis fewe lines concerninge bothe our cōmunicatiōs we haue accordingely written vnto yow/ referringe the reste to the discretion off oure Good frinde Maister Chambers/ who knoweth that we haue shewed oure selues moste conformable in all thinges that standethe in our powers and moste desirous off your companies accordinge to our former

letters,

XXII.

letters. The spirit off God moue your hartes to do that which shalbe most to his glory and the comforte off your brethern. At Franckford, this 15. off Nouember.

Your louinge frinds, &c.

The 28. off Nouember Maister Chambers came againe to Franckford from Strousbrough / and with him Maister Grindall with letters from the lerned men there / subscribed with 16. off their handes / whiche letter was as folowethe.

When we do consider what inwarde comforte it were for the faithfull people off Englande now dispersed for the gospell / and wandringe abroad in strange countries as shepe withowte pastor / to be gathered together in to one congregation / that with one mouth / one minde / and one spirit they might glorifie God: we haue at all tymes and do presently thinke it oure dewties / not only in harte to wishe that thinge / but also to labor by all meanes so muche as in vs lyethe to bringe the same to passe. And hauinge nowe perfit intelligence off the Good mindes / whiche the magistrats off Franckford beare towardes yow and others oure scattered countrie men / and also vnderstandinge off the free graunt off a churche vnto vs wherin we maie together serue god / and not dowtinge off their farther frinds hipp in permittinge vs franckly to vse our religion accordinge to that godly order setforthe and receaued in Englande: We bothe geue god thankes for so great a benefit / and also thinke it not fit to refuse so frindly an offre / or to let slippe so good an occasion. Therfore / neither dowtinge off their good furtherance hereunto / nor yet distrustinge your good conformitie and ready desiers in reducinge the Englishe churche now begun there / to it former perfection off the laste / had in Englande / so farre as possiblie can be atteined / least by muche alteringe off the same we shulde seeme to condemne the chieff au:tors theroff / who as they nowe suffer / so are they moste redie to confirme that facte with the price off

their

XXIII.

their bloude and shulde also bothe gene occasion to our adversaries/ to accuse oure doctrine of imperfection/ and vs of mutabilitie/ ād the godly to dowte in that truthe wherin before they were perswaded / and to hinder their cōminge hither whiche before they had purposed: For the auoidinge off these/ and the obtaininge off the other/ moued hereunto in conscience and prouoked by your ientle letters/ we haue thought it expedient to sende ouer vnto yow/ oure beloued brethern the bringers hereoff to trauell withe the magistrats and yow concerninge the premisses/ whose wisedomes lerninge and godly zeele / as they be knowen vnto yow/ so their doings in this shall fullie take place withe vs. And yff they obtaine that whiche we truste will not be denied at no handes : Then we intend (God willinge) to be with yow the firste off February next/ there to helpe to set in order and stablishe that churche accordingly. And so longe altogether to remaine with yow as shall be necessary/ or vntill iuste occasion shall call some off vs awaie. And we dowte not but that our brethern off Zurick/ Emden Duesbrough .&c. will do the same accordingly / as we haue praied them by oure letters trustinge that yow by yours will make like requeste. Fare ye well from Strasbrough this 13. off Nouember.

Your louing frinds,

Iames Haddon	Iohn Geoffrye	Arthur Saule.
Edwin Sands	Iohn Pedder.	Thomas Steward.
Edmond Grindall.	Thomas Eaten.	Chrst. Goodman
Iohn Huntington	Mighell Reymuger	Humphry Alcocson
Guido Eaten.	Augustine Bradbridge.	Tho. Lakin
		Tho: Crafton.

This letter was red to the congregation / at whiche tyme maister Grindall declared the occasiō of ther cōminge wh̄iche (amōge other things) was chieflie for the stablishinge of the booke off England not that they mente/(as he saied) to haue it so strictly obserued but that suche ceremonies / and thinges

ges whiche the countrie coulde not beare / might well be omitted / so that they might haue the substance and effecte theroff. Maister Knox and whittingham asked them what they mente by the substance off the booke / It was answered by the other that they had no comission to dispute those matters / but they requested that the congregation would answere to certeine interogatories / whiche were thies. First / that they might knowe what partes off the booke they woulde admit. The seconde was for a seuerall churche / and the thirde what assurāce they might haue for their quiete habitation. To the firste / answere was made that what they coulde proue off that Booke to stande withe gods worde / and the countrie permit / that shuld be graunted them. To the 2. whiche was for a church / it was tolde them / that they vnderstoode by the Magistrate / the tyme serued not to moue anie suche matter till the counsaile brake vp at Ausburge. To the third it was saied that a generall graunt was made at their first comminge thither / to the whole nation / and the fredome off the citie offred to all suche as were desyrous off it in as large and ample manner as they coulde require / whiche was to them assurance sufficient.

Theis 3. questions thus answered maister Chambers and Maister Grindall departe back againe with a letter from the congregation whiche was as followethe.

Grace, mercy and peace, &c.

AS it was euer moste true / so at this present we feele most ensiblie / that where so euer god layeth the foundation to builde his glory / there he continueth till he bringe the same to a present worke. All thanks and praise be vnto him therfore / that hathe moued your hartes so as in no point ye seeme to forslowe your diligence to the furtheraunce off the same. And as the worke is off moste excellencie. So the aduersaries cease not most craftely to vndermine it / or at the leaste / through false reportes and defacing off the worke begon / to staie the laborers / whiche shulde trauell in the finishinge theroff.
But

But truthe euer cleareth it selff/ and as the Sonne consumes the the clowds/ so misreportes by triall are confounded. Oure brethern sent from yow can certifie yow at lenght touchinge the particulers off your letter/to whom we haue in all thinges agreed whiche semed expedient for the state off this congation. As for certeine Ceremonies whiche the order off the countrie will not beare: we necessarily omit with as litle alteration as is possible (which in your letters ye require) so that no aduersary is so impudent that dare either blame oure doctrine of imperfection/or vs of mutabilitie/excepte he be altogether willfull ignorante/rather seekinge howe to finde faultes/then to amend them. Nether doo we discente from them whiche lie at the raunsome off their bloude for the doctrine wheroff they haue made a moste worthye confession.

And yet we thinke not that anye godlie man will stande to the deathe in the defence of ceremonies/whiche (as the booke specifieth) vpõ iuste causes maie be altered and chaunged.

And yff the not full vsinge off the booke cause the godly to dowte in that truthe wherin before they were perswaded/and to staye theyr comminge hither/accordinge as they purposed: either it signifieth that they were verye slenderly taught whiche for breach off a Ceremonie will refuse suche a singuler benefit/or ells that yow haue harde them misreported by some false brethern/who/to hinder this worthie enterprise/spare not to sowe in euerie place/store off suche poore reasons. Laste off all it remaineth that ye write/that the firste off February nexte yow will come to helpe to set in order and establishe this churche accordingly/whiche thinge/as we moste wishe for your companies sake and for that ye might se oure godly orders alreadie here obserued: So we put yow owte of dowte that for to appointe a iourney for the establishing off Ceremonies shulde be more to your charges then anie generall profit/excepte ye were determined to remaine with vs longer then 2. monethes/as ye write to our countriemen at Densbrorow and Emden/ whiche letters notwithstandinge are nowe staid and as apeareth we neuer the neere.

we

XXV.

We referre the reste to oure brethern maister Chambers and maister Grindall, who by their diligent inquisition haue learned so farre off our state as we wrote vnto yow in our former letters that is, that we haue a churche freely graunted to preach gods word purely, to minister the Sacraments sincerely and to execute discipline truly. And as touchinge our booke we will practise it so farre as gods worde dothe assure it and the state off this countrie permit. Fare ye well. At Francfort, this 3. off December.

         Your louinge frinds.

Gorge VVhetnall	Thomas VVood	Iohn Makebraie
Thomas VVhetnall	VVilliam VVilliams	VVilliam VValton
Iohn Knox.	Iohn Stanton	Mighell Gill.
Iohn Bale	Iohn Samford	Laurence Kent.
VVilliam VVhitingham	Iohn fox.	Iohn Hollingham.
Edward Sutton.	VVilliam Kethe	

The answere to this letter from Strausbrough was as foloweth.

Grace, mercy and peace, &c.

We haue receaued your letters, and also your answere in wrytinge concerninge certeine Articles, and do perceyue aswell by the same as by maister Chambers and Maister Grindall your state. But for so muche as your opinion is that the tyme do he not presently serue to moue the magistrats in those requests the obteininge wheroff was the principall cause of our sending vnto yow, we cannot at this present condescend vppon anie generall meetinge, at anie certeine tyme, ether to remaine with yow or otherwise. And therfore, iff yow shall certeinly perceaue a time conuenient, that the Magistrate may be traueled withe all aswell for the good and quiete habitation off the commers, and especially Studentes, as also a seuerall churche, and to knowe whither the exercise off the booke shall be vsed, suche we meane as no reasonable man shall

XXVII.

shall iustly reproue/ and that the certeintie off theis matters maie be knowen at the magistrats hands:

then/ (yff yow can let vs haue intelligence) we will farther consulte what is to be done on oure par, ye / trustinge/ god shall directe vs to do so as maye be moste to his glorie in the ende/ howe so euer the presente tyme shall iudge off it. From Strausbrough this 13. off December.

      Your louing frinds, &c.
      as in the letteers before.

When this letter was redd to the congregation/ they requested that for so muche as the lerned men/ coulde not condescend vppon any generall and certeine tyme off meetinge as nowe appeared by their letters/ they might conclude vppon some certeine order by common consent still to continue we and that wihowte farther delaye/ and also to haue the holie communion ministred/ whiche the moste part ernestlie desired. At lenght (it was agreed that the order of Geneua whiche then was alreadie printed in Englishe and some copies there amonge them) shulde take place as an order moste godly and fardeste off from superstition. But Maister Knox beinge spoken vnto/ aswell to put that order in practise/ as to minister the communion/ refused to do ether the one or the other/ affirminge/ that for manie considerations he coulde not consente that the same order shulde be practised/ till the lerned men off Strausbrough/ Zurik/ Emden/ &c. were made priuy. Neither yet woulde he minister the communion by the booke off Englande/ for that there were thinges in it placed (as he saied) onely by warrant of mans authoritie and no growonde in gods worde for the same/ and had also a longe tyme verye superstitiously in the masse byn wickedly abused. But yff he might not be suffred to minister the Sacraments accordinge to his conscience / he then requested that some other might minister the Sacraments/ and he woulde onely preache. Iff neither coulde be admitted he besought them

           D iij   that

XXVIII.

that he might be discharged. But to that the congregation woulde in no wise consente.

Whiles these things were thus in handlinge came maister Liuer (before elected) who / assemblinge the congregation requested that he might withe their consentes appointe suche an order / as shulde be bothe Godly withowt respecte off the Booke off Geneua or anye other / requestinge farther / that for so muche as that office was off so great importaunce / ād that he had not byn in the like before / that he might betweene that and Easter haue a triall off them / and they off him / and so at the ende off that terme either take or refuse / whiche time off triall / as it was willingly graunted him: so when they vnderstoode that the order whiche he woulde place and vse was not altogether suche as was fit for a right reformed churche / they woulde in nowise yelde to the same.

Knox / whittingham / and others / perceyninge that theis beginnings woulde growe to some what / yff it were not staid in time / drewe forthe a platt off the whole booke off England into the lattin tonge / sendinge the same to maister Caluin off Geneua and requestinge his iudgement therin / and shewinge him that some off their countrie men went abowte to force them to the same and woulde admit no other / sayinge / that it was an order moste absolute and that yff euer they came in to their countrie they woulde do their beste to establishe it againe. Nowe folowethe the description.

A description off the Liturgie / or boke off seruice that is vsed in Englande.

Firste off all / morninge praier offreth it selff. The minister hauinge put on a white garment (whiche they call a surplesse)

XXIX.

beginninge withe some sentence off holie scripture / as for example: yff we shall saie that we haue no sinne we deceyue oure selues/ tc. or some suche of like sorte. Then he takethe in hande the exhortation/ whiche stirreth vp to a confession off synnes/ whiche the minister pronounceth with a loude voice/ the people sainge after him. To this is added an absolution / and when these thinges are done / he rehersethe the lordes praier/ and afterward lorde open thow my lyppes/ and my mouthe shall shewe forth thy praise. O god be redie to be my helpe/ tc. Then/ come and let vs singe vnto th Lorde/ tc. By and by also there folowe 3. Psalmes together at thende of euery one. Then foloweth the first lesson/ whiche conteinethe a whole chapter off the olde Testament. After this lesson they saie or singe we praise the/ lorde/ or Blessed be the Lorde / tc. Then an other lesson owte off the Newe testamente/ vnlesse peraduenture the solemnization off some highe feast haue other set and apointed lessons. Nowe in cathedrall churches they vtter their lessons in plaine songe and the afterwards is Benedictus added. This booke warnethe that they keepe this order through owte the whole yere. Afterwards/ the crede is pronounced by the Minister/ (all the people in the meane tyme stāding vp) Afterwards fallinge downe vppon their knees / the Minister saithe/ The Lorde be with yow/ The answere/ And with thy spirite.

Then/ Lorde haue mercy vppon vs/ Christe haue mercy vppon vs/ Lorde haue mercy vppon vs/ tc. our father/ tc. pronounced owte alowde off all with all boldnesse. Then the Minister/ when he standeth vpp saithe/ o lorde shewe vs thy mercy. The answere/ and geue vnto vs thy sauinge helthe. O Lorde saue the king In the day wherin we shall call vppon thee. Indue thy Ministers w the rightcousnes. And make thy chosen people ioyfull. O Lorde saue thy people. And blesse thyne inheritaunce. Geue peace in our tyme o Lorde/ tc. At lenght 3. Collects are had in place off a conclusion / the firste/ for the daie/ the seconde for peace/ the laste is for the obteininge off Grace. Nowe/ the eueninge praiers are saide in a

manner

manner as the other are/ sauinge/ that after the firste lessen fo
loweth my soule doth magnifie the lorde. After the 2. lessen
Now Lorde/ʒc. and in steed off that collect/ God whiche arte
the Author off peace/ is vsed o God from whom all holie des
siers/ʒc. besides/ there is caution added that all Ministers
shall exercise them selues continually aswell in morninge
praiers as eueninge praiers/ except perhapp by studie in dy-
uinitie or some other busynes/ they be greatly and necessarely let or hindred. Besides/ vppon euery Sabothe daie/ wensdaie and fridaie there is yet in vse certeine suffrages deuised
off Pope Gregory whiche beginnethe after this manner.
O God the father off heauen haue mercy vppon vs miserable synners. O God the sonne redemer off the worlde/ ʒc. onely leauinge owte the inuocation off saincts/ otherwise we vse
a certaine coniuringe off God. By the misterie off his incar-
nation/ by his holy natiuitie and circumcision by his baptis-
me/ fastinge and temptation/ by his agonie and bloudie swe-
ate/ ʒc. yea/ it comprehendethe in plaine wordes a praier to
be deliuered from suddain deathe/ the people answeringe
to the ende off euery clause/ either spare vs good lorde/ or ells/
Good Lorde deliuer vs/ or we beseche thee to heare vs Good
Lorde. O Lambe off God that taketh awaie the sinnes off
the worlde is thrise repeated. Then Lorde haue mercy vpon
vs thrise/ and then the Lords praier with this praier also/ o
Lord deale not with vs after our sinnes to the same adioined/
passinge ouer some things least we shulde seeme to syfte all
those drosses which remaine still amonge vs.

  Nowe the manner off the supper is thus. The nomber
off three at the leaste is counted a fitt nomber to communi-
cate/ and yet it is permitted (the pestilence or some other common siknes beinge amonge the people) the Minister alone maie communicate withe the sicke man in his house. First ther-
fore/ the Minister muste be prepared after this manner/ in a
whit lynnin garmente (as in sayinge the other seruice he is
apointed (and muste stande at the Northeside off the Table.
Then is had the Lords praier after the custome/ then he reci-
ceth

XXXI.

seth the collect/ and after folowe in order the ten commaundements (but so notwithstanding/ that euery one off the people maye answere: lorde haue mercy vpon vs and inclyne oure hartes to keepe this lawe. After the rehersall off the commandements/ the collect off the daie (as it is called) and an other for the kinge is had. By and by the Epistle and Gospell folowethe/ to witt/ suche as the callender apointethe for that daie. And there in this place there is a note/ that euerie holy daye hathe his collect Epistle and Gospell (whiche fill vj. great leaues off the booke/ when the reste fill scarse fiftie. For all holy daies are nowe in like vse as were amonge the Papistes/ onelye verye fewe excepted.

Then he goethe forwardes to the crede and after that to the sermon (iff there be anie) Afterwardes the parishe priest byddeth the holie dayes and fastes on their eues / iff there be anye that weeke. And here the booke warnethe that none defraude the parishe priest off his due or right specially on those feast daies / that are dedicated to offrings. Then folowethe a praier for the state off the churche militaunte / and that not withowte a longe heape and mixture off matters vntill they come (after a certeine confession off sinnes) to lift vp your hartes/ the people answeringe/ we geue thankes to the lorde. Let vs geue thanks to our Lorde God/ the answer/ It is meete and right so to do. It is verie meete / right and our bownden dewtie/ ɛc. vntill they come to that clause: O Lorde holie father/ ɛc. and so the preface accordinge to the feaste is added. Afterwards he saithe: Therfore withe Angells and Archangells and so endethe with holy holy holy/ lord god/ till he come to hosianna in the highest. Nowe the priest bowethe his knee acknowledginge oure vnworthynes in the name off all them that shall receiue. And settinge owte gods mercye/ he beseche the God that oure bodies maye be made cleane by his bodie and that our soules maie be washed through his bloude. And then he againe standeth vp and takethe in hande a freshe an other praier appointed for this purpos/ in which are conteined the wordes off the institution / all whiche beinge donne/

E   he

XXXII.

he first communicateth/then/by and by he saithe to an other/ knelinge/Take/and eate this in remembrance that Christ died for thee and feede on him in thy harte by faithe with thanks geuinge.

Now abowte thende the Lordes praier is vsed againe/ the Minister sayinge it alowde and all the people folowinge/ to conclude/ they haue a geuinge off thanks in thende / with the Glory to god in the highest/ as it was vsed amonge the Papistes/yff it happen that there be no sermon/ onely a fewe thinges are omitted/but all other thinges are donne in order aforesaid.

In baptisme the Godfathers are demaunded in the name off the childe / wither they renownce the deuell and all his workes/the lustes off the worlde/etc. and they answere I renownce them. Then/wither they believe the Artikles off the faithe/whiche beinge confessed/wilte thow (saith he turninge himself to bothe the witnesses/ be baptized into this faithe/ and they saie yea/ I will. After a fewe things rehersed/ he taketh the Child and dippeth it in/but warely and discretly as it is in the booke / vppon whose forehead also he shall make a crosse in token forsoothe that when he is olde he shall not be ashamed to confesse the faithe off Christe Crucified. Afterward/sendinge awaie the Godfathers and Godmothers/ he chargeth them that they bringe the childe to be confirmed off the Bishopp as sone as he can saie the Articles off the faithe/the lordes praier/and the ten Comaundemēts. And seinge there be many causes/ as the booke saithe/whiche shulde move them to the Confirmation off Children/this/forsoothe/ off all others is the waightiest/that by imposition off hands they maie receiue strenght and defence against all temptations off sinne/ and the assaults off the world and the deuell/ bicause that when Children come to that age/ partlie / by the frailtie off their owne fleshe/ partly/ by the assaults off the worlde and the deuell they beginn to be in daunger : And leaste anie shulde think any error to be in this Confirmation/ therfore they take a certeine pamflett off a Catechisme/ whiche consi-

steth

XXXIII.

seth off the Articles off the faithe/the Lordes praier / and ten commandements / and all this is dispatched in lesse then two leaues.

To these is ioyned their manner off Mariage off whiche that we maie passeouer many petty ceremonies these follies who can suffer? The husbande laithe downe a ringe vpon the booke/whiche the minister takinge/he geuethe it in his hande and biddethe him to put it on the fourth finger off his wiues left hande/Then he vsethe this forme off wordes: withe this ringe (saithe he) I thee wedd/withe my body I thee worship withe all my worldly goodes I thee endue. In the name off the father/the sonne/and the holy ghoste.

A litle after the Minister saithe to the newe maried persons knelinge before the lordes table: Lorde haue mercy vppon vs Christ haue mercy vpon vs/Lorde haue mercy vppon vs. Oure father which arte/tc. Lorde saue thy seruannt and thy handmaide/tc. and so a few things beinge reherced they muste be brought to the Lordes supper. The visitation off the seke is after this manner. Peace be to this howse. The answere/and to all that dwell in the same. Lorde haue mercy vpon vs/tc. our father/tc. Lorde saue thy seruannte. Answere/ whiche trustethe in thee. Sende forthe thy helpe from thy holy hil/and withe spede saue him/tc. as in the other prefaces w:the questions and answers. Off the Buriall.

The Priest meetethe the Corse at the entraunce off the churcheyarde either singing or softly pronouncinge / I am the Resurrection and the liffe/tc. I knowe that my redemer lyuethe Job. 19. beinge comme to the graue it is sayed. Man borne off a woman Job. 9. When the earthe is throwen in / we committ (saithe he) earthe to earthe/duste to duste/ tc. The Lorde hathe geuen/ the Lorde hathe taken/ I harde a voice from heauen / sayenge / Blessed are the dead whiche die in the Lorde. Lorde haue mercy vppon vs/tc.

The purification of women in childbed/whiche they call

E ij   geuing

geuinge off thankes/ is not only in all thinges withe vs almoste common withe the Papistes but also with the Iewes/ bycause they are commaunded in stede off a lambe or doue to offre monie.

Knox and VVhittingham ashamed to opē some things
Other thinges/ not so muche shame it selff/ as a certeine kinde off pitie compelleth vs to keepe close/ in the meane season nothinge diminishinge the honor due to those reuerende men/ who partely beinge hindred by those times / and by the obstinacie and also multitude off aduersaries (to whom nothinge was euer delightfull besides their owne corruptions), beinge as it were ouerflowen / did alwaies in their minde continually as muche as they coulde striue to more perfect thinges.

Note, that this description is verye fauourably put downe, yf ye conferre it with the Booke off order in all points, and the vsage off the booke in many churches of this realme yow can confesse no lesse. And hereoff ye maie gather what M. Caluin woulde haue writen, yf they had noted all the abuses of the same.

The answere and Iudgemente off that famous and excellent lerned man Maister Iohn Caluin the late Pastor off Geneua/ touchinge the Booke off Englande after that he had perused the same faithfully translated owte off Latten by maister Whittingham.

To the godly and lerned men Maister Iohn Knox / and Maister William Whittingham / his faithfull brethern at Frankford &c.

This thinge trulie greueth me very muche/ and it is a great shame that contention shulde arise amonge brethern banished and driuen owte of their countrie for one faithe/ and
for

XXXV.

for that cause whiche onely ought to haue holden yow bounde together as it were withe an holy bande in this your dispersion. For what might yow do better in this dolorous and miserable plage/then (beinge pulled violently from your countrie) to procure your selues a churche/whiche shulde receiue and nourishe yow (beinge ioyned together in mindes and language) in her motherly lappe. But nowe for some men to striue as touchinge the forme off praier and for Ceremonies as thoughe ye were at reste and prosperitie/ and to suffer that to be an impedimente that ye cannot there ioyne in to one body off the churche (as I think) it is to muche owte off season.

Yet notwithstanding/ I allowe their constancie whiche striue for a iuste cause beinge forced againste their willes vnto contention. I do worthely condemne frowardnes/ whiche doshe hinder and staie the holye carefullnes of reforminge the churche.

And as I behaue myselff gentle and tractable in meane thinges (as externall ceremonies) So doo I not alwaies iudge it profitable/ to geue place to their folishe stowtenes/ whiche will forsake nothinge off their oulde wonted custome. In the liturgie off Englande/ I se that there were manye tollerable foolishe thinges/ by theis wordes I meane/ that there was not that puritie whiche was to be desired. Theis vices/ thoughe they coulde not at the firste daie be amended/ yet/ seinge there was no manifeste impietie/ they were for a season to be tollerated. Therfore/ it was lawfull to begin off suche rudimentes or absedaries/ but so/ that it behoued the lerned/ graue/ and godly ministers off Christe to enterprise farther / and to set foorthe some thinge more filed from ruste/ and purer. If godly Religion had florished till this daie in Englande/ there ought to haue bin a thinge better corrected and manie thinges cleane taken awaie. Nowe/when theis principles be ouerthrowne/ a churche muste be set vp in an other place / where ye maie freely make an order againe/ whiche shall be apparent to be moste commoditious to the vse and edification off the churche. I cannot tell what they meane whiche so greatly de-

Many tollerable foolishe things in the book by Caluins iudgement.

XXXVI.

lith in the leauinges off Popishe dregges. They loue the thinges wherunto they are accustomed. firste off all, this is a thinge bothe triflinge and Childishe. furthermore, this newe order farre differeth from a chaunge.

The booke triflinge and Childishe by Caluins iudgement.

Therfore, as I woulde not haue yow feirse ouer them whose infirmitie will not suffer to ascend an higher steppe: so woulde I aduertise other, that they please not them selues to muche in their foolishnes. Also, that by their frowardnes, they doo not let the course off the holie buildinge. Laste off all, least that foolishe vaine glorie steale them awaie. For what cause haue they to contende, excepte it be for that they are ashamed to gene place to better thiges. But I speake in vaine to them whiche perchaunce esteeme me not so well, as they will vouchsaffe to admitt the consaile that commethe from suche an authour. If they feare the euell rumor in Englande, as though they had fallen from that Religion which was the cause off their banishment, they are farre deceiued for this true and sincere Religion, will rather compell them that there remaine, faithfully to consider in to what deepe gulff they haue fallen. For there downefall shall more greuously wounde them, when they perceyue your goinge forewarde bejonde mid course, from the whiche they are turned. Fare ye well dearely beloued brethern, and faithfull seruants off Chrste. the Lorde defende and gouerne yow from Geneua this 20. off Jan. Anno. 1555.

Your Iohn Caluin

When this letter of Caluins was redd to them of the congregation, it so wrought in the hartes off many, that they were not before so stowte to maintaine all the partes off the boke off England as afterward they were bent against it. But nowe to returne. Whiles these thinges were in doyinge, the congregation (as yow haue harde afore) coulde not agree vpon anie certeine order, till after longe debatinge to and fro, it was concluded, that maister Knox, maister Whittingham, Maister Gilby, Maister Fox and Maister T. Cole shulde drawe forg

XXXVII.

we forthe some order meete for their state and time: whiche thinge was by them accomplished and offred to the congregation (beinge the same order off Geneua whiche is nowe in print) This order was verie well liked off many, but suche as were bent to the booke off Englande coulde not abide it, yea, cõtention grewe at length so hot, and theone partye which sought sinceritie, so sore charged, with newfanglednes and singularitie, and to be the stirrers of cõtention and vnquietnes, that Maister Gilby with a godly grieff (as well apeared) kneled downe before them and besought them (withe teares) to reforme their iudgementes, solemelie protestinge, that (in this matter) they sought not themselues, but onely the glorie off god, as he was verely perswaded, wishinge farther that that hande whiche he then helde vp were stricken of if by that a godly peace and vnitie might ensue and followe. In thende an otherwaie was taken by the congregation, whiche was, that maister Knox and maister whittingham, Maister parry and Maister leauer shulde deuise some order yff it might be, to ende all striff and cõtention.

The humblenes of Gilby and his godly zeale

Theis 4. assembled for that purpos. And first, Maister Knox spake to the reste in this wise. For so muche (saithe he) as I perceiue, that no ende of cõtention is to be hoped for, vnlesse the one parte somethinge relent, this will I doo for my parte, that quietnes maie insue. I will shewe my iudgement howe (as I think) it maie be beste for the edification off this poore flocke, whiche if ye will not accepte, nor followe (after that I haue discharged my conscience) I will cease and cõmit the whole matter to be ordered by yow as yow will answere before Christ Jesus at the laste daie, and to this his congregation in this liffe, &c. Wherupon after some conference, an order was agreed vpõ: some parte takè forthe of the Englishe booke and other things put to, as the state of that churche required.

The modestie of Knox

And this order by the consent of the cõgregation shulde continewe to the laste of Aprill folowing, yff anie contention shulde arise in the meane time, the matter then to be determined by theis 5. notable lerned mẽ, to wete, Caluin, Musculus Martir,

This order was taken the 6. off Feb.

XXXVIII.

Martyr, Bullinger, and Vyret. This agremente was put in wrytinge. To that all gaue their consentes. This daie was ioyfull. Thanckes were geue to God, brotherly reconciliation folowed, great familiaritie vsed, the former grudges seemed to be forgotten. Yea the holie communion was vppon this happie agremente, also ministred. And this frindshipp continued till the 13. off March folowinge, at whiche tyme. D. Coxe and others with him came to Frankford owte off Englande, who beganto break that order whiche was agreed vppon, firste in answeringe alowde after the minister, contrary to the churches determination, and beinge admonished theroff, by the Seniors off the congregation, he, with the rest that came with him made answere, that they woulde do as they had donne in Englande, and that they would haue the face off an English churche. And the sundaie folowinge, one off his compa ny withowt the consent and knowledg off the congregation gate vpp suddainly into the pulpit, redd the lettany, and D. Cox withe his companie answered alowde, wherby the determination off the churche was broken. The same sundaie at after noone it came to maister Knox his turne to preache, who hauinge passed so farre in Gen. that he was come to Noah as he laie open in his tente, he spake theis wordes folowinge.

D. Cox with others come to Frankf.

Th effecte of Knox ser mon.

As diuers thinges (saithe he) ought to be kepte secret, euenso suche thinges as tend to the dishonor off God and disquietinge of his churche oughtto be disclosed and openly reproued. And therupon he shewed, howe that after longe trouble and contention amonge them, a godly agremente was made, and howe that the same, that daie was vngodly broken, whiche thinge, became not (as he saied) the prowdest off them all to haue attempted, alleadginge furthermore that like as by the worde off God we muste, seeke oure warrant for the establisfhing off religion, and withowt that to thruste nothinge into anie Christian congregation: so for as muche as in the Englishe booke were thinges bothe superstitious, vnpure, and vnperfect (which he offred to proue before all men) he would not consent that off that churche it shulde be receiued, and

that

XXXIX.

that in case men woulde go abowte to burthen that free congregation therwith, /so ofte as he shulde come in that place (the texte offringe occasion) he woulde not faile to speake againste it.

He farther affirmed that amonge manye thinges whiche prouoked goddes anger againste Englāde, slacknes to reforme religion (when tyme and place was graunted) was one. And therfore it became them to be circūspecte, howe they laid their foundation. And where some men ashamed not to saie, that there was no let or stopp in Englande, but that Religion might be, and was already brought to perfection, he proued the contrary, by the wante off discipline. Also by the troubles which maister Hooper Sustained, for the Rochet and such like, in the booke commanded and allowed.

And for that one man was permitted to haue 3. 4. or 5. benefices to the great slaunder off the gospell and defraudinge off the flock off Christe off their liuely foode and sustenaunce. These were the chieff notes off his sermon, whiche was so stomaked off some, especially off suche as had many liuinges in Englande, that he was verye sharplie charged, and reproued so soone as he came owte off the pulpit, for the same.

The twesdaie folowinge, was appointed to talke off thies thinges more at large. When all were assembled earneste requeste was made that D. Coxe with his companie might be admitted to haue voices in the congregation. Answere was made by others that the matter yet in controuersie amonge them, ought firste to be determined, Secōdly, that they shuld subscribe to discipline as others had don before them, and farther yt was greatly suspected that they had byn (some off them) at masse in Englande, and others had subscribed to wicked articles, as one off them shortly after euen in the pulpit sorowfully confessed. For thei considerations and suche like, The congregation withstoode the admission off D. Coxe and his companie. Knox, at laste, began to make intretie that they might haue their voices amongst the reste, to whose requeste when certeine had yelded, they then became the greater parte, and

D. Cox sharply rebuked him.

But that they refused, and at lenght ouerthrew yt.

M. Iewell,

re and so were by them admitted as members off the churche. They thus admitted, by the moste parte, D. Coxe foorthwith forbad Knox to meddle anye more in that congregation.

Knox putt owt by tho se which he brought in.

The nexte daie beinge wensdaie, whittingham wente to Maister John Glauburge (who was the chieff meane in obtaininge the churche) and brake the matter vnto him, declaringe, howe that certeine, nowe come owte off Englande had forbidden their minister apointed, to preache that daie, and intended to set vpp an other, whiche he dowted woulde not be well taken. And therfore, leaste anie inconuenience shulde happe, he thought good to make him priuie therto. Whereupon the saied Magistrat sent immediatlie and gaue comaundement that ther shulde be no sermon that daie. Afterwarde he sent for Valeran the frenche Minister, commaundinge him that 2 lerned men shulde be appointed off either parte, and that he and they shulde consulte and agree vppon some good ordre, and to make report vnto him accordingly. Then were apointed D. Cox and leuer off the one side and Knox and whittingham on the other side. To decide the matter. Valeran was appointed to put downe in writinge what they shulde agree vpon. But when in this conference, they came to the order off Mattins and that D. Coxe saide, Ego volo habere, there coulde be no agrement amonge them, and so brake off, wherupon the congregation drew vp a supplication in latten and presented it to the saied maister Glauburge requestinge him to be a meane that the same might be considered off amonge the Senators, The Englishe wheroff was as folowethe.

The supplication to the Senate.

Let it not molest yow (moste graue and worthie Senators) that your affayers are letted with a fewe wordes. And leaste we shulde trouble yow with prolixitie, yow shall vnderstande the matter briefly. When your great and vnspeakable humanitie, through the prouidence of god had graunted vs a churche, we vndertooke forthwith (as became vs)

to com=

XLI.

to consulte aboute the orders off the same / and to set owt a Liturgie. And bicause we sawe that in the prolixe and Ceremonious booke of the liturgie of Englande / be manie thinges (that we maie speake no worse off it) not moste perfecte / it seemed beste to reduce it to the perfecte rule off the scriptures and to accommodate our selues to the ensamples off that churche wherein we teache / and to whom we haue subscribed. But when this enterprise offended some off oure countriemen (althoughe the greatest nomber agreed vnto vs) for that we woulde decline from the decrees off our elders / here vppon there grewe to vs for a fewe monethes no small trouble. *To weet the frenche churche.*

At the lenght / whē there appeared no ende / for peace and concordes sake we gaue place to their will / and suffred them at their pleasure to pike owte off their booke the chiefest or beste thinges vpon this condition that the same shulde continewe with owte alteration / at the leaste / vnto the laste daie off Aprill / at the whiche daie (iff there shulde anie newe contention arise) that then all the matter shulde be referred to these 5. notable men / Calvin / Musculus / Martir / Bullinger / vnd Viret. What nedethe manie wordes. This condition was willingly accepted / and the couenaunte rated on bothe partes. A writinge was also theroff to testifie the promesse made off the one to the other. Moreouer thankes were geuen to god withe great ioye / and common praiers were made / for that men thought that daie to be thende off discorde. Besides this / they receyued / the communion as the sure token / or seale off their mutuall agremente / whiche was omitted before / by the space off 3. monethes. Valaran also the frenche Minister was partaker off this communion and a further off concorde and a wittnes off theis thinges. Nowe of late daies / certeine of our countrey men / came to vs who haue indeuored by all meanes to obtrude that huge volume off ceremonies vpon vs to break the couenaunte and to ouerthrough the libertie off the Churche graunted by your beneuolence. And no dowte / this they enterprise and mindetodo vnder the

F ij   title

XLII.

title and name off your defence / Wherby they maie abuse the authoritie off your name to satisfie their luste. We are here compelled to omitte manie thinges whiche woulde make for oure cause / no lesse righ[t]ly then profitably / but we remit this to oure brethern for concordes sake.

Yow haue here / moste honorable Sen a brieff summe of oure case / and content on / wherby yow may easilie onderstande / what to iudge off the whole matter.

The letter a litle before.

What manner off Booke this is for the whiche they so cruellie contende / ye maie consider by the Epistle that Calvin lately wrote vnto vs / in the whiche he hathe signified his minde / aswell plainly off the booke / as also off the vprightnesse off oure cause. We coulde haue pointed owte vnto yow the foolishe and fonde thinges off the booke / but passinge ouer an infinite nomber off thinges / this one will we bringe for manie the whiche shalbe necessarie well tobe marked. within these three yeres arose a great conflicte betweene the Bishopps off the realme and the Bishoppe off Gloceter

This controuersie hath byn sithins kinge Edward his raigne as yete.

Maister Hooper / a man worthie off perpetuall memorie / whom we heare to be burned off late This man beinge made Bishopp By kinge Edwarde / there was obtruded by other B. off the same order (accordinge to this booke) a rochet / and a bishops robe this man being well lerned and a longe tyme nourished and brought vp in Germany / as soone as he refused thies proud thinges that fooles marveil at / he was caste into prison and at lenght by their importunitie ouercome / and relentinge / he was compelled to his shame to geue place to their impudency withe the common grieff and sorowe off all godlye mindes.

But wherfore speake yow off theis thinges will yow saie / that apperteneth nothinge to vs? yes verely / we thinke it touchethe yow verie moche / for yff this men armed by your authoritie shall do what they liste / this euell shalbe in time establishedd by yow and neuer be redressed / nether shall there for euer be anie ende off this controuersie in Englande. But yff it woulde please your honorable authoritie to decree this moderation betweene vs / that this whole matter may be referred

red to the iudgementes off the fiue aboue named, not we alone that are here present/ but oure whole posteritie/ yea oure whole englishe nation/ and all good men/ to the perpetuall memorie off your names/ shalbe bownde vnto yow for this great benefit. We might haue vsed moo wordes in this narration/ for we feared not/ that we shulde lake reasons/ but rather that tyme shulde faile yow/ letted with more serious busines. Therfore/ we by thes thinges/ leaue the reste to the consideration off your wisdomes.

The 11. off Marche maister Glauburge came to the Englishe Churche and shewed the congregation/ that it was commaunded them/ by the magistrates (when by his procurement the church was graunted) that they shulde agree with the frenshe churche bothe in Doctrine and ceremonies/ and that they vnderstood howe the fallinge from that order had bred muche dissention amonge them. Therfore/ he straitly charged and commaunded that from thence foorthe they shulde not dissent from that order/ yff they did/ as he had opened the churche dore vnto them/ so woulde he shutte it againe. And that suche as woulde not obey therunto shulde not tarie within that citie/ willinge them to consulte together owte off hande and to geue him an answere before he departed. D. Coxe/ then spake to the congregation in this wise/ I haue (saith he) redd the frenche order and do thinke it to be bothe good and godly in all pointes/ and therfore wished them to obaie the magistrates commaundement wherupon the whole congregation gaue consent/ so as before the Magistrate departed the churche/ D. Coxe/ leuer/ and whittingham made reporte vnto him accordingly. D. Coxe also at that presente requested that it woulde please him/ notwithstandinge their ill behauiour) to shewe vnto them his accustomed fauor and goodnesse/ whiche he moste ientlie and louinglie promised.

At the nexte meetinge off the congregation that order was put in practise/ to the comforte and reioycinge off the moste parte. Neuertheles/ suche as woulde so faine haue had the booke of England/ lefte not the matter thus. And for that they

f iij sawe

XLIIII.

sawe Knox to be in suche credit withe many off the congregation/ they firste off all assaied by a moste cruell barbarous and bloudie practise to dispatche him owte off the waie/ to thende they might withe more ease attaine the thinge whiche they so gredely sought/ whiche was the placinge of their booke. They had amonge them a booke off his intituled an admonition to Christians written in the English tonge/ wherin by occasion he spake off the Emperour/ off Philip his sonne/ and off Marie then Queene off Englande. This booke certeine off them presented to the Magistrates/ who (vpon receipte off the same) sente for whittingham and asked him off Knox their Minister/ what manner off man he was: whittingham answered that suche a one their was amonge them and to his knowledge bothe a lerned/ wise/ graue and godly man. Then one off the Magistrates saied vnto him/ certaine off youe countrie men haue accused him vnto vs Læsæ Maiestatis Imperatoriæ, that is off hightreason againste the Emperour/ his sonne/ and the Queene off England/ here is the booke/ and the places whiche they haue noted/ the true and perfect sence wheroff we commaunde yow (sub pena pacis) to bringe vnto vs in the latten tonge at one off the clock in the after noone/ which thinge he did accordingly/ at whiche time (after certeine communication amonge themselues/ they commanded that Knox shulde preache no more till their pleasure were farther knowen. The wordes concerninge the Emperour were theis/ spoken in the pulpit in a Towne off Buchingham (hee ein in the beginninge off Queene Maries raigne/ as by the saied booke apeareth) where it is saied: O Englande Englande/ yff thow wylte obstinately returne into Egipte/ that is/ yff thow cōtracte mariage/ confederacy/ or leage with suche princes as doo maintaine and aduaunce ydolatrie/ suche as the Emperour (who is no lesse enemie to Christ then was Nero) yff for the pleasure and frindship (I saie) of such princes thow returne to thine oulde abbominations before vsed vnder Papistery: then assuredly (O England) thow shalt be plaged and brought to desolation by the meanes off those whose fauour thow

Knox accused off treason.

The places in all were 8.

XLV.

thow sekeste/ and by whom thow arte procured to fall from Christe and serue antechriste. There were other 8. places/ but this was most noted/in that it touched the Emperour. But it semed the magistrates abhorred this bloudy/ cruell/ and outragious attempt/ for that when as certeine off Knox his enemies folowed hardly the Magistrates to knowe what shuld be donne with him/ they did not onely shewe most euident signes of disliking their vnnaturall suite/ but also sent for maister Williams and Whittingham/ willinge them/ that maister Knox shuld departe the City. For otherwise/ (as they saide) they shuld be forced to deliuer him/ yff the Emperour his counsaile (whiche then lay at Ausburge) shuld vppon like information send for him. *The banishment off Knox.*

The 23. off marche maister Knox the night before his departure made a moste comfortable sermon at his lodginge to 50. persons or there abowte/ then present/ which sermō was of the deathe and resurrection off Christe/ and of the vnspeakable ioyes whiche were prepared for Goddes electe/ whiche in this liffe suffre trouble and persecution for the testimonie off his blessed name. The next daie he was brought 3. or 4. mile in his waie by some off some off those vnto whom the night before/ he had made that exhortation/ who with great heauines off harte and plentie off teares cōmitted him to the lorde.

The verie same daie beinge the 26. off marche one Adulphus Glauburge (a Doctor off lawe and nephew to Maister John Glauburge the Senator) whom D. Cox and the rest had wonne vnto them/ sent for Wittingham/ and tolde him that there were presented to the Magistrates three Doctors/ 13. batchelers off deuinitie besides others/ and that the magistrates at their suites had graunted them the full vse off the Englishe booke cōmaunding and charginge him therfore not to medle any more to the contrary. for (as he saied) it was fullie concluded that so it shuld be. And supposing that Whittinghā woulde let it what he might/ the next daie againe he sent for him home to his howse where he gaue the like charge (D. Coxe and other present by whose procurement the same was donne) *Many off the lerned men were now come from al places.* *This Adulphus was before this tyme a greatt farther*

XLVI.

ver off the chur-che and the orders off the same how so euer he was tur ned.

ne) Whittingham answered, that yff it were so concluded, he woulde willingly obaie, not dowtinge, but that it might be lawful for him and others to ioine themselues to some other churche. But D. Coxe besought the lawier that it might not so be suffred, wherto whittingham answered that it woulde be to great crueltie to force men contrary to their consciences to obaie all their disorderly doinges, offringe, that if it woulde please the Magistrates to geue him and others the hearinge, they would dispute the matter against all the contrary parte and proue that the order whiche they sought to establishe, ought not to take place in anie reformed churche. The D. off lawe made a plaine answere that disputation there shulde be none, vsing his former wordes off charging and commaundinge not to deale farther in that matter.

Marck the placing off the Englishe book and off the reiecting thother.

When as the congregation harde off the cruell and more then tirannicall dealinges off this Doctor, Maister Gilby and others wythe him, were sente to maister John Glawburge (by whose commaundment as ye harde, they had receiued the frenche order) puttinge him in remembrance off the same and shewinge him that certeine lately come amonge them had sought (as they were crediblie enformed) to ouerthrowe their churche by placing the Englishe booke amonge them. To this maister Glauburg made answere, that he was enformed howe that bothe partes were full agreed and contented, and that theruppon he had committed the whole matter to the lawier his cousen. Then he asked for whittingham; it was answered that strait charge was geuen him that he shuld medle no more in that matter. The magistrate asked againe off whom he had that commaundement, and when it was tolde him that the Doctor his cousen had geuen him that charge, he then began, verie gentlie to perswade with maister Gilby and the rest that they shulde be contented, and he would se that nothinge shulde be vsed but that which shuld be tollerable, and so maister Gilby wythe the rest departed.

Marck this practise.

The 18. off marche D. Coxe assembled all suche as had byn Priests and Ministers in Englande to his lodging and

there

there declared howe the Magistrates had graunted them the vse off the Englishe booke, and that he thought requisite that they shulde consulte together, whom they thought moste meete to be Bishop/Superintendent or Pastor withe the rest off the officers, as Seniors Ministers and Deacons. Wherunto the maister Christopher Goodmā answered that his opiniō was, that they ought first to agree vpon some perfect an godly order for the churche, and therto to haue the consent of the congregation wherby it might appeere, that they contemned not the reste off their brethern: And farther, to proceade to the electiō which he thought also ought not to be attempted withowte the consent off the whole churche. To this was answered that for the order, it was already ditermined, and other order then the booke off Englande they shulde not haue, so that the perswasions off Goodman nothinge at all preuailed nether in one thinge or other, yea, the proceadings off sundrie personnes (whiche I coulde name) were suche as if there had bin nether orders, officers, or churche there, before their cominge, or any promes to be kepte off their partes, after they came, as maie more plainly apeere to the reader by this letter folowinge, writen by maister Whittingham to a frinde off his in Englande, whiche letter is (off his owne hande) to be seene. *At length they agreed vppon the name Pastor.*

Grace, mercy and peace throught Christ our lorde.

AS yow require a brieff answere to your shorte letter, so nether tyme permitteth, nor I intend to trouble yow farther then the verie necessitie off the matter asketh. And firste, for that ye seeme to hange in suche extreame perplexitie, partly, bicause of sundry talkes, and diuers letters off men off good credit which causethe yow not a litle to merueile, and partly, by reason off the Good opinion once conceyued and yet reteined off certeine persons bothe godly and lerned, which maketh yow to dowte; I think it beste, briefly and simplie *An answere to a letten sent him owte off Englande.*

XLVIII.

to open a fewe chieff pointes vppon the whiche the reste off the matter dependethe. After certeine monethes that we had here liued in great consolation and quietnes it chaunced that as oure nomber did increase / so some entred in / whiche busilie vndermined oure libertie and labored to ouerthrowe oure discipline/ whiche troubles grewe at length t in so great quantitie / that by the greatest parte it was concluded / that no man shulde neede here after to subscribe to anie discipline for as muche as they presupposed that none would come hither whiche shulde haue nede theroff. Whiche donne / they altered oure orders in praiers and others thinges / thinkinge to bringe in place the full vse off the great Englishe booke / whiche notwithstandinge / by reason off diuers imperfections we coulde not admit / so that to growe to a common concord it was agreed and the name off god inuocated that the whole matter shulde be referred / to maister Caluin Maister Musculus Maister Martir / Maister Bullinger and Maister Viret that bothe partes shulde drawe their orders and that to be receyued whiche by the iudgements off theis 5. excellent men shuld be thought moste agreable to a reformed churche. In the meane time euerie man to stand content withe that order whiche was then agreed vpõ and vsed. But within fewe daies after / this determinatiõ was broken. A stranger craftely brought in to preache / who had bothe byn at masse and also subscribed to blasphemous Articles / Many tauntinge bitter sermons were made (as they thought) to oure defacinge / in so moche / as maister Knox beinge desired therunto off diuers / was inforced to purge him self in sundrie pointes / and spake his mind freely in the pulpit / aswell in reprouinge certeine partes off the Englishe booke / as declaringe the punishmente off God whiche partly had light vpon oure countrie for slacknes in Religion / so as they seemed to take the matter so to harte that by their false delation in accusinge him before the Magistrates off treason againste the Emperour and the Queene in a certeine boke off his written to oure countrie men off England he was commaunded to departe.

And

XLIX.

And the Magistrates vnderstandinge their fetches/ and greedy cerchinge off their owne glorie(who seemed to spare no kinde off contention to purchase the same)commaunded that we shulde receiue the frenche order (whiche is accordinge to the order off Geneua the pureste reformed churche in Christendome(Wherupon all agreed and S. Coxe with others commendinge the same to the congregation)gaue thankes to the Magistrate in all oure names. Here yow maie note their double faces / who / bearinge the Magistrate in hande that they receyued his commaundement ioyfully / priuily practised/ and so laboured vnder hande / that they made this Magistrate vnsaie / and so obtained their booke / promisinge notwithstandinge/bothe to the Magistrate / and certaine off the congregation/ as well to proue by the worde off God so muche off the booke as they woulde vse / as also to set forthe the same in wrytinge/that they(before the forsaied order shulde be chaunged(might iudge off the equitie theroff. But preferringe the ioye off their vnhoped victorie before their promesse/ did nether the one bycause they coulde not / nether the other bicause they durste not. And yet haue they not made an ende off their triumphe. For beginninge in marche not onely to neglecte all orders in the election off their Ministers and other officers/but also to skoff and taunte others in their dailie sermons / do not yet ceasse as nowe appeareth by their slanderous and lyinge letters.

But to thende we might be deliuered from this vnsupportable yoke / God off his mercy hathe prouided better for vs/ and for this incommoditie hathe graunted vs a double benefit in so muche that contrary to their hope he hathe not onely at Basill moued the Magistrates hartes towardes vs in grauntinge vs a churche / but also at Geneua/ where as Gods worde is truly preached manners beste reformed and in earthe the chiefest place off true comforte. Thus in fewe lines J haue gon abowte to satisfie your requeste bearinge with tyme whiche hasteth and also folowinge mine owne Iudgement /. whiche perswadeth

G ij   me

me rather to geue yow a taste off thinges (whiche I moued in conscience wryte as moste true) then to fill yow with the whole discours/ whiche/ iff this maie not suffice/ yow maie by continuaunce haue at your commaundement. Pray for vs brother in this oure banishement/ that the frutes off this vncorruptible seede maie springe moste abundantly/ as we praie cōtinually that oure heauenly father woulde so strengtɦ hen yow with his spirite off boldenes/ that yow maie not ōꝛ nely resiste/ but also triumphe ouer all your enymies to the gloꝛ rie off God and the confusiō off the aduersaries. Knowe beꝛ fore yow iudge/ and beleue not all sleinge tales/ keepe one caꝛ re open and reporte the the beste.

       Your VVilliam VVhittingham.

Where as maister whittingham in this his letter makes the mention off a churche graunted them bothe at Basill and Geneua/ it is to be noted that he himselff was the man whiche the oppressed congregation required to trauel therin and through goddes great mercy obtained it with great faꝛ uour/ who (in his iourney) passed by Zurik to knowe off Maiꝛ ster Bullinger what he thought off the booke off Englande for that he (who had raported to maister Williams/ Whittinꝛ gham/ Gilbie and others/ that Cranmer Bishop off Canterꝛ bury had drawen vp a booke off praier an hundreth tymes more perfect then this that we nowe haue/ the same coulde not take place/ for that he was matched withe suche a wicked clergie and conuocation/ with other enymies) Euen he/ I saie/ yet stood in this that maister Bullinger did like well off thinglis he order/ and had it in his study. But when Whitꝛ tingham had demaunded that question/ Bullinger tolde him/ that indede Maister H and Maister C. asked his iudgemenꝛ te concerninge certeine pointes off that booke/ as Surples/ priuate baptisme. Churchinge off wemen/ the ring in mariaꝛ ge/ with suche like/ whiche/ (as he saied) he allowed not/ and that he nether coulde yff he woulde/ nether woulde yff he miꝛ

                  ght/

ght/vse the same in his churche/ what so euer had byn reported.

Whittingham passinge from thence to Geneua/ maister
Caluin shewed him a letter sent from S. Coxe and from 14.
more off Franck.in whiche letter/they partly excused them selues that they put order in their churche withowte his coūsaile asked/and partely reioycinge for that they had (as they saide)
brought the moste parte that had withstande their doynges
to their opinion/ which not withstandinge/ was farr others
wise.

They wrote also/that they had elected a pastour/2. Ministers. 4. Seniors. and 2. Deacons/ &c. but howe parciallie
they proceaded in their elections(those that were in office/neether discharged/nor yet their consents required)J leaue to the
consciences off them whiche sawe those disorders.

To this letter off thers the contentes wheroff are aboue
touched/maister Caluin answereth em in this wise.

To the worshippfull my louinge brethern in the
lorde maister Richard Coxe and the rest off the Englishemen whiche nowe remaine at Frankford.

PAraduenture J answere your letter(worship.frinds and
brethern) more slowlie then ether ye hoped or looked for/
but for so muche as ye knowe the wayes for a tyme so to be
beset withe theues that no messenger allmoste coulde passe
from hence to yow the excuse off my long delay towardes yow
shalbe the easier.

J expressed my minde frankly to oure beloued brother
Thomas Sampson/off that wheroff J was enformed by the
letters off certeine men as touchinge the contention vnluckelie stirred vp amonge yow. For certene off my frindes founde
thē selues greued that yow woulde so precisclie vrge the ceremonies off Englande/wherby it might appeere that ye are more geuen and addicte to your countrie then reason woulde. J
confesse that J harde certeine reasons alledged on your behalff
G iij   whiche

whiche woulde not suffer yow to departe from the receyued order / but they might be soone and easilie confuted. Nowe / as I counsailed mine owne frindes whiche dissented from yow / somewhat to yelde / yff they might conueniently / so it offended me that there was nothinge graunted or relented on your partes. Bicause there was no man named vnto me / I durste not entreprise to meble with the matter / leaste my credit shuld incurre the suspecte off rashenes. Nowe that ye are more mylder and tractable in this controuersie and that ye haue (as ye saie) stilled the matter withe quietnes / I am verie glad.

Verely no man well instructed or off a sounde Judgement / will deny (as I think that lights and crossings or suche like trifles / sprange or issued owte off superstition / wherupon I am perswaded that they whiche receine theis ceremonies in a free choise / or when they maie otherwise doo / they are ouer greedy and desyrous to drink off the dregges. neither do I se to what purpose it is to burthen the churche with tryfflinge and vnprofitable ceremonies / or as I maie terme them with their propre name / hurtefull and offensible ceremonies / when as there is libertie to haue a symple and pure order. But I keepe in and refraine my selff leaste I shulde seeme to beginne to moue a newe contention off that matter whiche as yow reporte / is well ended.

All good men will allowe the Pastoures and other Ministers elections with common voices / so that none complaine that the other parte off the churche was oppressed fraudulently and with craftye practises. For it standethe your wisedomes in hande to consider / that howe muche commoditie the goodnesse off the Senate dothe deserue / so muche enuie shall yow be giltie off / or charged withall / yf yow haue abused their lenitie or gentlenesse / whiche were so well affected towardes your nation. Yet / I woulde not haue this so taken / that I go abowte to be preiudiciall to anie man but I had rather shewe plainely what maie be saide / then to norishe an ill opinion by silence / or in holdinge my peace. But certenly / this one thinge I cannot

LIII.

I cannot keepe secret, that Maister Knox was in my iudgement nether godly nor brotherly dealt withall, iff he were accused by the subtill suggestion of certeine, it had byn better for them to haue taried still in their owne lande then vniustly to haue brought in to farr countries the fierbrande off crueltie to set on fier those that woulde not be kindled.

Notwistandinge, because it greueth me to speak sleightly off theis euells, the remembrance wheroff I woulde wisshe to be buryed in perpetuall forgetfullnes therfore, I onely counsaile yow (not withowt a cause) to be wounded, that ye applie your selues to make them amendes for the faulte committed.

When I harde that the one parte was minded to departe fro thens: I earnestly admonished them (as it became me) that iff they coulde not well remaine there, that the distance off place shulde not dissipate, or rent in sunder their brotherly agrement, for I feared muche least that some priuie grudge off the former contention remained. And certainely, nothinge coulde more comforte my harte, then to be delyuered from this feare. for iff anie haplie come to vs, it woulde grieue me that there shulde be (as it were) but a suspition off any secret debate betwene yow. *They begin pretely.*

Therfore as tonchinge that ye haue written off your agrement I desier that it maie be firme and stable that iff it chaunce the one parte to go to an other place, yet, that yow beinge so sundred by distance off places maie keepe sure the holie bande off off amitie, for the fault alreadie committed is to muche, although thorowgh discorde it creepe no further. Wherfore it shall well beseeme your wisedomes (that ye maie be frinds) to purge diligentlie what so euer remainethe off this breache. Fare ye well brethern, the lorde succour yow with his aide, and gouerne yow with his spirite, powre his blessinges vpon yow and mitigate the sorowe off your exile from Geneua this last off maie, Anno 1555.

Your Iohn Caluin.

LIIII.

Because that Maister Caluin in his letter maketh mention off lightes / some might gather that he was vntruely exformed/ that in the Englishe booke lightes were prescribed (the contrary wherof appeareth by the description before) where it is manifest to such as be lerned that he vseth the figure auxesis/ and that this is his argument/ a maiore ad minus/ for so muche as lightes and crossinges be 2. off the moste auncienstest ceremonies/ hauinge continued in the churche aboue 13 hundreth yere/ are yet for suche causes abolished: howe muche more ought all other/ that haue nor hadthe like continuance/ and yet abused/ be vtterly remoued.

And for that maister Caluin in this letter earnestly wished that all strife shulde ceasse/ and that yf anie were minded to departe their departure might be suche/ as all occasions off offence might be cut of and cleane take awaie: it was thought good to suche as were determined to go awaie with in s. weekes after/ to folowe his counsaile. And the rather for that some whiche too kethem selues/ to be lerned/ had openly termed their departure a sisme/ wherupon/ they wrote to the pastor Ministers / and whole congregation this letter folowinge and deliuered it in the open congregation.

For so muche as through the benefit off God/ we haue obtained a churche in an other place/ we thought it good to aduertise yow of the same. And to the intent that not onely slaunderous reportes maie ceasse/ but also/ if anie offence be either taken or geuen/ the same maie come to triall/ we desier that yow for your parte woulde apointe 2. Arbyters and we shall appointe other 2. Who hearinge our matters throughbly opened maie witnes where the faulte restethe/ at whiche time/ we will vndertake/ to defende oure departure to be lawfull contrary to the slanderous reportes off some which vnlernedly terme it a schisme. Thus farre brethern we thought good to signifie vnto yow/ thinkinge this to be the onely meanes of oure mutuall quietnes wherof howe desirous we are/ our tedious and chargeable iourney maie be a sufficient proffe/ beinge throughly perswaded/ that hereby stryfe maie be ended chari-

tie

be renued/frindshipe continued/Goddes glory aduaunced/ and oure brethern edified. Fare yewell this 27. off August.

VVilliam VVilliams   Thomas VVeed   Iohn Escot
VVilliam VVhittingham VVilliam Kethe.   Thomas Crofton
Anthony Gilby   Iohn Kelke.   VVilliam VValton
Christopher Goodman. Iohn Hilton.   Laurence Kent
Thomas Cole.   Christ. Soothous   Iohn Hollingham
Iohn Fox.   Nicholas Purfote   Anthony Carier.

When the Pastour had redd this letter openly to the congregation and was desired to knowe when they shulde haue an answere/ he saied vnto them that so farre as he perceiued/ it required none but that whiche might presently be made/ whiche was/ that they might departe seinge they were so minded. It was replied that for so muche as it was manifest that they had byn slaundered not onely by letters into diuers partes / but also/ by some that then were present/ who had affirmed their departure to be a schisme/ and farther/ that they coulde finde no indifferency at their handes: it was thought necessarie to commit the hearinge off that controuersie to lerned and indifferent iudges/ by bothe partes to be chosen wherby the faulte might appear where it was in dede/ and so they either excused or founde giltie.

D. Cox/ at lenght/ tolde them that their letter shulde be considered off/ and an answere shulde be geuen them the fridaie after. On fridaie the 30. off Auguste bothe partes mette: The Pastor (accompanied with the Ministers and elders) spake this vnto them. It seemeth very fonde that arbytrers shuld be apointed to take vpp strife that maie come hereafter/ as your letter signifieth. And furthermore / ye write/ yff anie offence be taken or geuen/ whiche semethe as strange/ for this worde (yff) importethe a dowte/ so that yff ye dowte it is but follie to apointe arbitres. fynally / to excuse your departure/ yow call them vnlerned whiche iudge it a schisme but (saithe) he) he) terme it as yow liste yet can yow not let men to think. And yff arbitres shuld pronounce it to be none/ yet mennes opinions will be diuers.

Now therfore/your answere shall be/that iff anieman be offended either with any priuate mā/ or publiquely/let him or them complaine to vs/ or yff they refuse vs/to the Magistrat.

As for Arbitres/we will appoint none. Then spake Whittingham and saied that it was to him no small wonder that men of suche lerninge and wisedome shuld so shrink in a moste equall requeste/and so/ withowte all reason to cauill where no matter was offred. For/ as concerninge (saithe he) the firste pointe/it was not vnknowen to them that at that time/ thorough their occasion/their was no small contention/ and that seinge they had geuen such offence it coulde not be but that mennes mindes were moued.

And therfore/to thende that contention shulde growe no farther/ Arbytres were very necessary/who neded not to deliberate (as he saied) off thinges to come whiche were vncerteine, but as the letter truly purporteth/ off iniuries longe agoo begonne/yet continued/and hereafter not like to be ended excepte some good meane were vsed to staie their slanderous letters and false reportes / to the vtter perishinge and lose off mennes Good names. And where ye seeme to be offended that the letter shulde call them vnlerned/whiche terme oure departure a schisme (yow omitt saide D. Coxe the 2. pointe/whiche is off no small importaunce) to whom he answered that he thought he did them a pleasure in omittinge thinges of so small value/notwithstandinge/ he woulde obaie his will but (saithe he) as touchinge this worde vnlernedly/it was not vnaduisedly placed. For either they be withowte lerninge/and therfore maie be so called in dede/ or yff they beare the name off lerninge/yet in this they shewed their vnskilfulnes for as muche as euery departure from a congregation was not a schisme/nether were anie that departed for iuste causes schismatikes as we (saith he) will proue vnto yow/yff yow will take oure

Vvittinghā here interrupted.

LVII.

to oure reasonable and moste equall offre. Naie/saithe the pastor/ Arbitres in this point can litle availe for be it they iudged it none/yet mennes thoughtes are free / and we knowe that all men be not off one mynde in sacramentes and predestination/shulde men therfore take arbitres? Also saith he maister Caluin and Bullinger/are against yow. To this was answered/that thoughtes/yff they were not growned vpon Goddes worde/were euell/neither was this controuersie off like force with the matter off the Sacramentes and predestination / notwithstanding / woulde to God that not onely the difference in those articles but also in all other which be off waight and importaunce might be decided by the authoritie off Goddes worde and arbytrement off godly lerned men. But men maie iustly suspecte your cause to be nought which refuse the iudgments off the wise and godly.

And where yow saie that Caluin and Bullinger are against vs/ yow abuse your selff and there names/ for we knowe bothe what they and other wryte as touchinge this matter.

Then the Pastor asked what schisma was but a cuttinge off from the body/and that it was Caluins definition. To this Whittingham answered that he woulde vndertake firste/to proue that definition to be false/ and secondly to be no none off Caluins definition for yff euery cuttinge off from the body shulde be a schisme/ then yow and all other which once had sworne to the pope and now haue refused him are schismatiques. Then the pastor added/ from a churche well reformed. Answere was made that a churche well reformed muste be builded vppon the doctrine off the Prophetes and Apostles / the vnitie whereoff S. Paule comprehendeth in theis wordes: one god/one faithe/one baptisme/ not beggerly ceremonies and obscurations / although that sundry causes besides moued them to departe. Then Maister Treher: en/ asked whither the donatists were not schismatiques.

Yee/saith Whittingham and also heretiques/but yow are deceiued yff yow thinke that they seperated them selues

H ij for

for ceremonies. It is manifest said Treherren, that the churches off Asia were excommunicate as schismatiques for that they kepte not Easter at the same time that the Romaine churche did. And it is no lesse euident said Whitthingham that Ireneus and other godly men aswell off that time, as sithens haue sharply reproued and condemned Pope Victor for the same.

Here D. Coxe put Whittingham in remembraunce that he had not answered to the faultes off the letter. Whittingham tolde him, that as touchinge that poore worde (yff) he marueled howe it coulde Minister anie cauillation, seinge the text ioininge therto was so plaine, whiche declareth bothe the offences by yow geuen and by vs taken. And also your consciences beare yow witnes, the thinge to be moste true excepte a man will be wilfully blinde, and finde a knot in a rushe, so that that worde (yf) mente not that we do, dowte who were oppressed with infinit wronges, but iff they woulde dissemble so farre that they might seeme to dowte theroff, yet at the leaste, they woulde abide the tryall theroff before their Arbitres. But here the disputation brake vp with this plaine and finall answere that arbitres they shuld haue none, and that yff they founde themselues greued, they shulde seeke remedy where they thought Good and he the Pastor with the reste off the congregation woulde answere them.

The nexte daie the Pastour, D. Coxe, maister parry and maister Asheley sent for Whittingham, Thomas Cole, John Fox, William Kethe, Roger harte, John Bilton with certeine other, demandinge off them what shulde be the cause off their departure. Whittingham made answere that the daie before they had declared sufficiently, and yet woulde farther shewe reasons, yff they would permit the controuersie to Arbytrement. And to the intent they shulde not counterfait ignorance (amonge other) theis were some causes: firste, their breach off promes, established with inuocation off goddes name: 2. Their ordreles thrustinge themselues in to the churche. 3. Takinge awaie the order off discipline established before their re their comminge and placinge no other. 4. The accusation off maister Knox their godly Minister off Treason and seekinge his bloude 5. Their ouerthrowinge off the common order, taken and commaunded by the Magistrate 6. The displacinge off officers withowte anie cause alleadged. 7. The bringing in off Papisticall superstitions and vnprofitable Ceremonies whiche were burthens yokes and clogges, besides other thinges, whiche, yff they woulde abide the triall they shulde heare at large. When he and some off the rest had rendred their reasons for their departure to this effecte, certaine warme wordes passed to and fro from the one to the other, and so in some heate departed.

Not many daies after the oppressed churche departed from Franck. to Basill and Geneua, some stayinge at Basill as maister Fox with other. The rest came to Geneua where they were receiued withe great fauour and mutche curtesie, bothe off the magistrates Ministers and people. So soone as they entred their churche, they chose Knox and Goodman for their Pastor, and Gilby requested to suplie the rome till Knox returned owte off France.

The lerned men whiche came from all places to Frank. abowte this matter (when they had donne that whiche they came for, they returned againe from whens they came, and some to other places, where they might saue charges, and not to be either burthened or bownde to the excercises of the congregation, so that, the exile whiche was to many a poore man full bitter, greuous and painefull, was (to some off the greatest persecutours off their poore brethern (as it were, a pleasant progresse or recreation.

But nowe it shall be necessary to declare what order was taken in this newe erected congregation for the prosperous continuance off the same, whiche thinge to do, I cannot by a better meane then placinge here this letter folowinge whiche maister Cole (late deane off Sarum) wrote to a frinde off his, whiles yet he staied (behinde his company) in Franck. amonge them, his letter is yet to be seene.

B iij   The

The holie spirit off God that guideth the children off God in truthe and godlines be your comforte thorough oure mercies seate Jesus Christe, now and for euer Amen.

The tempeste off the swellinge seas whiche in timespaste threntned ship wrack to euery vessell that sailed with a faire winde and full sailes to the porte off blessed truthe, whiche off her selffe is stronge ynoughe, with owre anye barr or wall off mannes inuentions, are somewhat (the lorde be praised) caulmed to me warde, so that withowt farther reasoninge they permit me to my conscience as touchinge their ceremonies.

The cause I iudge is not for that they beare lesse loue to them then in tymes past, but that they perceiue the sturdy defendinge off them, to worke them that they looke not for, or rather, that whiche they are lothe to se, namely, the decreasinge off their companie: yet they labour with policie what they maie or can, to preuent this daunger but yet that whiche they feare, I suppose will fall vpon them, vnlesse god geue them to repent their olde faultes and humble them more to knowe them selues.

They haue set vp an vniuersitie to repaier againe their estimation by mainteinance of lerninge (whiche surely is well done) that was fondly brought in decaie by willfull ignorance, in defendinge off ceremonies, to the whiche Maister horne is chosen to be the reader off the Hebrue lecture, Maister Mullings off the Greke, and Maister Treherren when he is stronge, shall take the diuinitie lecture in hande. Maister Whitthead was appointed therunto but bicause he woulde escape the labour off the lecture (for iuste causes as he saide) he forsooke the pastorall office also, slowtly (as yow knowe) denyinge to be in office anie longer. Great holde there was abowte this matter in the congregation, in so muche as they hasted to a newe election, and verie fewe (as it semed) were off a contrary minde, no, not his owne frindes sauinge
Maister

Maister makebray and Maister Sorby, who desired him to take respit / and the congregation to geue it. But some lookinge for the office themselues woulde not in suche a matter suffer delay/ but againe demaunded off Maister Whithead whither he woulde keepe his office or no supposinge that he whiche had so stowtely denied it in worde/ woulde not soone be flexible to the contrary. But he perceauinge that some woulde haue had him owte one the one side / and by leauinge off it/ his estimation was like to decaie on the other side/ (for many rough wordes were geuen him) when occasion off interte was offred/non respuit conditionem by that meanes bringinge to him selfe wittily/ a triple commoditie/ one / the preuentinge off them whiche looked for the office/ an other/ the refusall off the diuinitie lecture / Thirdly/ a faster growndinge him selff in that office / whiche he lefte in mouthe/ but as it semed/ not in harte. Thus ended that comedie.

But shortly after (notwithstandinge a vehement sermen made for the purgation from mannes inuentions) the seas begin againe to swell/ (so fickle an element is water) for Maister Bent hauinge a childe to Christen purposinge to haue it done simplie/ withowte the bewtifinge off mennes traditions/ came with his childe accordinge to the frenche order whiche we once receiued/ and one to holde it there to professe his faith yff it were required/ but the pastor denied the Christening/ vnles 2. Godmothers were had after the order off the booke/ as concerninge the Godfather/ Maister Makebray (who is nowe comme to that office) supplied it. A lucky matter is attained at Wezell in Westphalia / an open churche for oure Englishe men/ to whiche bicause off nighnesse) they feare many will go from hence / but moo wil come owte off Englande to yt. I pray yow commende me to M. Tell him that Maister wisedom railed on them that were gon to G. Callinge them mad heades with many pretye names / I will not saie vnwysely /. But I maye well say vncharitably / in whiche Sermon / he shewed him

him selff an Antagonist for the booke off Englande/ etc.

Your Thomas Cole.

Shortly after thies thinges to wete/ the 6. off Jan. When as maister Whithead gaue vpp off his owne good will/ as he saide/ the pastorall office/ Maister Horne was in the election to succede him/ who protested that he woulde not medle therwith/ till he were cleared off certeine suspitions which some had bruted to the discredit off his ministerie/ and obtaininge his requeste/ he withe the Seniors entred the churche the first off marche Anno Domini 1556. were they receiued all such persons (as members off that churche) which were contented to subscribe and submit themselues to the orders off the same. From whiche tyme forward the troubles and contions were so sore amonge them/ that who so shall well waie it with due consideration/ I ween/ he shall think it to be the iuste iudgement off our righteous God that fell vpon them/ for supplantinge a churche there before them in great quietnes and off muche sinceritie.

The historie of that sturre and strife which was in in the Englishe church at Franckford from the 13. daie off Jan. Anno Domini 1557. forwarde.

There fell a certeine controuersie the xiij. daie off Jan. at supper betwene Maister Horne the Pastor and Maister Asheley whiche controuersie was handled/ with somewhat more sharpe wordes then was meete/ but yet they so departed/ by the industrie and labour off some certeine persons/ that they dranke wyne one to an other/ and all that strife and contention was thought to be wholie taken awaie. Afterward/ to witt/ the 16. daie off Jan. at one off the clock in the afternoone/

LXIII.

no one/ thre off the elders sent for Maister Asheley in to an howse off one off the Elders and they began to debate the matter with him touchinge an iniurye done/ not to the pastor alone/ but to all the Elders (as they affirmed) and to their ministery which thinge/ Maister Asheley denied that he euer did at any tyme.

The next daie beinge the 17. off Jan. After that publique praiers were ended/ Maister Asheley was by the Pastor and all the Elders called into the churche/ and there/ in the name off them all it was obiected vnto him/ that he had spoken vpon the 13. daie off Jan. in supper while/ certeine wordes tendinge to the slander off them and their ministery.

Asheley answered that he perceiued and vnderstood that they all were offended as in their owne matter/ and that therfore he would not answere before them as competent iudges off the cause/ but would referre the cause/ that he had against the Pastor and them (seinge they shewed them selues an aduersarie parte to him) to the whole churche and Ecclesiasticall discipline. Then the Pastor exhorted him that he would not so proceade/ for yff he so did/ that then they were minded to seeke and demaunde helpe off the magistrate agaynst him After that the 24. off Jan. Asheley himselff handled his owne cause in his owne name before the pastor and elders/ and then in the afternoone/ he sent 2. mē of the churche who/ in his name require the pastors and elders that they would not proceed against him in that cause/ wherin they themselues were a parte/ and therfore not fitt or competent iudges/ but to geue ouer the whole matter to 8. or 10. men vpright in conscience and incliuinge to neither parte/ by whose iudgementes/ iff he were founde in faulte/ he woulde willingly submit himselff to all Ecclesiasticall disciplne. Answere was made him by the Pastor in the name off them all/ that they had receiued their authoritie from the whole churche and woulde reteine and keepe the same till such time as they from vvhom they had receiued it vvoulde againe demaunde it. And in the meane vvhile/ they purposed to proceede thereafter againste

J   all

all suche as had offended and so muche the more seuerely and sharplie against Maister Asheley / by howe muche it might be more profitable for the whole churche / to make him beinge a worshipfull man / an ensample to others to take heed and beware by asheley (that answere beinge receiued the 16. off Jan. Which was a daie off solemne praier) fearinge those thinges whiche Horne had saide before / threateninge him with the Magistrate / when common praier was ended declared the whole matter to the churche and desired that the churche woulde vnderstand off the whole matter betwene the pastor and elders / as the one partie and him selff as thother.

Wherupon certeine men did in the name off the whole churche demaunde off the pastor and elders whither they were a parte against Asheley. The pastor answered in all their names that they were not a parte against him / but that Asheley had slandered them all. Againe / it was demaunded in the name off the churche who were his accusers / to whiche / vvhen the pastor answered nothinge / neither in his owne name / nor in the name of the seniors: Asheley was comaunded by the churche publiquely and openlie to reade those thinges whiche he had comprehended in vvrytinge concerninge his cause. Afterward the pastor and elders were asked vvither those thinges vvhiche Asheley had redd vvere true. The pastor answered in all their names that they would not ansvvere either more largely or anie othervvise / to anie questions then they had ervvhile ansvvered and so the congregation vvas dismissed vvithowte ansvvere / yet not vvith ovvte cōtempt as was thought. The same daie at afternoone / Maister Hales / vvho vvas absent when theis thinges vvere done) vnderstanding that this matter tended to more greuous striffe and contention / did vvryte his letters to some certeine personnes that semed desirous off the peace off the churche / and desired / that they would come together the nexte daie after to the churche / to consulte / and deliberate what were the beste vvaie to pacifie this trouble and turmoile before it waxed more stronge / or shulde be more publisshed abroad and made better knowen to the senate or magistrate. The

LXV.

The very dryfte and purpos off the letters/together with them that were called/ as them also whiche came to the place appointed/dothe appeere by the letters themselues/ the copie whereoff insewethe.

The superscription.

To his brethern off the Englishe churche.

Maister Crawley	Maister Nowel	Maister Dakies
Maister Railton	Maister Carell.	Maister Benthame
Maister warcope.	Maister Kente	Maister Brikbeke.
Maister Faulconer	Maister Kelke	Maistee Sutton.
		Maister Christ. Hales.

Iohn Hales sendethe greetinge in the lorde.

Deare brethern / that whiche is to me greuous to heare/ to witt / that striffes are arisen in oure churche/ whiche tende either to the dissolution off the churche/or to the hurte and destruction of the poore/wherefore I pray yow whose names are in the subscription off the letters/that(if yow shall so think good) we maie meete to morowe in the morninge in oure churche/there to consulte and take aduise what maie be the beste waie to quiete this styrre/ to the glorie off God and our owne quietnes. god geue vs his peace. This 26. of Jan. 1557.

Your louinge brother
Iohn Hales.

I pray yow/that so many off yow as will mette at the tyme and place apointed to put downe your names/ lest some parhap maie come in vaine.
Nowe all those whose names are before rehersed came except maister warcope.

I ij   After

After consultation and aduise taken/ it semed best to al them that were called together and mett there/ that the nexte daie after/ one off them in all their names shulde deale withe the Pastor and elders/ that sith Ashley complained that they were aduersarie parte vnto him/ they woulde suffer the churche/ or some suche certeine persons as the churche shulde appoint/ to take knowledge off the cause/ and to heare firste wither they were an aduersarie parte to Ashley whiche if they were not founde to be/ then the knowledge off the matter shuld be put back againe to the and that withe the ignominie and shame off him that had appealed from them. But yff they were founde to be aduersary parte/ that then it shulde seeme vniuste/ that they shuld sit in their owne cause as iudges/ but more meete and vpright it would be/ that then the churche shulde knowe and vnderstand off the whole matter/ wherupon the next daie after/ that is to saie/ the 15 off Jan. when praiers were ended/ the matter was proposed to the pastor and Elders/ by one apointed for that purpose. When this counsaile was once knowē/ the minister by the consent off the Elders drew owte off his bosome a decree whiche the magistrate off that city had made/ and redd it with a lowde voice before the whole churche. The decree beinge redd he added in graue wordes/ that theis oure assemblies and meetinges woulde be verie daungerous not to vs onelie but to all the congregations off strangers. for it was greatlie to be feared least the magistrate beinge offended withe such meetinges/ did not shut vp the gates off oure churche alone/ but also off all the strange churches. And therfore that he (to thend he might in good season prouide for suche daungers) would surely by Ecclesiasticall discipline handle according to his deserte/ maister Gales (who then by occasion of sicknes was absente) the author of that assemblie/ and that he woulde pronounce of vs generally/ that if it were not schismaticall/ yet/ that it did withowte dowte ted to schisme/ how so euer we excused oure mindes ād purposes. moreouer he affirmed/ that we had don verie yll/ in that we had excluded/ and shut owte certeine

which

which came into the churche in the time off oure consultation and meetige. Anſwere was made in the names of the churches/ that that decree off the magiſtrate was by them before, bothe read ouer throughly/vnd also verie diligentlie waied/and that they iudged that decree to be moſt vpright and iuſtlie to be feared off wicked and lewde men/ſuch as were ſectaries and factious perſons and that they did aſſuredly knowe that the threats of that decree did nothinge at all concerne them who were mett together to make peace and vnitie/ and that they for this deede did ſo litle feare the angre and diſpleaſure of the magiſtrate that they truſted the magiſtrat woulde praiſe them for this matter/yff parhappes he knewe off the thinge it ſelff and that therfore they were aſſembled and comme together that the whole matter might be quietlie ended amonge themſelues and not brought before the magiſtrat. for where we (ſaie they) were baniſhed men/and had by the meanes off a very good magiſtrate/receiued that ſinguler and moſte excellent benefit off reſte and quietnes/we ſhulde do that whiche ſhulde be moſt vnfit and vnſeemly for vs/iff we ſhulde by occaſion of our ſtriffes and hurley burlies/trouble the magiſtrate/and to render vnto that verie good Magiſtrate vnquietnes/ troubles and ſtirrs whiche ſhulde be verie euell thankes/for ſo great a benefit off quietnes and reſt as we haue receiued. And we affirmed that we ſo muche the more diligentlie and wilingly labored in pacifiynge and endinge this controuerſie bicauſe there were amongeſt vs certeine/who raſhly and withowte aduiſe/brought vnto the Magiſtrat all light and ſmall controuerſies/whiche might eaſilie haue bin determined and ended amonge our ſelfes/herein deſeruinge no fauour at all either at the the handes off ſo Good a Magiſtrat/whom they oftimes withowte cauſe troubled/or of their countrie men whom they by thies their priuie complaints and accuſations did amonge ſtrangers ſlander as vnquiet and troubleſome men/and that they had done no leſſe diſpleaſure to the goſpell we profeſſe/ (whiche by occaſion off ſuche accuſations/is comonlie euell ſpoken off amonge the aduersaries) then to that so good a magistrate and to their owne countriemen. And that we therfore (to thende the Magistrate might not be troubled/ nor our nation slaundered as vnquiet and troublesome/ nor the worde off God through vs euell spoken off) met together to take counsaile and auise howe ai the matter might be peaceably ended and for no other cause or purpose. And where it was obiected that in that decree off the Magistrat there was no mention at all made/ either off the whole churche/ or off the authoritie off whole churche: We answere (say they) that we do not so interprete the Magistrate decree/ as though yt were the Magistrats minde and pleasure to take from the churche the right and authoritie due to the Churche and make the whole Churche subiecte to some certeine persone. For we bothe well inoughe knowe by the example off the frenche churche in a like controuersie / and we haue tried that so verie good a Magistrate hathe very great care off the churche. And as concerninge Maister Bales/ yt was answered/ that he was then absente/ by reason off his sicknesse/ and not for seate/ or that he was giltie to him selff off any ill.

And concerninge oure whole purpose and business/ bycause 't was said thoughe oure myndes parhaps were vpright/ yet the dede it selff was/ yff not schismaticall/ yet verelie tendinge to schisme/ answere was made in all our names that we woulde render accompte aswell off oure myndes and purpose before God/ as off our dede before the whole churche / and that vnder perill and paine off the laste punishement that Ecclesiasticall discipline can apointe/ or yff the matter so require/ before the ciuyll Magistrate in paine off oure lyffe. And as touchinge them that were not admitted in to the churche/ to our consultation/ it was answered that we were vniustlie accused/ for that it was not a publick and common assemblie of the whole churche. But a meringe of some certeine persons to consulte of that whiche might be profitable/ and that therfore they had no greater iniurie done the in not beinge at the consultation to whiche they were not called or sent for/ then if

they

had not byn admitted in to some certeine priuate stoue or howse. for as touching the churche / seinge it was then emptie and voide off people/ it was/ as it were/ a priuate howse. Neither is euery assemblie mett there to be counted the churche. For when the pastor or some other readeth there a lecture / or moderateth the disputations/ it is not then a church but a scoole. And therfore/ not the place/ but the company off men gathered together did make a churche or congregation. Afterwards/ it was skarcely by many wordes obtained off the pastor and Seniors / that the churche might withowt their fauour and good will meete together for the finishing and takinge vp off this controuersie/ and vprightly determine whether the said pastor and elders were an aduersarie parte to ashley yea or no which thinge yet at the lenght the pastor and elders graunted to the churche. And the pastor and Elders beinge required and desired that they would together be present with vs in the congregation / they answered that there was no suche nede/ nether that they would at anie hande hinder vs. The next daie after/ to wit/ the 29. off Jan. the pastor and Elders agreinge therto/ as is saide before / when the whole churche was mette together/ maister hales/ who then was somewhat better/ and was present when they began to take aduise and coũsaile/ rose vp and spake to this purpose. My brethern (saithe he) seinge J am accused of the pastor before the whole churche/ as the author of schisme or of a schismaticall facte/ or at the least tendinge to schisme/ if yow also iudge of me in like sorte J will departe oute off this companie/ as one beinge vnmeete to tarie amonge yow in this assemblie. This beinge saide/ he addressed himselff to departe/ Afterwardes/ he was called back by all the men there assembled and intreated to abide amongest them. Afterwarde he drewe foorth those letters by whiche he had called certaine men together to make peace and ende the stirre/ as is before saide / and preferred them to the church to be openly redd. Whiche letter beinge redd/ that/ his dede was iudged off all them that were present/ be the honest and most meete for a Christian man ne-

ther

LXX.

ther that anie man that had called either others to make peace by their meetinge/ was for suche a facte to be accounted a schismatick. Then they were all desired/ that seinge they had so iudged and determined/ they would appoint this their sentence to be registred and put downe in writinge / that it might stande in steed off a recorde and testimonye/ not for Maister Hales onely but for all other in the like case/ and with all/ that this newe and present vpstartinge matter might by their iudgemēts be decided and ended least it might bringe forth and stirre vp new contentions amonge them. Wherupon it was put downe in wrytinge to this effecte. Iff two/ foure/ eight/ twelue or mo or lesse/ meete in the churche when it was voide off people/ praier and other exercises/ or els in priuate howses to make peace betwene some members off the churche/ or to consulte off anie other thinge profitable for the church that that their dede and acte shulde not in anie case be iudged or esteemed vnorderlie/ seditious/ schismaticall/ or tendinge to schisme.

Neither that he whiche either by writinge or worde off mouth had so called them together shulde be thought to be the author off anie schisme or a schismaticall facte or tendinge to schisme and diuision. And bicause nowe no place off speakinge in the congregation withowte offence did seeme anie more to be left to anie man / it was ordeined the saide 29. off Jan. that it shulde be lawfull for any man hauinge before desired/ off the pastor / elders / and whole churche licence and libertie to speak/ to shewe his iudgement and opinion in the churche witowt any reproch off a disordered dede therfore/ so it be, that he did it godly quietlie and soberlie. Yff he shulde speake anie vngodly thinge that thē it was lawfull for the pastor and Seniors/ or anie eff them foorth with to commaunde him to holde his toung. The laste daie off Jan. beinge the Sabath daie after morninge praier was ended/ pardon was offred of all priuate offences/ by the pastor in his owne name and the name off the elders to all the people off the churche ād in like sorte the people were desired to pardon them yet in sus-

che

che sorte this was done that the Pastor and Elders woulde reserue to themselues suche causes as concerned their Ministerie/ to be pursued and followed off them. It was answered againe in oure names off the churche/ that we in like sorte did pardon all men/ all priuate grudges/ yet/ that the churche did accordinge to their example reserue vnto it selff publike causes belonginge to the churche and the libertie theroff quietlie and Christianly to be pursued and folovved/ vvhich ansvvere althoughe it were measured by the rule off that pardon and forgeuenes vvhiche the pastor had before offred/ yet/ it did no white at al please him whiche thing also I warrāte yow he did not dissemble. Afterwards/ the pastor and elders suffered that the same daie in the afternoone/ the church shulde againe meete/ and shulde trie owte and knowe the matter betvvene them and Asheley/ to vvit/ vvhither they vvere an aduersary parte/ to Ashley yea or no/ But the Pastor and Elders beinge desyred that they also vvoulde be present/ they vvoulde not therto agree. Wherfore the churche beinge gathered together in the afternoone/ it was iudged by the testimonie off some meete mē and by this also/ that in the vvhole churche there coulde no other be founde that woulde accuse Ashley but the pastor and elders (for it vvas 3. times verie diligently enquired of and published amōge the people/ that if their vvere anie in the vrhole churche whiche either vvould or coulde accuse maister Ashley/ he shulde then vter it) It vvas I saie iudged and determined that the Pastor and Elders/ vvere an aduersarie parte to Maister Ashley and that therfore they vvere not fit and competent iudges in that matter. Furthermore/ it vvas fullie decreed that the Pastor and elders in suche causes as in vvhiche they vvere an aduersary parte were not fit arbitres or iudges/ but that suche causes did apperteine and belōge/ either to the knovvledge off the congregation or off such as the congregation vvoulde appointe to that purpos. And bycause the pastor and elders haue bene oftētimes desyred to be present vvithvs and yet vvoulde not (notvvithstanding that they themselues suffred the congregation to meete together) leaste parhapp some deceite might be amonge many of the congregation as

B   thoughe

LXXII.

thoughe it were not off it sellf lawfull, or to small purpose to apointe anie thinge withowte the pastor and elders (whiche thing afterwarde tried) it was decreed that iff the pastor and elders were required to be present at an assemblie and woulde not come, that the assembly was lawfull notwithstandinge their absence, and that those thinges whiche they decreed shulde be had and esteemed as a lawfull decree. Theis Ecclesiasticall decrees and ordinaunces, whiche euen nowe were rehersed were subscribed vnto with the names off 33. persons whiche is a great deale the bygger parte off the churche, and the 2. off February were offred vpp to the pastor and Elders in the name off the whole churche with this protestation folowinge. We present vnto yow theis oure decrees and ordinaunces agreing with the right and reason and not contrary to the holie scriptures, desyringe to haue yow knowe them and further requiring that yow woulde with vs consent, yelde and subscribe to the same. Or yff ye will not so do, shewe we praye yow vpright reasons and good causes why ye refuse. For we are ready to correcte and amend oure faultes yff they be shewed vs, at the monition off any priuate person, but muche more at yours the pastor and Elders. For as we desier their wisedomes to come to perfecte truthe: so we will not thorough stubbernes defende anie errour, beinge shewed vnto vs to be an errour in dede. Yet notwitstanding, afterward vpon in the aforesaie daie off February, the Pastor did in his owne name and in the name off the Elders, openly reade certeine written letters to whiche he and the Seniors had before in the presence off the churche subscribed their names. The summe theroff was this. Seinge the churche had left vnto them a vaine shadowe onelie off authoritie withowte anie other matter, that therfore they did in oure presence shake off from themselues and vtterly forsake all Ecclesiasticall ministerie and seruice to the churche.

Maister Nowel was the mouthe for the rest.

Amonge other thinges they added this that we had geuen them a cause to complaine off vs to the magistrate, but that for oure sakes they wolde not do it. Afterward some of them

them departed and sate downe in private mennes places, neither woulde they suffer so muche as to be called by the name off pastors and Elders. Then one in the name off the whole, hauinge fullie shewed before, that there was no iuste cause geuen them by the churche, so to forsake their ministerie, did afterward in the name of the whole churche verie earnestly desier them that they woulde not in suche manner forsake and leaue the churche that had deserued no suche thinge at their handes.

This was with moste earneste and effectuall wordes required off them, thre or foure tymes in the name off the whole churche, but they remained willfull and obstinate in their purpos, not so muche as once suffringe themselues to be called by the name off pastors and elders. Then at the lenght, it was shewed vnto them in the name off the whole churche, that the churche woulde not admit that their forsakinge of their ministerie, but would stil take and esteme them for their pastor and Elders. And when one in the name off the churche did accuse the pastor and Chambers to be suche as had abused the churche, leauinge it and forsakinge it in suche manner withowte anie cause or reason shewed, and did in the name off the churche desier them to make answere vnto him concerninge this their dede, they vtterlie refused the same. But horne who then was Pastor, hastely takinge a penne, wrote to this purpos in a pece of paper in his owne name and in the name off the elders. Where as we are vrged and pressed by one in the name off the churche to make answere, we generally answere, that whensoeuer we shal be ordinarelie demaunded before the churche or them whiche the churche shall apointe, we will then answere, or if we shall be called before the ciuill magistrate we will ther answeare. other answeare then this they woulde geue none, to anie off the questiõs whiche we had proposed in all oure names of the churche. (and they assigned this writinge by puttinge to their names) where as indede this was not onelie to answere nothinge at all, but also to pretẽd a cloaked cause of answeringe nothinge at all. Moreouer, they were desired in the name of the churche that they woulde deli-

K ij uer

uer to the churche the letters signed withe their owne hādes / by whiche they had shewed their renounsall and denyinge of the ministerie: or if they woulde not do that / that thē against a certeine daie they woulde graūte and giue to the churche a coppie therof. But neither woulde they geue them the letters whiche they had in their bosome neither woulde promisse any coppie to the churche / who moste earnestlie required the same off thē. At the laste / the pastor and elders departed / some certeine fewe folowinge thē / but the multitude remained and so farre forthe as they coulde remember / committed to writinge the actes off that daie and the summe off those letters (by whiche the Pastor and Elders had willingly put them selues from the ministerie) ād for witnesse subscribed thereto with thirtie and there names. The next daie after / that is / the 3. off February the Pastor and Elders beinge called off the churche by the Deacon / to intreate off makinge peace / they came together ād met. But the Pastor and elders set them downe in priuate places. Afterwardes / the pastor (because one speakinge in the congregation did not by and by so soone as he bad him holde his peace) fayned that he woulde departe. But when he perceyued that verie fewe folowed him / and by some consailed / he returned / and suddanly placed himselff in the pastors place / and called the elders to him / whiche thinge / before he had refused to do although he were by the whole churche verie instantly and ernestlie required therto. Then / he spake to this effecte: we in dede (saith he) did displace oure selues from the ministerie / notwithstandinge / absolutely and fullie we did it not / but vnder this condition onely / yff yow shulde proceade to deale in suche sorte as yow haue done against the olde ād receiued discipline. Nowe then / yff ye goo forwarde as yow haue appointed and purposed / then will we wholie and alltogether displace oure selues from oure Ministeries / but yff yow will obaie the olde discipline then will we continew pastor and elders as we are. Answere was made that there was nothinge at all conteined in the olde discipline / wherby they might medle with / or proceed againste the pastor and elders / iff parhapps they ps they were founde faultie and in some offence. Moreouer/ that there was nothinge put downe concerninge suche causes/as in whiche the pastor and elders were an aduersarie parte/and therfore it was desired that they woulde suffer the discipline in that behalff to be amended and to be made more perfect. Nowe the pastor beinge offended as it shuld seeme/ with so free speeche wolde imediatlie againe haue bin gone/ and rann euen to the churche dore/but yet seinge but fewe folowinge him/by the counsaile and aduise off certeine persons he returned/and sat him selff downe in the pastors place with the seniors.

And in like sorte/ by and by againe vppon the suddaine/ he ran for the thirde tyme/ but within a litle while after he returned and planted him selff in the pastors accustomed place. Afterwards intretie was made with the pastor and elders in the name off the church/ that they would suffer Ashleis cause (in whiche matter they themselues were founde at the lenght to be an aduersarie parte) and the hearinge theroff to come before the churche/ And that the churche woulde (yff Ashley were founde faultie) verie sharply and seuerely punishe him/ and in this behalff aboundantly satisfie the pastor and Elders and all good men. But the pastor and Elders would at no hande suffer that. And as concerninge the amendinge off the discipline/the pastor saide that he and the elders with certeine others by the authoritie off the church beinge ioined vnto them woulde (yff the churche so thought good) amende the discipline. But answere was made vnto bothe/ in the name off the churche. First that it was verie vniust that/ the churche shuld not be suffred to haue iudgement and determination. For therby the authoritie and right off churche was wholie as it were/taken from the churche. To the seconde it was answered that sith suche ordinaunces and decrees were to be made/as by whiche the Pastor and Elders shulde be hereafter deteined in ditie (some off them also beinge already accused) it shulde be vniuste dealing to admit them to the framinge and makinge off suche decrees. And when they affir-

B iij med

med they would answere no other thinge/ and they were desired to suffer thos things to be committed to writinge whiche were done alreadie/ they woulde not agree/ but the pastor saynge he was a colde made himself ready to departe/ and goinge his waie a fewe folowinge him/ he pronownced/ that he dissolued the assemblie. But the companie that taried in the churche and wrote the doings of that daie by their decree/ and appointed 8. men to amend the discipline/ and Afterward to offre it the churche to be seene of the/ did also apointe other 8. men (of whiche 8. three/ allwaies stuck the pastor) arbitres and iudges to decide the cause betweene the pastor and elders/ and Ashley. Theis are their names, maister Railton/ maister Warcope/ M. Beike M. faulconer/ M. Bentham M. Cockroft/ M. Carell and M. Wilson. Three off theis were addicted the to pastor but M. Bentham and M. Beike alwais shewed themselues indifferent and equall to bothe sides. From that time forwarde the pastor and elders and certaine others beinge often times called of the churche/ by the Deacons and certeine other to intreate of makinge peace and agrement/ would neuer apere or be present.

  Morouer the pastor and the Deacons/ and certaine painefull poore men/ ceased bothe from preachinge and also the Ecclesiasticall lectures and other ordinary functions and charges whiche they ought to haue executed/ neither woulde they come to solemne and publick praiers in the churche. notwithstanding the churche yet thorough Gods fauour obserued bothe publike praiers/ sermons and Ecclesiasticall lectures/ and all other things accustomed and minded to keepe them so longe as the godlie Magistrats shulde suffer and graunt the same. And no other matter did so muche spread abroad throughowt the citie as the fame and reporte off oure striffes and as the dede off maister Horne and Maister Chambers. For when they off themselues had forsaken the churche and had by their example stirred vp some other with their families to do the like/ and some off theis nowe frequented and went/ partely to the frenche churche/ and partly to the Germanie churches/

churches/the matter nowe coulde not anie longer be hyd and in secret seinge it was published, and knowen not thorowe the citie alone, but the same theroff ran to other strangers also, whiche matter and busines withe their brethern, woulde to God they had chosen, rather to haue had it ended quietlie and peaceably in their owne churche, then in such troblesome sorte to haue consulted so greatly, bothe to their owne dishonestie and oures. The fourth daie off Februarie, which was Thursdaie and appointed for publick praier, the pastor who that daie shuld haue preached, and all the Elders were absent. Nowe the pastor beinge before by the Deacon desired in the name off the churche that either he himselff would preache or apoint some other in his place, made answere, that neither woulde he preach him selff nor apointe anie other. For that matter did nothinge at all belong vnto him. After praiers were ended some there were that disputed and reasoned in the pastors behalff and saide, that that assemblie whiche remained after the pastors departure (in as muche as he had authoritie to call together the churche and to breake vp the assemblie and he goinge his waie saide, that he brake vp that assemblie) was no lawfull assemblie. To whom it was (in the name off the churche) answered, that Maister Horne had put owte himselff from his pastorall dewtie, and therfore, both for that matter and manie other recited before amonge the Act. of the 2. daie of Feb. he had not anie authoritie, or any maner of right either to gather together or to breake vp the assemblie. And although it were graunted that he were their lawfull pastor, yet it was affirmed that the churche was aboue the pastor and not the pastor aboue the churche ād that therfore thowghe the pastor departed, before the actes off that daie were confirmed, and pronounced that he brake vp the assemblye yet was the assemblie whiche remained ād taried behind a lawfull assemblie, ād had authoritie to make effectuall decrees, by whiche they might binde all ād euery mēber of the churche without exception. And that this question (whither the pope was aboue the churche or the churche aboue the pope) was stirred vp in the councelles off Constance and Basill, and was decided

LXXVIII.

ded also by the authoritie off the schole off parise ioyned ther to. Nowe they whiche reasoned in the pastors behalff did seeme by the space off certein daies after, to approue thes 2. councells, for they placed the pastor aboue the churche. They brought foorth openly all the olde store and howsholde stuffe of Pighius and Eckius of the primacie of the pope, vnder the name off the Pastorall authoritie and for the proffe theroff. The actes and disputations off that daie were in testimonie, signed and confirmed vvith two and thirtie names. The 5. off Februa. Maister horne and the seniors beinge required off the congregation by a deacon to come and treate off reconciliation woulde not appeare. After this there were 3. Messengers sente from the congregation vnto them, off whom, one was to be specially reuerenced off all that be off the congregation bothe for his age and grauitie, the other 2 specially well lerned, to the intent they shuld be moued by theis so honest a company off Messengers sent by the congregation. Theis men, whē they had in the churches name instantly desired and praied them that they woulde come to the congregation and there common brotherly amonge themselues for a quyete agrement to be had, so as the matter might not come to the magistrates eares, nor be bruted anie farther abroade to the great infamie of oure nation, coulde do no good with them at all, for they saide they woulde not come vnlesse they were ordinarily called. As for other answere at that present they would make none. When this answere was declared to the congregation, it was determined that for asmuche as R. Horne had openly put himselfe owte off his pastorship by writinge subscribed with his owne hand, and confirmed the same by wordes and deedes in lōge absteining from preachinge and other pastorall functions, and affirminge that suche matters were no point off his charge: In as muche as now beinge called of the churche, he will not appere, and so absteinethe all together from publicke praiers and all Ecclesiasticall meetigs: And for asmuche also as the Seniors come not at the meetings of the churche, leaste the congregation thorough the forwardnes of

the

the saied Robart Horne and absence off the Seniors/ beinge voide and destitute off common praier/ preachinge/ and reading the scriptures shulde be vtterly dissolued/ that certein men shuld take charge off the churche and for all things to be done in the congregation as it hathe by Gods goodnesse byn yet hitherto done.

Other decrees also whiche are specified in the Acts off the 5. daie off Februa. they establisshed: all whiche everie one that was present confirmed by his name subscribed with his owne hande/ as they were wont to do in other actes and decrees. And to the decrees off that daie subscribed 33. hands. But in this behalff bothe maister Horne and maister Chambers and other in their behalf did finde verie muche faulte with vs/ for that we had proceaded vnordinarilie/ that is (yow must vnderstand) contrary to the olde discipline. For where they coulde not iustly finde faulte with those thigs that the churche had done/ they made cauillation at the manner off doinge off things as an vnordinary mañer. And we answered as well manye other things grewe now by occasion off that matter/ as this chiefly: in case Maister Chambers or anie other man/ either woulde or coulde shewe anie ordinarie waie in the olde discipline wherby the congregation / or anie other might commence matter/ and proceade against him or againste a Senior or Seniors beinge accused: or howe we might proceade ordinarely according to the olde discipline in causes/ wherin he ãd the seniors were the one parte as they nowe were proued to be: And yff Maister Horne/ or anie other man either woulde or coulde shewe the tytle or wordes in the ould Discipline/ wherin this ordinarie waie is set forthe and conteined: Then we would confesse that we had gon amisse owt off the ordynary way and olde discipline. But yff neither he nor anie other woulde or coulde shewe in deede / that they would not be discontent at vs that reduced the congregation to their right authoritie and amended that olde discipline as a thinge amisse/ or filled it vp as a thinge vnperfect and broughte the matter to the hearinge off the churche as it ougyt to be:

L And

And that they woulde at length geue ouer, to vaunte them selues so off the order which they neuer had, or to blame vs hereafter for proceading vnordinarely. The summe off this anfwere, we dryued into certein Articles, and sent them pryuately to Maister Horne to peruse, requiring his answere to the same vnd also we sticked them vpon the pulpit in the churche where they remained a great many daies. And where it was required in that same writinge, that Maister Horne, or the Seniors or some other man shulde make answere vnto thes matters, there is no man yet hitherto that hather made anye answere, either by worde or by writinge, sauinge that Maister Horne fallinge to his olde generall answere, saide, he woulde make answere when he were ordinarely called or questioned withe for by this shift he thinkethe he vndoeth all dowtes at once, where as in dede, to answere after that sorte, is to answere nothing at all, but to pretend false causes to holde his tonge when he is able to shewe no reason for himselff. For this was his meaninge that he is not ordinarely called nor questioned withall, nor accused ordinarely, sauinge onely before himiselff, and the Seniors as Iudges, Where as they bothe in their geuinge ouer off their ministery, and in the principall cause against maister Asbley were the aduersary parte so that by his iudgement there is no ordinary waie to medle against the pastor and Seniors excepte they call themselues to be hearers of their owne cause and their owne Judges themselues. For other ordinary waie against the pastor and Seniors in that olde discipline off theirs, neither he nor anie other shall be hable to shewe.

After this, when those 8. Persons which were appointed by the Churche to heare the variance betwene Maister Horne and Maister Chambers one thone side, and Maister Asley on the other side, shulde preceade in the hearinge off that matter, Maister Horne and Maister Chambers whiche had absented themselues nowe 11. daies from the churche were commaunded by the Magistrate the 12. off February (for that daye) they and certeyne others were seen with the Magi

Magistrate) that they shuld in no wise comme at our church, when we harde off yt / we had maruell / fyrste that the matter was comme to the Magistrats eare (for Maister Horne and the reste testified the 2. off February by their owne hand writinge / that they would neuer open it to the Magistrate) and secondarely / seinge Maister Horne and Maister Chambers coulde by no meanes be intreated to come to the churche yt semed a wonder that yt was commaunded by the Magistrate that they shulde not come / as though they had byne desyrous to come / whiche in dede neded not.

Therfore / the moste parte thought that that commaundement was obtained by their owne sute / at the Magistrates hands / both that such persons as knewe not the matter / shuld be perswaded that yt was longe off the Magistrats commaundement that they did not their offices in the Church. Where as before this Commaundement was geuen they had off a purposed frowardnes absented themselues now allready more then ten dayes from the congregation. And also besides / that the congregation might not proceade agaynst them seinge the Magistrate commaunded them that they shulde not appeere. And this was the very let in dede why the congregation proceaded not in hearinge and determining off the varyance betweene Maister Horne and Chambers off the one partie and Ashley on the other.

And in this they burthen vs maliciously with owr cause / As thoughe we woulde haue Ashley ridd from Judgment off that maiter / and as though that were the onely thinge whiche was sought in oure contention / where as in deede yt was longe off them that his cause was not determined. We therfore / hauing knowledge off this matter / for feare least we shulde be falsely accused / as though we had vttered ytto the Magistrate / and had seemed / first to haue accused our brethern vnto the Magistrate / whiche we might not abide to do / assembled toge

L ij ther

LXXXII.

ther in the churche the 13. off Februar. and there was openly recited in writing, this that folowith. Forasmuche as oure contention is alreadie bruted abroad not onely through this citie but also come to the Magistrats eare. (for we heare saie that maister Horne and maister Chamber were commaunded by the magistrat yester daie that is the 12. off Febr. that they shulde in no wise come at the congregation till the magistrate had fuller knowledge off the matter) we professe that neither Maister Horne nor Maister Chamber nor no man els was complained vpon to the magistrate by vs or any off vs, or by oure meanes / but that we sought rather by all diligent endeauor / that the matter shuld not come abroade / but that all matters might haue byn secretly agreed amonge oure selues and that we woulde all men shulde vnderstand by this oure writinge. This done / those that knewe themselues to be of an vpright cōsciēce in this behalf were requyred to set their handes to that writinge / and so there were 37. handes subscribed as appearethe in the actes off the 13. off Febru. And were Maister Horne and Maister Chamber beinge so often desyred by all instant means off the congregation that they woulde be content to haue all matters pacified amonge vs by brotherly communication / did neuer suffer themselues to be talked with all off anie matter / leaste they shuld afterward alleadge to suche as knewe not the matter / that they did it off force bicause off the magistrates commaundement / whiche forebad them to come to the congregation. All the tyme wherin they absented themselues / and contemned so manie desires and intreties off the churche to haue met vpon agrement makinge / before anie commaundement was geuen them off the magistrate (whiche commaundement notwithstandinge maie seeme that they at lenght for the causes before mentioned procured themselues) was recorded amonge the Actes off that 13. off Febru and confirmed by the testimonies off 37. names subscribed as in the acte appearethe more at large.

The 14. off Febru. those 8. whiche were appointed the 5. off Febru. by the congregation to amende the discipline / presented

sented the booke off the Discipline to the congregation agayne and the congregation allowed it. And those matters that were altered or augmented in the discipline were such as specially perteined to those causes / wherin the pastor and seniors were the one parte / and howe it muste be proceaded against the pastor and seniors / in case anie off them were accused. For concerninge theis thinges there was neuer a worde in the olde discipline. And where in the olde discipline there was no certeine mention / howe the churche shulde be gouerned / and seinge maister Horne and other had now vtterly forsaken the congregation / who in leauinge there offices had drauen away with them the moste parte off them that were appoynted preachers / and disposinge off the churche monie / were more largely and more trulie set forthe and expressed.

For where maister Chamber had authoritie to gather all godly mennes almese for the poore off the congregation confirmed vnto him (as he him selff required) in writinge / signed by the pastor and seniors and certeine other off the chieff men off the churche with their owne handes / and had exercised the same gatheringe nowe a yere and halfe / that he alone / shulde receiue all / he alone distribute / and be accomptable to no man and he alone to be priuie to the mony / (that matter) were he neuer so faithfull a man) semeth verie suspitious to him and hurtefull to the churche / yff he shulde dye suddanly as the state off man is casuall: And the example also shulde seeme pernitious to the churche least parhapp an other man off small fidelitie shuld by the same reason drawe all the churche mony in to his owne onely handes.

And for as muche as the Deacons (vnto whom the charge off the churche monie semeth to apperteine by the worde of God / and by the example off all rightly instituted churches) in oure congregation had not a mite to bestowe: for their were made Deacons honest men in dede / but yet such as for their pouertie semed not fit men to whom the common mony shuld be comitted: and by that coulour Maister Chamber thought he might with owte controlinge receiue all the comon

A iij   monie

LXXXIIII.

monye in his owne handes alone. The congregation thought good to haue a deaconshipp appointed more vprightly accordinge to the rule described in the Actes off the Apostles / and the example off other Godly instituted churches / and to the intent the Church mony might be medled with all by the Deacons with owte all suspition it is prouided in the amendinge off the discipline that suche men shulde be chosen Deacons / as be not onely off a most aproued Good fidelitie / but also suche as were able hansomly to liue off their owne withowte anie nede off the Churches Almes. And in dede this seemed to be nowe so muche the more necessary / for that many complained : some that the almes whiche they receyued before priuatlie off priuate frindes was taken vpp by the waye / sythens Maister Chamber began to gather / as in dede Maister Horne then Pastor threatned openly owte off the pulpit in his Sermon sayinge that he woulde stoppe all mennes vente (as he termed it) and receiptes. Againe / some complaine that they coulde haue nought at Maister Chambers hande / but after beseching and vnreasonable longe delais / some that they coulde haue nothing withowte byter vpbraids and some / that they could obtaine nothing off gyfte but onely off loane / and other some that they coulde gett nought at all. So that nowe it semed requisite off necessytie to seeke some remedie for theis mischeues. All whiche complaints we shall be constrained off extreamie necessitie to put in to one seuerall peece off worke touching the whole matter and communicatinge it to good men. And concerning the Discipline / seinge there was no certeine expresse waye in the olde discipline how the congregation shuld be gouerned / ne ther coulde anie longe quietnes indure so longe as Maister Horne had the gouernement by that discipline. And seing nowe Maister Horne and Maister Chambers haue vtterlie forsaken the Churche / not onely themselues / but also haue drawen awaie with them many other / and of them / the most parte such as were appointed preachers and readers off the Scriptures : so as they might plainely appeere to seke nothinge els but that

the

the congregation beinge destitute off preaching and reading (as thoughe it coulde not stand withowt those men) shulde be vtterlie broken vpp: the congregation was off necessitie enforced to deuise and prouide for some certeine waie for the gouerning off the churche, wherby the congregation might be set at a fyrme and a constant quietnes.

After this 14. off Februa2. preachers off the frenche and Fleinishe Churches and Maister Valeran pullain came to the congregation with the Magistrats Edicte. The meaninge off the edicte was, that Maister Horne, Maister Chambers, Maister Isaac and the reste off the Seniors shulde be restored into their former full authoritie and that Maister Horne shulde do the office off pastor, and they off Seniors in our churche till the Magistrates might haue the hearing and determining off the matter more at large. And yt was commaunded, that all suche men as had anie thing to saie against Maister Horne and the reste, shulde exhibit the same to the Magistrate in writing. Maister Horne, the decre beinge red consulting first with some off his complices, as in a newe matter that he neuer knewe before, said to this effectet that he was ready to obeie the honorable Magistrate, as concerninge other functions belonginge to the Pastor, that is to saie consultations with the Seniors and administration off discipline, but he woulde not medle with preaching, bicause his ministerie was infamed by some men, he coulde not do yt with owt the offence off himselff and off many. Answere was made in the Churches name for that the honorable Magistrate had sent the Seniors againe to the Churche, the churche was glad off it. For they were all sory for their departure and nowe were verie ioyous off their comminge againe. Concerninge Maister Horne for so muche as he refused the chiefeste parte off the Pastors office wherin he hathe behaued him selff well (yff in anye thinge well) that is, in the office off preachinge. Againe, where he woulde take vppon him that parte wherin he is iustly reprehended, as wantinge discretion, and sobernes therin, that is, the administration off

LXXXVI.

off Ecclesiasticall discipline with the Seniors, he ouer showeth him selff in bothe thes pointes.

Therfore in as muche as he exempteth himself from that office wherin he might profit the congregation: the congregagatiō in like case will not admit him to that office wherin he bothe ill behaued him selff before, as the congregation (yff nede be) shall declare vnto the Magistrats: wherin likewise the congregation cannot admit Maister Chambers to the office off Senior for certein Causes. And for the rest off the Seniors, We (saie they) geue vnto the Magistrats right humble thankes.

This done, those 3. men whiche came vnto them with the Magistrats edicte, did earnestlie exhorte, firste in the magistrates name and eftsones in their owne, to fall to a quiet agremente amonge them selues, for that were more honestie then to accuse one an other vnto the congregation: Whiche thinge, as it is most vnworthly off Christen men, so is it vnto vs specially that professe our selues banished for the gospell sake. Answere was made in the name off the churche as foloweth. We wishe for a brotherly peace from the bottome off our hartes praing Maister Borne and Maister Chambers instantly to bend their mindes vnto quietnes, and moste hartely besechinge theis 3 men our bretherē, and banished for the same gospell that we are, that they will helpe with their authoritie to set a quietnes amonge vs, so as the matter shulde come no more to the Magistrats eare. Theis 3. answered that they woulde heare what answer Maister Borne and Maister Chambers would make, hereto Maister Borne answered, seing the matter is allready before the M the magistrat shall haue the hearing and determining off it. Iff anie had ought against him let them put it vp in writing before the magistrate, for he was ready to answere all men and either he woulde trie his innocencie or (being founde faultie) suffer punishement for the same. Maister Chambers made like answere for him selff.

Then, for as muche as there could be no other ende, the congre congregation requested those 3. graue and lerned preachers/ to make reporte to the magistrate off their desier. And readines to haue agrement. And so they (as soone as theis things were put in writinge) departed. And the churche also made an acte off that daie subscribing with their hands to the same. The same daie at after noone the Magistrates hauing more plaine intelligence off the matter/commaunded by theit edicte/subscribed with their handes/that Maister Horne and Maister Chambers shulde medle no more the one with the pastorshipp and the other withe the Seniorshipp till all the controuersies were throughly harde and decided. And commaundement was geuen/that the eight daie after (whiche was the 3. off marche) suche as had to saie off anie parte shuld be present. This matter was greuous to the church (as maie be thought) that things shuld growe to suche extremitie.

When they had gathered certeine matter/they exhibited it to the Magistrates when as they came to the Englishe churche where all the company were assembled before them whiche was the last off February. Where the Magistrates made an ende (by their owne authoritie) off the controuersie as shall be saide here after.

The laste off Feb. the Magistrate came to oure Temple a litle before ten off the clock and there off his authoritie reconcilied certeine off the congregatiō that were at variaunce amonge them selues / and tooke order that all former offences shulde be vtterly extincte and buried in the graue off forgetfulnes. Wheruppon at the commaundement / and in the presence off this Magistrate/the parties ioined handes together in token that they were reconcilied and were Good frinds and lovers. Afterwarde / the pastor / Elders and Deacons/ were put from their Ecclesiasticall functions by an Edict signed and subscribed with three off the Magistrates handes and were all made priuate men / as the rest off the congregation. And by the same edicte off the Magistrates it was decreed that that congregation might freely / when they woulde

M chuse

LXXXVIII.

chuse either them or other ministers. likewise/it was permitted and graunted/that accordinge to the abilitie off the congregation they might chuse one/ or many ministers off the worde or doctors. Moreouer/order was taken by the same Edicte/that the treasure or common monie off the congregation shulde be kept and distributed by the Deacons. And that the Deacons shulde at certeine appointed times geue vpp an accounte off it before the Ministers off the worde and Seniors.

We were licenced by the same Edicte off the magistrate, to drawe owte an Ecclesiasticall Discipline wherby the congregation shuld be gouerned. Afterward/there was thankes geuen to the magistrate in the name off the whole congregation for his singuler good will and affection to the congregation. And the magistrate departed/wisshinge well in like sorte to the companie. But by whose meanes the magistrat came thus vnto vs and toke such order/ or whither the Magistrate off himselff wrought this deuise we cannot certeinly saie, But that we off the churche were not the cause / that anie suche thinge was done/we take God and oure consciences/and the magistrate to witnes/who knoweth the whole matter.

The morowe after/ whiche was the firste off marche the Magistrate gaue vs Counsaile by a fewe lynes that he wrate vnto vs to drawe forthe the Ecclesiasticall Discipline owte of hande/ whiles we were as yet all priuate men and therfore might best take counsaill/for that that shulde be moste behouable for the whole companie: leste/ that yff we differred the doinge off it vntill the Ministers were chosen and appointed/ oure cōsultation shulde be more troublesome/ whiles the ministers on the one side and the congregation on the other/ might pluck and force more vnto them selues then off right they ought. This most wholsome and profitable counsell off the Magistrate was the nexte daie after/ whiche was the ij. off marche proposed in the congregation/and it liked and pleased the whole company. not withstanding bicause Maister

Horne

Borne made some matter/for that some were absent the mater was differred vnto the nexte daie.

The thirde off marche / by the aduise off that Good and godlie magistrate/eight and thirtie off the congregation chose by voices 11. men to write Ecclesiasticall lawes. Maister Horne and Maister Chambers and almoste to the nomber off 14. moo sat by and woulde geve no voices / notwithstandinge that we requested and intreated them: But they required they might haue leaue to put downe there mindes in writinge. So then beinge requested to write downe their mindes Maister Horne rose vpp and wrate in the paper in their wordes folowinge. My minde is that the olde discipline be kepte still and not mended. Maister Chambers and Maister Isaac and other to the nomber off 14. wrote downe their mynde to the selff same purpose. Nowe when we saw farr beyounde oure expectation and otherwise then we looked for that there was a newe dissention arisinge betweene vs/being set at one and recōciled one to the other/not scarse 3. daies before and in witnesse therof had geué handes eche to other (we coulde not otherwise doo but be greued and sorowe greatly/ to se the growndworke of mo troubles and dissentions laide.

And bicause those. 14. gaue to vnderstande by their handes put downe vnto it in writinge that they thought it not Good to alter their olde discipline / to the ende that it might euidently appeare / howe many we were that had consented vppon the choise off 11. men whiche shulde set downe in writinge a forme off discipline accordinge as the magistrate had commanded/we on the otherside trusted / that we thought it for the behouff and profit off the congregation that a forme of discipline shuld be made and put downe as the magistrate had commaunded. And to this determination and sentéce beinge put in writinge/we in nomber eighte and thirtie subscribe doure names/ with protestation that we did nothinge but that was Good and lawfull and accordinge to the magistrates will and mind requestinge them to geue their consent and to agree with vs.

M ij   Bus

XC.

But they/ after muche debatinge and many wordes to and fro for their olde discipline/ that it neded not to be displaced or altered/ came to this passe at the lenght/ that they saide (we had to consulte off correctinge but not off makinge a discipline and verie instantly vnd earnestlye vrged the same vpon the wordes off that aduice and councell whiche the magistrate had geuen touchinge the spedie dispatche off the discipline of the churche before the election of the ministers. we therfore which thought it not muche materiall whither it were termed a newe made/ or a corrected discipline to haue no occasion of dissentiō/ chaunged/ oure copie and put in in steade of the is wordes/ discipline shulde be made/ shuld be corrected. And so those 14. whiche made as hewe before as though they wolde not suffer anie one iote of the olde discipline to be altered/ ād chaunged/ callinge to minde (I suppose/ either their fewnesse off their nomber or the oddes off the matter bycause it at olde discipline was vtterly taken awaie by the Magistrates edicte/ the laste off Februa. as the chiefest cause off oure controuersies: or ells foreseinge/ that the magistrate would be offended with that their dissention: they all ioyntly together Maister Borne and Maister Chambers beginninge the daunce put their hands to oures/ for the correction off the discipline.

The simple sutteltie off b. factious bead.

Then did Maister Borne request that seinge nowe they had consented vnto vs/ for the wrytinge downe off the discipline/ he and the residewe for that fourtene might freely geue their voices for the chosinge of those fourtene whiche they had alreadie appointed or some suche other as they woulde. But we bicause we had before requested them to geue their voices and three refused/ cōsidering that those fourtene drew all one line and were fullye bent in all pointes to do one as the other/ beinge all like affected and by that meanes/ might off purpos wholie bestowe their voices vpon some certeine/ and so oure throw oure election whiche they knewe already/ denied to graunt and suffer them. and yet we saide, that yff they wolde we wold not refuse to appointe an other daie/ to chuse the sayde 14. men or other, yet geuinge Maister Borne in the meane while

Horne and his companie subscribs to the other parte.

XCI.

while to wit/ that that matter whiche might haue bin quietlie dispatched in three houres / would scarsly by his meanes be fynished in three daies.

At the lenght Maister Horne / after consultation had with certain/ spake alowde in the name off the fourtene in this wise.

Although (saide he) it were meete that we all seuerally geue oure voices/ yet that we maie be no longer an hinderance/ I pronoūce in all their names/ that we all do by our voices chuse those 14. men. Whom yow haue alreadye appointed. When the residew were asked whither they consented to this or no: Maister Isaac/ answered that all agreed: otherwise/ yff anie were contrarie minded he woulde speake. And thus by a generall consente off all not one man excepte fiuetene men were chosen to write Ecclesiasticall lawes the thirde off marche.

The 15. Elected agreed betwene themselues to assemble and come together the fourth of marche at one of the cloke at afternoone. Whē they came together ther was muche adoo a great while whither the olde discipline shulde be corrected or a newe made. We (of the churche) alleadged that all occasions off olde controuersies (wheroff the olde disciplie but vnperfecte and naught was one) were vtterly taken awaye by the magistrates Edicte. some vrged this worde corrected/ or amended which was in the aduise and counsaile that the Magistrat gaue vs for the spedie dispatche off discipline. For/ saide they/ that is not corrected whiche is cleane taken waie. At lenght/ the booke off the olde discipline and an other off the newe discipline/ whiche was corrected in the absence off maister Horne and others were read / and so they departed for that daie appoynting to meete agayne the 3. off marche the same houre.

M. Horne came not till two.

The book of discipline brought foorth and read.

The 8. off marche the 15. men assembled againe and they reagreed vpon articles for makinge off discipline / whiche were set downe in a paper and subscribed all vnto them / sauinge that maister Horne/ Maister Chambers and Maister

M. Horne came at 3.

M ij   Isaac

Isaac and Maister Bentham woulde not subscribe to that Article concerning the hauinge off two ministers off the worde, and yet notwithstandinge they all agreed vpon it, so that it was a matter indifferent whither there shulde be one or many ministers off the worde, for it is not defined in the scriptures but left free. Afterward Maister Hales gaue to Maister Chambers a booke off discipline (which was writen in the absence off maister Horne and others, and was off the same Articles as the congregation had made and agreed vpon) that maister Horne, and he, and maister Isaac might reade it ouer, and if they allowed ought therin that it might be annexed to the discipline that was in hande. But afterwarde, when maister Horne through occasion off talke abowte the correctinge off the discipline, saide that there had byn no other discipline in the churche, but that olde discipline, and that therfore the magistrate spake off correctinge off that not off the vtter abolishinge theroff, and that it was answered, that that same other booke off discipline beinge written when he was absent might as well be vnderstoode to be ment, as that same olde discipline: bothe for that there was more equitie in it and also was suscribed vnto off so many as well as that olde discipline whiche he so extolled. Then maister Horne brake owte in to most spitefull wordes against all his countrie men that had agreed to that discipline which were at the leaste 36. persons, affirminge that all they that had thus conspired together for the establishing off those articles (accordinge to the shornes off the time wherin they met) that they were in a certeine degree, giltie off treason againste the magistrat, against the Senate, and (to be shorte) against the whole citie.

Then maister Hales, vnderstandinge by maister Hornes wordes that nothinge was sought but newe trouble, and beinge put in minde also aff maister Bentham) reherseth agayne that booke off discipline which a litle before was offred to maister Chambers affirminge that he vnderstode, they went abowte to seeke rather an occasion off chalinginge at the booke by readinge off it, then a way off makinge a new discipline.

The

XCIII.

The eleventh off marche the fiftene men meete againe vpõ certeine Articles to whiche (excepte one whiche maister Horne and M. Chambers would not subscribe) they al subscribed.

A litle before our departure it was thought profitable that those thinges which we had collected and agreed vppon shulde be brought in to a certeine forme of a booke, adding either owte off the olde discipline, / or by occasion / as we were gatheringe theis thiges together such thinges as might seeme profitable. Maister Horne, and maister Chambers beinge intreated, that they would gather those thinges in suche sorte, or elles be present to conferre withe other that reade: Maister Horne answerethe that he woulde not, neither that there was any suche neede. The 16. daie of marche they met againe in the churche and there a certeine bill (in whiche were writen certeine articles tendinge to discipline) is exhibited vnto them that amonge the fiften it might be deliberated vpon and debated. maister Isaac spake many things verie sharplie against one Article as verie daungerous and perilous againste those good men through whose liberalitie the poore off the church were susteined, and makinge wise as thoughe he woulde knowe the matter better, he requested the bil, whiche, beinge reached vnto him, he putteth it vp in his bosome, neither woulde he geue it againe. And so by this meanes, he tooke away the matter for vs to worke vpon sith that we had no other copie.

Afterwarde, the booke in whiche those thinges were writen that were agreed vppon amonge the 15. and certeine thinges owte off the olde discipline, and other also were gathered into some order was brought owte amõge them to be consulted vpon, and beinge redd, maister Horne and Maister Chambers fyrste off all complained, that booke was gathered they not wittinge theroff, and had byn longe beatten vppon amonge certeine of them, and therfore that it was reason that a copie shuld be geuen to them, and to maister Isaac and a farther tyme also to delyberate, maister Isaac affirmed that he neded 2. monethes, or one at the leaste to consider off that boke. It was answered that although Maister Horne and

Chambers

Chambers complained that they were not admitted to the collectinge off the booke) in that they did vs wronge/ for beinge of vs therunto required they refused it and left it to others. In that they required a copie/ it semed vniuste/ (seinge that the church had decreed/ that we the 11. shulde debate together as concerninge the writinge off the discipline) for that thinge tended againe to a newe dissention. Againe/ that they required so longe a tyme to deliberate/ and especially Maister Isaac/ it was moste vniuste. For seinge the marte was nowe at hande/ it was profitable or rather necessarie that oure churche shulde with spede be established and oure ministers elected leaste/ to oure great infamie/ men comminge hyther owte off all Europe/ they might also se the broyles off oure churche and so spread them farr abroad amoge all nations: more ouer: that it woulde fall owte to the great hurte off the poore/ yff godly men being offended/ with oure dissentions/ (beinge before beneficiall to the poore) withdrawe nowe their liberalitie/ and that therfore there was nede off spedie helpe in pacifiynge and quietinge the churche before the marte beinge nowe at hande. Maister Borne answereth/ that he requireth not to muche tyme 2. or 3. daies shulde be enough for him to deliberate/ notwithstandinge that the copie ought to be graunted for no lesse tyme/ seinge many thinges were conteined in that booke/ and some also darke and dowtefull thinges and to him before that tyme vnharde off/ or/ at the least/ vnknowen: and that therfore he requested that all shulde be asked mā by mā whither they thought not this reasonable ād iuste that he required. For if to the moste it shulde seeme reasonable he would at anie hande haue a copie off that booke. Euery man therfore was asked/ beginninge at Maister Beniham: he/ aswell for the causes before alleadged as also that no occasion off wranglinge might arise off the booke / and leaste the booke shulde come to the handes off anye other before it were brought to the congregation/ and for certeine other causes/ thought it not meete that anie copie shulde be geuen to anie/ but that the booke shulde be brought foorthe amonge them/ and
all

XCV.

all they hearinge it that were appointed off the congregation/ it shulde be after read and that tyme enoughe/shulde be geuen to stande vpon euerie decree and sentence and more exactly to examin them, and that this seemed to him very iuste and reasonable. And this iudgement is condescended to off all the reste/and so Maister Horne leaueth off from requestinge the copie. Afterwardes/ the booke is begonne to be redd from the beginnige/and in examininge off euerie off the decrees longe time is spente/and off some articles in the beginninge muche disputation and debatinge is had. But Maister Horne/ Maister Chambers and Isaac beinge asked their iudgementes would not answere/no/not in the moste plaineste materes/and knowen of all men/ either to allowe or disalowe/ as for exaple: There was one article: we professe the selffame doctrine which is conteined in the Canonicall bookes off all the holie scripture/to witt/in the bookes off the olde and newe Testamente/in whiche is conteined fullie all doctrine necessary for oure saluation. To this and suche other beinge moste plaine and manifeste, maister Horne answered as to all thother that he woulde answere nothinge with owte great deliberation. By whiche his doinges/he gaue occasion to all men to wonder. And so/some other decrees off that booke beinge examined a meetinge off the 15. was appointed againste the nexte daie/ and so they departed. The nexte daie beinge the 17. off march and againe the daie folowinge beinge 19. twelue off the 15. mette. For Maister Isaac/ Maister Horne and Chambers came not. Vpon bothe daies the discipline was more diligently read and examined/ and off eleuen off them whiche were appointed/ alowed and subscribed vnto. Vpon the 20. daie off marche the discipline was offred to the whole congregation/ that it might of them either in the whole or in parte be alowed or disalowed/and the same daie was it twise reade ouer.

After the readinge Maister Horne and Maister Chambers require a copie off the discipline/ that at their leasure they might farther deliberate vpõ it. It was answered that it was to be opely read and reade againe/bothe to them and o=
thers

Yff maister Horne tooke such deliberatiõ before he would subscribe to that article: what meaneth this that poore ignorant men and wemen must thus subscribe vpõ the sudden or ells to newgate.

thers/as often as they woulde/with time ynough geue to euery man more diligently to examine euerie Article/ but seinge the Magistrate had commaunded that we shulde exhibite to them a copie off the discipline turned in to latin/ so soone as possible might be/Therfore we durste not scater any copies before the Magistrate had seene it. Besydes that we feared leaste Maister Horne and Maister Chambers (Who were amongethe 15.(appointed) off the churche for the writinge off the discipline who might also when they woulde not onely heare the discipline but also examine the same diligently, and yet woulde not meete with the others at the appointed time) would requeste a copie not so muche to knowe the discipline as to sturre vpp newe broiles. Neuertheles when the Magistrate had once seene it / leaue to be geuen to anye man that woulde to se it. Wuthe this answere they and some others beinge offended/at the second readinge off the discipline they departed awaye and abstained agayne with their whole housholdes from the churche/from publick praiers and sermons whiche thinge blewe vp and increased the reporte off our disagrements and striffes. Neither woulde they from that time forwarde vnlesse they were commaunded by the magistrate come to the churche when as notwithstandinge they could not shewe vs anie iuste cause to be giuen them why they shulde so departe from the churche and refraine the publicke prayers and godly sermons/ as yff we had byn Ethnickes or publicannes.

The 15. daie oure discipline was read the 3. time/and the 16.daie it was read the forthe tyme by the commaundement off the Magistrate at the reading wheroff all Englishe men that were off the churche were commaunded to be present. The 30. off marche it was read the fyfte tyme and so at diuers times there subscribed 42. in the good allowance theroff whiche was the greater parte by a greate deale off the churche. For the whole churche at that present had not aboue: 62. And bycause nowe the marte was at hande/ that there might be some better forme off a well ordred churche ; siue were appointed

pointed off the churche the 10. off marche to nominate certai
ne from amonge whom/ accordinge to the Magistrates de
cree shulde be chosen/ the Ministers off the worde/ Seniors
and Deacons. The 11. off marche the names off twentie men
or there abowte were proponed to those fiue appoynted off
the churche and therwithall declared that yff anye woulde or
coulde reproue anye off them that were named / either
in doctrine or manners / they shulde shewe it the 12. daie af
ter. Upon the 13. daie/ none fyndinge anie faulte in anie of tho
se whose names were propounded / it was agayne decreed
that yet/ yff they had anie thinge to saie against anie man they
shulde declare that the 15. daie folowing.

The 15 off marche Maister Chambers/ maister Binkes
Maister Ade/ Maister Brikbek maister Bentham/ who were
amonge them that were named/ tolde the churche/ that yf pa
eaduenture they shulde be chosen / for certeine causes they
coulde not serue the churche / and that they signified this to
the churche in time leaste the election were frustrat. But w
hen no man coulde obiecte anie faulte in theis or other that
were named: the election off the Ministers was made the 19.
off marche/ and the ordeininge off them that were chosen
was appointed of the churche the daie folowinge. In the me
ane season Maister Borne and Maister Chambers and cer
taine other leste not off to sue to the Magistrates that bothe
oure election might be hindred/ and also that it might be law
full for them to be off our churche / and yet not to subscribe
to oure Dysciplyne / the thinge that they them sel
ues notwithstanding would neuer graunt to anye o
thers.

The 20. off Marche after dinner it began to be
muttred off certeyne that the Magistrate had forbydden
that we shulde go forwarde in the election/ the whiche thin
ge surely greued vs: for by that meanes we sawe that we shul
be haue no forme of a Churche before the marte and that the
erfore we shulde become a reproche to all men/ which seemed

shulde

shulde be spred amonge all nations. But this rumor was altogether vaine/for the 28. of marche which was the daie before the election shulde be/after the sermon/the decree of the Magistrate was openly reade in the churche/wherin it was commaunded that we shulde take in hand and performe the election off the Ministers in the same order and vpon the same daie that we had apointed/and that all Englishe men that were off oure churche shulde be present the same daie / at the election/and geue their voices.

The 29. daie off Marche after praiers / the sermon and publique faste/a litle before twelue/the election off the Ministers began to be made and when we were in the middeste off the election: Maister Horne Maister Chambers/ and others to the nomber off 18. men/ (who before were neither with vs at the sermon/nor at praiers/but had kepte themselues in some howses not farre from the churche/beinge warned of their side that had watched vs in the churche) came in suddanlie on a troupe together in to the churche and there eche one striue the who shall caste in his bill firste / vpon the table standinge in the middeste off the churche/all whiche bylles conteined one matter and writen almost with like wordes / to witt / that they coulde not geue their voices in the same election / bicause they coulde not off their consciences alowe that discipline by whiche the election was made. And that they might enlarge their nomber/they brought with them 2. billes off those that were absent and off some others whiche neuer were accompted off the churche. And so after they had troubled oure election/and after Maister Horne also / walking with an other a litle while ouerwhart in the middest off the churche / all in a manner departed againe.

Afterwards the election was fully ended/ at one off the clock at afternoone/ there were chosen 2. Ministers off the worde, 6. Seniors, and 4. Deacons. Nowe the Deacons were (besides the wonted custome off oure churche) off the nomber off those that coulde lyue of their owne/for that the common treasure might seeme withowte all suspition to be committed

mitted to suche rather then to the poorer sorte. Nowe/ in that maister Borne neither anie off the other that were before in the Ministerie (excepte onely maister Willforde) were chosen againe to the Ministerie/ was specially through their owne faulte. For Maister Borne neuer almoste ceased for certeine daies to professe openly that he woulde neuer exercise againe anie Ecclesiasticall ministerie in that churche/ and beinge before appointed by the magistrate to preache in oure churche he would neuer so muche as once preach. And maister Chambers/ when his name amonge the reste to be chosen/ was propounded/ the 25. off marche he professed openly in the churche/ (all men hearinge it) before the election/ that though he were chosen off vs to some Ministerie/ yet that he woulde neuer vse it. And therfore that we shulde not in anie case chuse him vnlesse we woulde haue oure election to be frustrate.

Wherfore/ it is no maruell / yff they were not chosen/ who/ leaft they shulde be chosen did themselues openly denounce it. And therfore/ in this/ they do vs great wronge/ that would seeme to beare men in hande/ that they were at the firste thruste owte off their ministerie by vs/ or longe off vs they were not chosen in againe.

Maister Isaac in like manner / Maister Binks Maister Brickbet and Maister Escote openly professed that they woulde in nowise vse any publique ministerie in oure churche. And here vpon it came specially to passe that onely Maister willsord/ (who had not made anie suche exception) was from amonge thē/ which were before in the ministery chosen agayne.

The thirde off Aprill the Magistrate/ who desired that their churche dissentions off oures might be pacified and quieted/ and he now bicause off the marte had no leasure to do the same/ writeth his letters to S. Cor/ S. Sandes and maister Bartue in whiche he exhorteth them/ that they/ yff they coulde by anie conueniente meanes/ as arbitres off some estimation ende this striffe amonge vs.

Nowe when either side was come before them and all we in the name off the churche (for all had graunted oure controuersies

N iij

trouersies to be harde and determined with owte anye excep=
tion at all to them and to other arbytrees/what so euer/ whom
they shulde call vnto them) and had offred this thinge to
the arbytrees written and all oure names subscribed vnto it:
Maister Horne/Maister Chambers and others firste reque=
sted that maister Horne might be restored to his office off
pastorshippe/Maister Isaac Maister Chambers and others
into their offices off Seniors and the olde discipline into his
former place and autoritie/so as they were in the beginninge
off their controuersies. For then (said they) will we leaue all
controuersies to the arbitres. When we had refused this as
moste vniuste and vnreasonable/ then they requested that see
inge we woulde not restore the olde discipline/ and them to
their former authoritie/that then we would suffer oure disci=
pline and Mynisters to be none otherwise then their olde wi=
thowte all authoritie and no minister at al/nor discipline to be
in oure churche but that the matter shulde remaine in that sta
te and condition that it was in the last off February/ when
the Magistrate hauinge put all the ministers from their offi=
ces departed frō vs/and so shuld the mater be lefte to arbitres

Whan we remembred what and howe great trauelles
that discipline/election off Ministers had coste vs and sawe
that by this meanes oure churche shulde be made destitute of
Ministers and a large windowe to be opened for newe con=
tentions/and had also denied that thinge/Maister Horne re=
quested that it might be lawfull for him to goo a litle a side and
to consulte with some off his side abowte the whole matter.
A litle after returninge againe and sainge/that they woulde
leaue no waie vnsought after/wherby peace might be got=
ten/although they yelded muche from their right. Then he re=
adeth a certeine bill to those 3. (appointed off the magistrate)
and to vs written in his owne name and the names off others
which I haue added vnder here writen worde for worde/least
anie man shulde thinke that anie thinge off purpose were al=
tred by vs.   *The Bill off maister Horne and Others.*

WE offre and permit with moste willinge myndes (hauin=
ge

ge the licence of the magistrate as it maye well be for this purpose) that all oure controuersies and contentions / whatsoeuer / whiche haue byn sowne and brought in amonge vs sithes the beginnige of this breache / and synce the firste daie we began to striue / vntill this present time and houre: to be debated decided and determined by Arbytres / beinge none off this oure congregation / and yet from amonge the brethern / oure countrie men / equally and indifferently / by the parties disagreinge / to be chosen vpon this condition / that not onely the election off Mynisters and besides all others thinges don by the order off the saied discipline / stande in suspence / to be allowed or disalowed by the determination and iudgemente off the arbytres to be chosen as is aforesaide writen the 5. off Aprill. Anno 1557.

And that the indifferent reader / maie / by comparinge their offre and oures / se whiche is moste resonable / we haue added oures also / writen owre worde for worde as we offred it vpp before the forsaied Maister Bartue / D. Coxe and D. Sandes and to the dissentinge brethern.

The copie wheroff is this.

WE submit our selues and are contented to commit all maner off controuersies that haue heretofore rysen amongest vs in the churche / to suche Arbitres as the magistrate has theapointed and to all suche as they call vnto them to the hearinge ād determininge therof / accordinge to gods word and good reason. And thus symplie and plainely withowte anie manner off exception or condition. In witnes wheroff we haue subscribed oure names the 5. off Aprill / Anno 1557.

Thow maiste se here / gentle reader / that albeit we had oure Discipline writen and allowed off a 11. off the 15. men whom the congregation by the Magistrates authoritie had apointed / to wit / the Dyscipline / and therupon confirmed with the hands off 42. men which was the greateste parte off our churche by a great deale: Albeit we had also / all eccleasticall ministers / by the magistrats decree / and the authoritie of the con

gregas

CII.

gregation lawfully elected/yet for quietnes sake/we put all to the Arbitres wholie/either to be allowed or disalowed withowte anie manner off exception. But maister Borne and maister Chambers/and others/sekinge more their owne will then anie quiete agremente/woulde not at the first admit those three Arbitres appointed off the magistrates. For Maister Borne made exception againste some off them. And afterwardes woulde abide no order or offre/vnlesse we wolde with oure subscriptions suffer and commit oure discipline/the election off ministers/and all other matters off oure churche to stande in suspence (as they call it) so that by their dryfte we shulde haue had no discipline/no certein ministery/no order and so consequently no churche. They would that thies Arbiters shulde be chosen indifferenly from amonge suche as were oure countrie men/But not of oure congregation/so that it

Theis three arbytres had their beinge owte from the Englishe churches.

shulde be lawfull for them to chuse where they lyste and whom they liste. Nowe consider with me/who so euer thow arte (indiffent reader) yff we/firste hauinge geuen and sealed oure writinge in the name off the whole churche had granted our discipline/ministers/and all other orders off oure churche to stande in suspence/vntill they shulde either be allowed or disalowed of the arbitres chosen in suche sorte/and till maister Borne and Maister Chambers accordinge to their canuasinge craftines/nowe ynough and more then ynough knowen vnto vs/had chosen Arbitres for their parte owte off farr places/who either coulde not or ells woulde not meete together abowte this matter/or (whiche was moste certeine to come to passe) yff Maister Borne/and Maister Chambers wheresoeuer at lenght they had choosen arbitres/had not for all that chosen suche for their side/who vnlesse thinges were don accordinge to their owne minde/would decree nothinge at all. But the Arbitres disagreinge on bothe sides/the matter shulde be lefte vndon: what then shulde haue become off oure churche/with thies their suspensyue ministers/and withe the discipline and all other thinges? For the condition offred vpp off Maister Borne, and Maister Chambers was declared

clared to be this/that so longe all shulde remaine in suspence till they shuld be allowed or disalowed by the arbytres: so that yff the arbyters shulde haue bin deuided equally (as many times it comethe to passe) the Ministers off the churche might determine nothinge / but the Discipline and all other thinges muste continually hange in suspence. Againes the churche (thoughe it were in great perill and daunger/yet/ least it shulde leaue anye waye vnproued for the obtayninge off peace (bicause they thought that some off those three were not meete whom the magistrates had appointed for Arbitres/ offred vpp an other bill conteining alltogether the sclff same matter/and write withe the same wordes/that they woulde stande to the Iudgement off any other Arbitres who so euer beinge chosen indifferently by the other partie from amonge oure countriemen/and leaue all thinges to them plainely and symplie withowte anie exception or condition to be determined and decided. But they wonld allowe no condition offred off vs vnlesse we woulde firste/ by the subscribinge off oure names allowe that moste vniuste and vnreasonable condition off thers / and by oure preiudice condemne oure Mynisters/ oure Discipline and all other thinges that we had donne. And so by this meanes had opened a gapp to them to ouerthowe oure churche. And when they had thus behaued themselues before Maister Bartue D. Cox and D. Sandes/ yet certeine off them (when nowe the marte was in the chieff flowre) reported throughowte the whole cytie that we had reiected their most iuste and paeceable requestes and that we were alltogether troublesome men / and plainely bent to suffer no peace nor quietnes/ howbeit/ we had rather that they shuld shewe theis thinges that are false off vs to others/ then that they together with others shulde openly deride oure follie (yff we had yelded to such requests) as they that with oure great toile and trauell had (to the quiete off the churche) establyshed some churche / and nowe vppon a suddaine by the subscribinge off one bill thorough headinesse and foolishe facilitie shulde haue ouerthrowen the whole. But they/ when they

O   conlde

coulde not obtaine this, went abowte this verie busilie, that the whole churche might then be dissolued and broken vpp. For Maister Chambers for halff a monethe space and more would geue nothinge to anie man that remained in the churche, and folowed not maister Horne and him departinge from the churche.

To certeine other also he woulde geue nothinge at all whiche were in the publique Ministerie, to preache the word and reade lectures, and also in the exercise of disputinge by his owne appoyntemente and the order taken by Maister Horne alwais from the time sithens they came to oure churche, when nowe they were for their bourde in debte to their hostesses for 4. monethes, neither had don anie other faulte, vnlesse it were bicause they remained in their functions off preachinge and readinge lectures in whiche they were placed by Maister Horne and Maister Chambers, leaste the churche shuld altogether be destitute bothe off sermons and lectures: Onely bicause in this dissention they agreed not with them and toke their partes, and had with them withdrawen them selues from the churche that it might be vtterlie scattered, whe as notwithstandinge (whiche is moste vnhonest) they had promised to geue 3. monethes warninge before they woulde forsake them: whiche, notwithstandinge Maister Chambers affirmed they woulde neuer do vnlesse it were that they were constained by extreame necessitie. Abowte the middest off the matte or a litle after ther began a rumor to be spread off the departure of maister Horne and maister Chambers from this citie, but whither they woulde go, or whither they woulde at all departe, it was yet vncerteine. For neither was it likely that maister Chambers hauinge gathered so muche common mony, and that by the authoritie and in the name off the churche seinge he had bin here so longe with owte makinge off as nie accoumpte to the churche, woulde go awaie. in suche sorte, Neither was it credible that M. Horne, who had gouerned in his pastorall office and charge so longe (no reconciliation ner pacification beinge made for so great offences) woulde so
departe

departe/yea/not so muche as haue taken his leaue of the churche. In the meane time it is incredible to be spoken/but more shameful to be hearde/what reportes certeine had spred that marte tyme secretly and especially amonge the rycher sorte that were able to helpe the poore off oure churche/forsooth they that there were certeine traitors amonge vs. That we desired to knowe the names off those persons that were liberall towardes the poore off oure churche/to the ende to betraie them and vndoo them: That we had caste our Pastor and Ministers owte headlonge from ther ministeries and offices. In all whiche thinges/ they went aboute nothinge ells but to stirre vp newe braules and contentions. And that they maie alienate the hartes off the welthie sorte from vs/ and so bringe the poore of oure churche/ first to famine and then vs into deadly hatred off them/as thoughe they were by vs throwen into theis miseries / But forasmuche as all theis thinges are vaine and vntrue/and fained by the secret sleightes off those priuie whisperers/ who dare speake nothinge openly: we haue thought them rather to be contemned then to be answered: hopinge that at laste when they are weary off lyinge/they will be quiet. But iff they go forwarde still to belie vs so impudently and outragiously / surely we will not neglecte oure fame and honest estimation: but we wil diligently wipe awaie all their slanders with one spunge/ and there withall will open to the worlde/their wicked endeauors against oure churche. In the meane time nothinge distrustinge the lordes mercie (how soeuer the deceites off men would let it) hopinge/ that neither liuinge nor foode shall euer want to oure poore congregation/ who also feedeth the rauens/ and that he will allwaies be present by his spirit to vs and to oure whole churche continually which thinge that it maie please him to bringe to passe / we beseche the good reader (who so euer thow art) praie vnto god togither with vs/and fare well.

CX.

Here folowithe the exhortation off the Magistrate for the amendinge and establishinge off the Discipline.

The Englishe Thus.

Me think it Good and profitable for the establishinge off peace and tranquilitie off your churche, that yow altogether consulte and determine, as concerninge the amendinge off discipline, nowe, whiles ye all be yet priuate men and withowte anie Ecclesiasticall ministerie. For whiles none off yow doshe yet knowe, wither he shallbe a priuate person or ells shall haue anie authoritie Ecclesiasticall, euerie man man will applie his minde, and studie to that whiche shall seme moste reasonable and profitable aswell for the cōgregation as for the Mynisters. But after that the Mynisters be once elected, it is to be feared leaste they will drawe some what more then reason to themselues, and in likewise the congregation to it selff. And so, your consultation maie chaunce to be somewhat troublous whiche we woulde not shuld happen. Wherfore that all thinges maie procede aswell as maie be to to the establishing off sure peace we exhorte yow that with all spede ye take in hand this consultation abowte the amendinge off your Discipline with mindes and meanes moste aplyable to tranquillitie, which Almightie God graunt, ye maie happely bringe to passe. The first off marche, 1559.

John Glauburg.

Nowe

CXI.

Nowe, folowith the discipline both the olde, and that which was by the Magistrats appointement, corrected.

The order off the olde discipline in the Citie off Franckford.

There be 2. partes off the order off Discipline in the churche. The one perteininge to the whole churche. The other perteininge to the ministers and Elders alone. *The olde Discipline.*

Off the firste parte.

In the Discipline perteininge to the whole church, is firste to be apointed the order off receivinge men in to the congregation whiche is this.

The manner off receivinge off all sortes off personnes into the saide congregation.

Fyrste, everie one aswell man as woman which desireth to be receyued shall make a declaration or Confession off their faithe, before the pastor and Seniors shewinge himselff fully to consent and agree with doctrine of the churche and submittinge themselues to the discipline off the same.

Iff anie person, so desyrous to be receiued into the congregation, be notoriously defamed or notid off any corrupt or euill opinion in doctrine or slaunderous behauior in liffe, the same maye not by the pastor and Elders be admitted till he haue either purged himselff theroff, or ells haue declared himselff to the pastor and Elders penitent for the same.

The good behauiour and godly conuersation required off such as are receiued.

P   Secondares

Secondarely all the members off the churche so admitted and receiued shall diligently obserue and keepe all suche godlie discipline and orders apoointed within the churche whiche tend to the increase off knowledge and godlynesse off liffe/as the appointed times off praier/ preachinge/ and hearinge goddes worde/the administration off the Sacramentes/with submission to all godly discipline off the churche.

Thirdly/ such also as beinge in England after knowledg receiued/haue communicated with the popish messe contrary to their consciences by reason of feare/weaknes/ or otherwise/may not be receyued till they haue confessed their fall before the pastor and seniors/and haue shewed themselues penitent for the same.

This article I finde rased in the copie, what they mēt by it, I know not.

How the youthe shalbe Catechised.

Also for the increase off godly knowledg and vertue/ all the youthe shall resorte to the churche euerye satterdaie at 2. off the clock at afternoone/and when we haue a seuerall churche/at one off the clock on the sundaie at afternoone/ there/ to be instructed in the Catechisme/ and not to be admitted to the communion till they be able to make profession off their faith before the whole congregation. And also to haue an honest testimony off towardnes in godly conuersation/ and that euery member off the churche do not refuse to reade a declaration off their faithe before the pastor and Elders when so euer they shall be therto required.

Thorder off correction/ for priuate and priuie offences.

Fourthly/for as muche as no charge is so perfect but offences maye arise / for godly charitable redressinge and reforminge off suche/ this order is to be obserued.

Firste/yff anye off the congregation be offensiue in maners or doctrine to anie off the brethern/so that offence be priuate vate and not publickly knowen/ther can be no better order deuised then that which Christe himselff hathe apointed/which is/firste brotherly to admonishe him alone/yff that do no preuaile/call/one or 2. Witnesses/yff that also do not profit/then to declare it to the pastor and elders/to whõ the churche hath geuen authoritie to take order in such cases according to the qualitie and greuousnes off the offence and crime.

Off the order off correction for publick and open crimes.

But yff anie person shalbe a notorious knowen offender so as he is offensiue to the whole churche/then shall the pastor and elders immediatlye call the offender before them and trauel with him to reduce him to true repētance and satisfyinge off the congregation whiche/if he obstinately refuse to doo: then the pastor shall signifie his offence and contempt to the whole congregation desiring them to praie for him/and further to assigne him a daie to be denownced excommunicate before the churche/except in the meane time the offender submit himself before the pastor and seniors to the order of discipline

Finally/in case any person of this congregatiõ be knowē to be an hinderer or a defacer of anie of the godly vsages nowe excercised in the same congregation/either priuely or apertly by worde/letter/or dede: the same shall acknowledg his offence with satisfaction to the churche/according to the true order off Discipline.

The 2. parte off discipline concerninge the ministers and elders/and their elections.

Firste for the election of ministers and Elders/the qualities of the same are to be examined and considered according to the rule off S. Paule 1. Tim. 3. Wheroff this is the summe That no man be elected whose doctrine or liffe can iustlie be reproued and condemned. As concerning the order and forme off Electing/the same is to be obserued whiche hathe already bin practised and is here vnto anexed.

Off ther offices and functions.

The pastor, according to the commaundement off the holye ghoste in the scriptures, ought withall pastorall care diligently to attende to his flock, in preaching goddes worde, in ministring the Sacramentes, in example off Good lyffe, in exhortinge, admonishinge, rebukinge, and as the chieff mouthe off the churche, to open and declare all orders taken by him and the elders whiche are to be opened and publis hed: to whom no man mayen in the face off the congregation reply. But yff anie think himselff to haue cause to speak let him come before the elders in the place appointed for their meetinge and there to open his mynde, and to be hard with all charitie indifferently.

The office off preachers and suche as are lerned in the congregation.

The office off preachers and such as are lerned in the churche is to assiste the pastor in preachinge the worde, ministringe the Sacraments and in all consultations and meetinges off him and the Elders especially in causes off Doctrine, and also at other tymes when they shall be required.

The office off Elders.

The office off Elders is to be (as it were) censors, ouerseers off manners and disorders. And to be with the pastor in all consultations, for the publick order off the churche, and that all corrections and exercises off discipline be done with their common consaile.

Deacons.

Consideringe also the present state off the churche, it is thought requisite that the Deacons besides the speciall office appointed in the Acts off the Apostells in caringe and provi-
dinge

dinge for the poore / do also visit the sick and be assistant in Carechisinge the youthe yff they shall be thervnto required.

The same order and forme is to be vsed for reformation off offences and crymes in ministers and Elders whiche is described for other offenders / and to be donne towardes them rather with more seueritie.

Now folowith the Discipline reformed and confirmed by the authoritie off the churche and magistrate.

It is moste cumlie and godly / that Christian people resorte together in place and tyme / therunto by common consent appointed (yff the persecution off the vngodly will suffer the same and they themselues haue no vrgent cause to the contrary) there to heare the pure doctrine off Godsworde taught / and themselues openly with their presence and voice to declare the consent off their hartes to the same / and to confesse with their mouthe agreablely their beleeff and faith vpon god and his holy worde according to the scriptures.   **1.** *The new discipline.*

The congregation thus assembled is a particuler visible churche such as maye be in diuers places off the worlde verye manye. And all theis particuler churches ioyned together not in place (for that is not possible) but by the coniunction off true doctrine and faithe in the same / do make one whole churche in this worlde. And the electe off God that be in this whole churche and euery parte theroff with all the elect that hath byn from the beginninge off the worlde and shall be to the ende theroff doo altogether make that holy catholike and Apostolike churche / the spouse off oure sauiour christe whiche he hathe purified to him selff in his blood wheroff mention is made in the creede. I beleue one holie Catholike and Apostolike churche. But at this present oure consideration muste be off the visible and particuler churche.   **2.**

p ij   The

The signes and notes off a visible churche are thies. Firste/ true and godly doctrine. Secondly/ the right ministration and vse off the Sacramentes and common praier: Thirdly: honest and godly liffe/ yff not in the whole multitude/ yet in manie off them: fourthly/ discipline/ that is/ the correction off vices/ but the 3. firste notes are suche as withowt the whiche no forme off anie godly visible churche can possibly be. Wherfore/ they be the principall and chieff notes. And therfore we define a particuler churche visible/ to be the congregation off Christen men whither they be fewe or many assemblinge together in place and time conuenient to heare Christes true Doctrine taught/ to vse his holy Sacramentes rightly and to make their common praier together/ in the whiche their appeareth a studie off honest ād godlye liffe/ and which hathe in it a godly discipline/ that is to saye/ ordinaunces and decrees Ecclesiasticall for the preseruation off comely order and for the correction off vices.

Off the doctrine off the churche which is the first note.

The Doctrine whiche we holde and professe in oure church is the same that is taught in the canonicall bookes off the holie bible/ conteininge the olde testamente and the newe in the whiche is conteined the true and liuelie worde off god and the doctrine off helthe bothe as concerninge faithe and godly liffe / at full / sufficient for the saluation off all the faithfull that vnfainedly beleue therin: The summe off the whiche as concerninge faithe is briefly and truly comprehended in the 3. creeds/ the common creede commonly called the creed off the Apostells/ the Nicene creed and the crede off Athanasius: And as concerninge godly liffe/ in the ten commaundementes/ written in the 22 chapter off Exodus.

Off the Sacramentes/ and common praier the second note.

We obserue ad kepe the forme and order off the ministra 5.
ȟ off the sacramentes and common praier/ as it is set foorh
by the authoritie off the blessed kinge Edwarde off famous
memorye/ in the laste booke off the English seruice: Wherof
notwithstanding in the respecte off tymes and places and o-
ther circumstances certeine rites and ceremonies appointed
in the sayed booke/ as thinges in different/ maie be left owte/
/as we at this present doo.

The times and houres for the teachinge and hearing off 6.
goddes worde and the ministration off the sacramentes/ and
and saying and hearing of the comon praier/ such as be nowe
vsed/ or shall heare after by common cōsent be thought moste
meete to be vsed/ are to be kept and obserued off all men not
hauing lauful cause to the contrary.

Off the Ministers off the worde/ Sacra/
mentes and common praier.

It is thought expedient for the churche at this present/ A.
to haue 2. Ministers or teachers off the worde elected/ off doc
trine and godly liffe/ such as the rule off the scripture dothe requyre as muche as maie be/ And that the sayde 2. Ministers
and teachers off the worde shall in all thinges and points be
off like authorite and neither off them superior or inferior to
other.

Item that the saied/ 2. Ministers shall by themselues/ B.
or fit persons by them and the Seniors in the name off the
whole congregacion to be appointed/ when necessarie cause
shall so requyre/ preach the ordinarie Sermons on wens-
daies/ thursdayes and sondaies before noone/ and after noone instruct and heare the examination off the youthe in the
Catechisme/ on sondaye in the after noone at the howre ac-
customed/ and shall by them selues or other appointed persons as is afore sayed Minister the Sacramentes dewly/
saye the common prayers distinctly viset and comfort the
sick specially at their last tyme and howre off deathe/ bury the dead comely/ and obserue all other comely rites and v-
sages

ges in the churche directing all their behaviouractes and life according to the rule off off their vocation/ set foorth in the holie scriptures.

9. Item that sixe/ either fewer or more / (as the habilitie off the churche will beare) such as be godly and haue nede off the helpe off the churche / be appointed by the Ministers and Seniors in the name off the whole congregation: Wheroff 4. to be well lerned/ who shall reade and expownde the chapters/ and shall helpe the two ministers off the worde/ when nede shall require in the doctrine off the worde/ Catechisinge off youthe/ Ministringe off the Sacramentes/ sainge off common praier and the other two or moo/ shall ayde also the sayed ministers Seniors and Deacons in visitinge off the sick and seinge to strangers and in callinge off the congregation when nede shall be/ and in all other necessarie and comelie thinges and rytes to be done in the churche. Notwithstandinge/ an other godly and lerned men whiche lyue off themselues / and be not burthenue to the churche maye helpe the Ministers off the worde in the aboue named Ecclesiasticall functions/ iff they themselues so will/ and be ther vnto called by the saied ministers and Seniors.

10. Item/ for the further instruction off youthe and seruants it is thought good/ that besides the examination off children in the Catechisme ordinarely vsed / the said children and seruants with the whole congregation/ shulde be all presente at oure ordinarie sermon/ to be made purposely for them on sondayes at afternoone/ so lernedly that it be yet for their capacitie most plaine and with all possible perspecuitie/ and that one tenor off Christian doctrine from the beginninge to the ende be obserued and kepte in the saide sermon/ off the whiche no better forme in oure iudgement can be then Caluins Catechisme/ receiued in so manye churches and translated into so manie languages. Yt is thought good therfore that the preacher off the saied Catechisinge sermon followe the good order off that Catechisme in his sermons and confirme the godly doctrine off the same by the scriptures / and after the same

CXIX.

me sermon the common praier/and seruice to be exercised and fynished as at other tymes.

11. Item/that the one preacher beinge sick the other shall doo or see donne by other fit persons/ as is before saied all the dewtie and dewties to the other so sick belonginge.

12. Item/ that a lecture off diuinitie and disputations for the exercise off students/ yff it maie be/ be mainteined/ or ells that prophesie be vsed euery fortnight in the Englishe tong/ for the exercise off the saied studentes and edisinge of the congregation/or bothe disputations and Prophesie also/ iff it so shall seeme good vnto the ministers and Seniors.

13. Item/that such as shall therunto seeme moste meete off the congregation shall be appointed to translate into Englishe some such bookes/as shall be profitable either for the instructiō or for the comforte off oure countrie in this oure exile and affliction off oure countrie.

14. Item that the common bookes or librarie off the churche/be at the appointment off the minister and the seniors in such place as all the studentes maie moste conueniently come vnto.

The thirde note/that is Christian liffe/and Good workes the frutes off godly doctrine.

15. Item/we teache that such goode workes are to be done as are commaunded by Goddes worde in the scriptures/ such euell deedes to be auoided as are forbiden by the same.

16. And where as concerninge the frutes off godly doctrine none is more commaunded in the scriptures then the relieuinge off the poore whiche either is donne priuately by euery persone or ells by the common treasury off the churche/for the good and right vse and order off the same/it apeareth as well by Goddes worde as by the examples off churches rightly reformed/that bothe the keepinge vnd also the distribution off the treasure of the churche apperteineth to the Deacons: who be so necessarie Ministers in the churche off Christe that

Q.   w.th

CXXI.

withowte them it cannot well be. For Christe saith yow shall haue alwaies poore men amonge yow. Wherfore they ought to be honored of all men, and they them selues ought to haue this opinion, that they highlie please god in that ministery.

17. Wherfore we think it expedient for the churche that 4. men of speciall grauitie, auctoritie, and credit, in the churche, such as off them selues be able to lyue and will do this godlie office rather for Christes sake and the loue they beare to him and his poore flock, then for anie there owne necessitie or worldly rewarde, be chosen to be Deacons, whiche 4. Deacons shall haue the custodye off the treasure and distribution off the same, and other almes off the churche remaininge in their handes and kepinge, in suche sorte as it shall seme good to the ministers, seniors, and Deacons for the most saftie off the said treasure.

18. Item, that although the Deacons haue in their custodie the treasure off the churche, yet the ministers and seniors shall haue knowledge of the whole summe off the sayd treasure.

19. Prouided allwaies that neither the said 4. Deacons, ministers, Seniors, or anie of them shall haue anie knowledge or make anie inquisition of the geuer or geuers of anie Almes to the poore off the sayed churche, otherwise then the messinger or bringer off the said Almes shall of himselff declare, to whom and as he hathe commission from the geuers so to doo, but that the gyfte be receauid and knowen and the geuer and geuers names vnknowen and kept close with all possible secresie.

20. Item, that the said Deacons once in a monethe, that is the last daie of euery monethe shall make there accounpts before the ministers and senyors, howe the said treasures be bestowed, and that all the said companie, so appointed to make the accounpt shall note the remayns of the said treasure at the date and yere in the whiche euery accounpt shall be taken.

21. Item, we thinke good and do decree, that there beinge a schole in the said churche (seing the said scoole is a member of the said churche, as of the whole bodie) the treasure for the

mains

CXXI.

mayntenance and for the maintenance off the other poore also be all one and ioyned togither: that neither in the procuring off the saied treasure or in the distribution theroff, anie occasion off diuision, emulation, or contention do happen amonge them, who ought to liue togither lyke bretheren, and members of one bodie in all concorde, coniunction and vnitie: otherwise, the schole whiche is of it selff so worthie a member off the bodie, maye by abuse, cause, not onely the hinderance, but also the destruction off the whole body.

Item, that in the distribution off the saied treasure a speciall regarde be had of the saied studentes that be poore. first, for that they be poore, and againe, for that they be destinate to be workmen in the lordes vineardе, and so worthie members in the bodie. And that as they be studious of the scriptures specially, and yet with all of other liberal artes also, as mynisters and handemaides to the settinge foorth off goddes worde, so they maye be liberally handled and receyue goddes blessinge, whiche is the liberalitie off the godlie withowt the shame and abashment as the gyft off god, who geueth to all men and vpraideth no man.

Item, it is decreed and also the whole congregation desireth the Deacons monthlie to visit, and speake priuately with the saied studentes, that be poore, and other poore also, and to examin their states frindly and charitablie and according to euery mannes necessitie, as the treasure of the churche will beare, to offre to euerie one off them with obtestation to them, that yf they haue no nede theroff they receiue it not. For that were nothing ells but to robbe the nedie. for so shall bothe the shamefastnes of the honest, and liberall natures be saued and the treasure of the churche willingly spared. For he that vpon suche obtestation will not refraine to receiue that is offred, when he hathe no nede: will not be ashamed to begg and craue when he hath no nede, and that not onely lyinge, but also with periurie yf nede be.

Item, yf anie by euident profes, such as cannot be gainsaied, be founde to haue taken or vsed the treasure of the chri-

Q ij che

22.

23.

23.

24.

che, hauinge no nede hereof that they not onely be exempted frō anie more partakige of the saied treasure til it appeere that he haue euident neede but also that he doo make therfore publique satisfaction, before he be admitted to the communion.

25. Item, that the Seniors and Deacons se that the poore off the congregation be not ydle but diligent in well doeinge.

26. Item, that yff ther be anye off the poore, sick, that then foorthwith one of the Deacons resorte to them and presently succor their necessitie, and the needy straungers off our nation be holpen towardes their traueill and iourney, yff the treasure off the churche will beare it.

27. Item, that in case the treasure off the churche do faile or wax thinne, that then such as be off the welthey sorte off the congregation, shall quarterly contribute accordinge to their habilitie and godly deuotion for the maintenaunce off the ministerie, poore, and studentes off the congregation. And the same at euerie quarter daye to be deliuered into the handes off the Deacons.

28. Item, we think Good that declaration be made by the preachers off Goddes worde diuers tymes as iust occasion will serue, how comely and profitable for Christes churche, that al mennes liberalitie towardes the poore, do come to the handes off the saied 4. Deacons, by them publickly in the name off the whole churche to be ministred to the poore: for by this rule, let not thy left hande knowe what they right hande dothe, maye beste be obserued: And the blowinge off the trumpet before the almes geuer, and all wordly reward off vaine commendation maie best be auoided: and so our heauenly father, who seethe in secret, will rewarde euerie man more abundantly in the daie off the reuelation off the thoughts off all men.

29. Item we think good that certeine letters in the same sence be written with an exhortation and hartie praier to all such as will relieue the poore off oure congregation with their godly liberalitie, that they will deliuer or send their charitable reliffe to the saied 4. Deacons, commonly to be bestowed off them

them vppon all the poore/whither they be studentes or other
according to euerie mans necessitie: whiche the saied Deacons
and the churche here present can best knowe and Iudge/
rather then to committ the allmes to anie one person, han∫
de / to anye priuate vse / for the auoyding off sundry su∫
spitions / and many other inconueniences / that maye be
the presently, and here after arise and ensewe off the same:
And the sayed letters subscribed w.th as many handes off
the congregation as shall seme good / with a generall super∫
scription to all such as will charitably relieue the poore off ou
re congregation with owt anye naminge off any persons / to
be sent where the Ministers Seniors and Deacons / or the
more off them shall think good by a most faithfull and discre∫
et messinger, to all places where such good men, by whose libe
ralitie the churche is releiued, doe or maie resorte / that the sa∫
yed letters maye by the sayed messinger be shewed as a testi∫
monie off credit to the said godly men in places and at tymes
moste conuenient.

This article folowing 29. I also fynde in the Copie.

Item/as concerning the relieffe to be had at strangers —30.
handes/who be not off oure churche: such order is to be taken
as shall seme most expedient to the ministers of the worde and
Sacramentes. It semeth that this article was put in/in place
off the former whiche they could not agree vppon.

Item we thinke it expedient that the said 4. Deacons   31.
be charged neither with the helping off the Ministers in the
preaching off the worde neither in the Catechising off the y∫
outhe/ neither in ministring off Sacramentes / or saing off
common praier: or specially the visiting off the sick/ other then
the poore for the releyuing of their necessitie/ as with thinges
perteininge to the office off deaconshipp: nor with any other
offices other then is expressedly declared in gods worde apper∫
teine to the Deacons: according to the rule off the whiche/
O iij   they

they shall by all meanes possible direct their dooinges: The summe wherof is/ diligently to receiue and kepe all/ and all manner off publik and priuate almes/ and the same faithfully to bestowe vpon the poore off Christes churche accordinge as euery mannes necessitie shall requier and by all meanes possible/ as well by worde as by writing/ to procure the mainteuaunce off the saied treasure off the churche/ so to their credit committed. Notwithstandinge/ it is not ment hereby/ but that anie off the sayed Deacons/ being lerned/ when good occasion shall therto serue/ may preach or instruct the youthe in the Catechisme/ or doe anie other godly function wherunto they shall be called.

Item/ that where there is no godlier acte then to succor such as be bothe sik and poore for that their burthen is moste heauy/ we think good/ yff the habilitie off the churche will extend therunto that there be 4. graue and honest wemen either widowes or wyues (such as haue nede of the helpe of the churche) appointed and chosen with the consente off their husbandes/ to kepe the poore/ when they be sicke/ and to watche with them by course one after an other: and that they haue therfore cut off the treasure off the churche a certeine stipende quarterly payde vnto them.

Off the Discipline off the churche which is the 4. and laste note.

33. Furste/ in all matters touchinge conscience/ gods worde/ is the perfect rule/ as well for those thinges whiche Christen men ought to doe/ as for such thinges as they are bownd to abstaine from.

34. Item/ in all controuersies ciuill/ the ciuill or municipall law off the countrie or citie where the churche is/ is a sufficient rule to be obaied.

35. Item/ all matters touchinge the congregation/ or the members off the same directly apperteining to neither off the two former partes/ Ecclesiasticall ordinance and discipline of the

CXXV.

the faied churche / ought by all members off the same to be obaied.

Item / although this worde Discipline generally doth conteine all Ecclesiasticall orders and ordinaunces / yet in this place it is properly taken for the rule off owtward honest orders and manners and off the punishment and correction off vices. 36.

Item / for the execution off the whiche discipline to the mainteining of all comely order and vertue in the churche / and correction off disorder and vice / it is agreed / that 6. men off speciall grauitie / authoritie / and wisdom / suche as the rule off the holy scriptures dothe set foorthe as muche as maie be shal be chosen to be seniors / whiche 6. seniors with the two Ministers off the worde shall haue the execution off the Discipline and gouernement off the churche / and shall be reuerenced / and in all thinges godly and reasonable obeied and reuerenced of all persons in the congregation vnder paine off moste sharpe discipline. 37.

Prouided alwaies that the saied Ministers and seniors seuerally and ioyntly / shall haue no authoritie to make anie manner off decree / or ordinances to bynd the congregation or anie meber therof: but shall execute such ordinaces and decrees as shal be made by the congregatio and to the deliuered 38.

Off the election off all Ministers.

Item it is agreed that all seniors / Deacons and all other ministers (what so euer they be) the preachers and ministers off the worde onely excepted / shall ones a yere that is the first daie off marche take an ende off their ministerie / what so euer it be: And they from that daie / till a newe election be made / which shalbe within one forthnight after the saied fyrste day off marche (vnles some great causes incident do let the same) shall be all priuate persons / as other mebers off the congregation and so continewe still / till they be newe elected / to the same / or other ministerie or office: euerie one off them yet notwithstanding in the meane tyme / from the saied first daie 39.

off

off marche/ till newe ministers be elected/ doing the dewtie and dewties to your office belonging.

40. Item that publick praier and fast be made before/ and at the election off all ministers / in time and continuaunce/ as to the congregation shall seme good.

41. Item/ that before the election off the ministers/ Seniors and Deacons the places off the scriptures for that purpos most fit be openlye redd/ and a sermon to be made vppon the same/ As for the present purpose shall be most conuenient.

42. Item/ that election be made by bills/ euerie man bringing a litle bill rolled vp / the names off such persons appointed/ as they shall think moste meete for the office wherunto the election is then made.

43. Item/ that imposition off handes with praier be vsed at the institution off the saied ministers/ seniors/ and Deacons/ according to the doctrine and examples of the scriptures.

Off the callinge and assembling off the congregation.

44. Item that the ministers and seniors thus electe / haue nowe authoritie as the principall members of the congregation / to gouerne the saied congregation accordinge to goddes worde, and the discipline of the churche as is aforsaied: And also/ to call together and assemble the saied congregation for causes and at tymes/ as shall to them seme expedient.

Prouided alwaies that yff anie dissention shall happen betweene the ministers and the seniors/ or the more parte off them and the bodye off the congregation or the more parte off it: and that the saied ministers and Seniors in such controuersie/ beinge desired therto/ will not assemble the congregation/ that then the congregation maye of it selff cum together/ and consulte and determine as concerninge the saied controuersie or controuersies and the saied assembly to be a lawfull congregation/ and that which they the more parte of them so assembling

sembling shall iudge or decree/the same to be a lawfull decree and ordinaunce off sufficient force to bynde the whole congregation and euery member off the same.

45. Item/ that no man being sommoned or warned either by the ministers and Seniors or in the name off the congregation so as afore is saied assembled/to appere in the congregation shall absent himselff but vppon a lawfull cause/vnder paine off discipline: And that none shall departe owt off the said congregation so assembled till it be broken vp/ without licence off the whole or the more parte remaining/vppon paine of discipline before the whole congregation therfore.

46. Item in case some do departe/that yet notwithstanding those whiche still remaine (yff they be the greater parte) to be a lawfull congregation: and that whiche they or the more parte off them shall decree/to be a lawfull decree/ off force to bynde the whole body/ministers/seniors/Deacons and euerie other member or members theroff withowt exception.

47. Item/ that no checkinge or taunting be vsed in the saied congregation / by anie persons / vnder paine off Discipline/ and that in speakinge/ all other shall holde their peace and keepe silence: absteining also from priuate talke that all thinges maie be donne comely and in order.

48. Item/ that it shall be lawfull that euerie member off the congregation/ making protestation off licence before / to the ministers/seniors/ and the whole congregation / maie speake his mynd in the congregation / so he speake quietly and not against goddes truthe/for in case he speake vngodly/that then it shall be lawfull for the ministers/ seniors/ or anie off them to commaunde him silence by and by.

The manner or receauing all sortes off persons into the saied congregation.

49. Firste/ for the auoidinge off all heresies and sectes in oure churches euery one aswell men as wemen which desier to be receiued shall make a declaration / or confession off their

R faithe

faithe before the ministers and elders / shewinge him selff fully to consent and agree with the doctrine off the churche and submittinge them selues to the Discipline off the same / and the same to testifie by subscribing therto yf they can wryte.

50. Item / yff anye person so desyrous to be receyued into the congregation be notoriously defamed / or noted off any corrupt behauiour / or euill opinion in doctrine / or slaunderous behauionr in liffe / the same maie not by the Ministers and Elders be admitted / till he haue either purged himselff theroff or ells haue declared himseiff to the ministers and elders penitent for the same.

Off admission to the holie communion.

51. Item / that none off the youthe be admitted to the communion till they be able to make profession off their fa the before the whole congregation / and also to haue an honest testimony off towardnes in godly conuersation.

52. Item / that none openly noted as an heretickke / sectarye Idolater or other notorious offender / shall be admitted to the communion / before he either purge or reconcile himselff publiquely before the whole congregation / And that euery member off the congregation do not refuse to render a declaration off their faithe / before the Ministers and Elders / when so euer they shall by them be therunto requyred.

Thorder off proceadinge to the execution off the Discipline and correction off offences.

53. For as muche as no churche is so perfect / but offences may rise / for godly and charitable redressing and reforming off suche / this order is to be obserued: firste / yff anye off the congregation be offensiue in manners or doctrine / to anie off the brethern / so that the offence be priuate and not publicke

lickely knowen, there can be no better order devised then that whiche Christe himselff hathe appointed: whiche is firste brotherly to admonishe him alone. Iff that do not preuaile, to calle one or two witnesses: yff that also do not profit: Then to declare it to the Ministers and Elders: To whom the congregation hathe geuen authoritie to take order in suche cases accordinge to the Discipline off the churche.

Item, that it maye be the better knowne, what is ment by this worde discipline or correction off vice, we thinke that there be 3. degrees off Ecclesiasticall discipline: The first, that the offender acknowledg his faulte, and shewe himselff penitent before the Ministers and the Seniors: The seconde, that yff he will not so doe, as well his originall cryme as also his contempt off the Ministers and Elders who haue the authoritie off the churche, be openly declared by one off the Ministers before the whole congregation, and that he therfore make satisfaction, bothe for his originall crime and also for his contempt off the Ministers before the whole congregation and that he be not admitted to the communion before he haue satisfied. The thirde, that yff he remaine still obstinate before the whole congregation after a tyme to him by the whole congregation limited to repent in, he then shall be openly denounced excommunicate which excommunication, seing it is the vttermoste penaltie off Ecclesiasticall power, shall not therfore be executed, vntill the matter be hard by the whole churche or such as it shall specially appoint therunto.

Item, yff anie person shall be a notorious knowen offender so as he is offensiue to the whole congregation, then shall the Ministers and elders immediatly call the offender before them and trauell with him to reduce him to true repentaunce and satiffyinge off the congregation. Whiche yff he obstinatly refuse to do, then one off the Ministers shall signifie his offence and contempte to the whole congregation, desyring them to praie for him: and further to assigne him

CXXX.

a daye to be denownced excommunicate before the congregation: except in the meane time the offendor submit himselff before the whole congregation to the order off the discipline.

56. Item, that neither the Seniors and Ministers, nor the whole congregation shall medle in anie ciuill matters, as iudges or determiners off the same, but onely as arbitres for peace makinge, that the magistrates be troubled as litle as maye be with oure controuersies: but in case the Seniors and first, and afterwardes the congregation, or such as the congregation shal appoint, can make no peaceable ende, by waye off arbitrement, then the iudgement off the saied matters to be referred to the Magistrates off the citie and there to be ended.

57. Item, we thinke good for oure quietnes sake and for the conseruinge off the good reporte of oure nation, that all matters and controuersies amonge oure selues, yff they cannot priuately be pacified (whiche firste ought to be attempted) be brought before the Seniors and Ministers and there to be harde; And in case they cannot ende them, then afterward to be referred to the whole congregation or such as the congregation shall apoint to the hearinge and determininge theroff yff they can: and that no matter be brought vnto the magistrate or senate, to hinder, derogate, or let the authoritie off the churche or the discipline theroff, before theis waies be proued vnder paine off discipline before the congregation, vnlesse the thinge appeteine directly to the state off the citie, or offence againste the lawes, Senate, or magistrate, off the same. In whiche cases euerie man maie and ought forthwith to complaine to the magistrates.

58. Item, whereas the best waie off Christian reconciliation is, that the parties priuately betwene them selues agree: and the next, that agrement be made by mediation off some paceable and godly men: We decree that in case 2. 4. 6. moo or lesse do consult amonge themselues, or trauell with the parties, for peace makinge quietly and charitably, then the saied parties, in so doinge, do nothinge against good order off discipli-
nes

ne/but according to the dewtie and office off Christian and peaceable men.

Item that the ministers and Seniors shall haue authoritie te heare and determine/on the behalff off the whole churche all offences (determinable by the congregation) committed by any person in the congregation: vnlesse the partie called before them haue iust occasion to take exceptions to the sayed ministers and Seniors: or to appeale from them as not competent iudges. 59.

Item/yff anye haue iust occasion to take exception to some off the Ministers and Seniors/and not to the more parte: that then those off the Ministers and Seniors / to whom the exception is made/in this case shall not be iudges / but in this case for the tyme remoued / from the ministery and that the rest off the Ministers and Seniors to whom no exception shall be made / with as maine off the congregation ioyned to them/ as they be in nomber whiche shall be excepted/ shalbe arbitrees and iudges in the saied causes: and that the saied persons so to be ioined to the Ministers and Seniors/ shalbe appointed by the congregation/the Ministers and seniors not excepted/geuinge their voices as others off the congregation. 60.

Item/yf exception be taken/ to the more parte of the ministers and Seniors/ that then the churche shall appointe 6. moo to be Iudges with the reste off the ministers / agaynst whom exception is not made: the same reste off the ministers hauing their voices in the election off the 6. as other members off the churche. 61.

Item yff all the ministers and Seniors be suspected or founde parties/ or yff anie appeale be made from them / that then such appeale be made to the bodie off the congregation. The ministers/seniors/and parties excepted. And that the body off the congregation maye appoint so manie off the congregatiō to heare and determine the sayed matter or matters as it shall seeme good to the congregation. 62.

Item/iff anie person doo vniustly take exceptions to anie 63.

B iij   off

off the Ministers or appeale from the whole ministery: that then such persons/ besides the punishement for the principall cause shall also be punished as a contemner off the ministerie and a disturber off the churche.

64. Item/ yff all the ministers and seniors from whom it shall be appealed/ as is aforesaied/ shall saye and chalenge the more parte off the congregation as not indifferent iudges/ that then they maye appeale from the congregation to the magistrate. provided that iff any minister or senior appeale to the Magistrate and be founde to haue done it with owte iuste cause that then/ by that facte/ he shall be remoued from his ministerie and shall neuer after be admitted in the ministery before he hathe made publick satiesfaction for the same.

65. Item/ that the Ministers and Seniors and euerie off them be subiect to Ecclesiasticall Discipline and correction/ as other priuate members off the churche be. And that in case anie person or persons accuse anie off the Ministers or elders or the more parte off them/ or them all/ of anie crime or crimes the same order off proceadinge in all pointes be vsed as it is heretofore particulerly expressed in the making off the exception/ to summ/ or the more part / or all/ the saied Ministers and Seniors/ as parties/ or otherwise incompent arbitres.

66. Item/ that no accusation against any off the Ministers and Seniors be admitted vnder 2. Witnesses at the leaste. And that yff anie do vniustlie accuse the Ministers and Seniors or any off them/ that he or they shall therfore be moste sharply disciplined as a contemner and defacer of the ministerie and a disturber off the whole churche.

67. Item/ yf anie controuersiebe vppon the dowtfull meaning off anie worde or wordes in the discipline that first it be referred to the ministers and Seniors. And yff they cannot agree therupon/ then the thing to be brought and referred to the whole congregation.

68. Item/ for the auoyding off occasion off contention hereafter that bookes of discipline cocerning this churche hereto fore made be of no effecte hereafter/ but voyde and Canceled.

Item

CXXXIII.

Item, that all bookes and writinges off recorde concerning actes and orders in this churche, be deliuered, and remaine in the custodie off the ministers and elders for the tyme being.

Item, that a Register booke be kept by the ministers and Seniors off all suche names as be in the congregation and such as shall be hereafter admitted to be writen in the same.

Item, that mariages Christenings and buriells with the daye and yere therof be registred in the same booke.

Item, for the auoyding all controuersyes, that hereafter maye happen, it is ordeined, that all testamentes and willes made, by any off oure nation, dyinge in this congregation, shall be brought foorthe and exhibited to the Seniors off this congregation for the tyme being, for a perpetuall testimonye off the truthe in that behalff.

Item, that bicause all mennes doinges be vncerteine and chaungeable, the discipline and orders off the churche shalbe read openly once euery quarter, and warninge therof before, shall be geuen to the whole congregation bothe, that euerie member therof maye knowe their dewtie, and that euerie man maye with libertie, quietly speak his minde for the chaunging and amending of it or anye parte therof, according to goddes worde, and the same exhibited in writinge with the argumentes and reasons off that his requeste.

The names off suche as subscribed to this discipline, and were off the churche.

Thomas Crawley
Christopher Hales.
Thomas Ashley
Edmond Oldsworth
Edmonde Sutton
Thomas Asworth

Richard Alvair.
VValter Franch
Richard Leiler.
Richard Mason
Richarde Beesley.

Richard

CXXXIIII

Richard Nagors
Robert beste.
Henry Reignoldes
Perciuall Harrington.
Richard Porter.
Magnus Elyot.
Henry Perryus
Iohn Browne.
Dauid VVhithead
Iohn Mullins.
Iohn Pedder.
Iohn Hales
Gre. Railton
Alexander nowell
Iohn VVilford
Iohn Fauconer
Thomas Serbis
Thomas VVilson
Iohn Bedell
Iohn Olde
Iames Peers
Thomas Sandes
Edward Parpoint

Thomas VValker.
Iohn Kelke
Thomas VVatts.
Leonarde parry
Robarte Crowley.
VVilliam Master
Laurance Kent.
Thomas Knolle
Peter sade
Iohn Vates
VVilliam Raulinges.
Thomas VVater
Thomas VVillobie
Edmond Tomson
Richard Luddington.
Thomas oldsworthe.
Edmond Harries.
Philipp Adishe.
Gawin dixson.
Iohn Geoffrie.
Anthony Donninge
Edward Colton.
Iohn Turpin.

The 21 off December 1557. theis were added to the churche.

Sir Frances Knolls
Edward Boyes.
Iohn Browne.
Frances VVilforde.
Thomas Knot.
Thomas Donnell

Arthure Saule
Richard Sandell
Robart Ioyner
Henry VVood
Richard Lynbrougbe
Ralfe Selye.

Henry

CXXXV.

Henry Knolls
Thomas VVilford.
VVilliam Dausge
Reignolde Baker.
Robarte Hodgston
Iohn Penteny

Mighell Coke
Thomas Tod Chamber
Alsxender Nowell
Iohn Ade
Thomas Bagster.
Daniell Rogers.

Now that yow haue harde bothe the olde discipline/ and that whiche was by the authoritie off the magistrate deuised, order requireth that I place here the reasons whiche Maister Horne and the rest off his side brought against the newe discipline established.

And to the ende this volume shuld not excede measure in greatnes/ I think it expedient to do here/ as I haue done allready/ and minde to do throwghowt the whole story/ whiche is/ off a leafe/ to take/ (as I might saie) a lyne or two/ as one lothe too weary yow sith a taste maie suffice.

To the 7. Article off the newe Discipline.

VII.

13. Sept.
Horne.
Isaac.
Chambers.
VVilford.
with diuers others.

To the Article off 1. Ministers off like charge and authoritie we think we haue good reasons to require that there be no moo in the speciall burthen and charge pastorall then one/ to whom the others ioyned with him for preachinge off the worde and ministringe the Sacraments shall not incure and charge / gouernment and preheminence / bein all respectes coequall.

The Reasons.

Firste/ the scripture speakinge or treatinge of the office of a Bishopp or minister/ so speaketh as it wereto be presupposed and as an order receiued/ that one shuld in cure and charge be burthened aboue other/ and in gouernement/ for order sake/ in preheminence.   S   Item/

CXXXVI.

2. Item the expositions off all anncient Authors and Wryters vpon the scriptures that toucheth that matter do alltogether as they seeme/to gather owte off the texte/conclude/declare/ and teache one Minister or pastor in respectes aforesayde preferred and charged aboue other and thus doth the newe also.

3. Item this order off one in cure / charge/ and gouernement preferred/ haue all the churches to be red off/planted by the Apostels and all others in the primatiue churche obserued/ whose examples off vs are not to be neglected.

4. Item/like as good reason off it self forceth and concludeth/so all good autors both the newe and olde doo freely teache that for conseruation off vnitie aud concorde and for auoidinge off schismes and discorde/it is requisite and necessarie that a prerogatiue and preheminence for cure/ charge /and gouernemente be committed and geuen to some one /to be (as it is afore saide) charged aboue others.

5. Item/ all the reformed churches off Germany for the moste parte/be off that iudgement/and therfore obserue that order.

6. Item/ yff Nicene conncell decreed and ordered/for good order sake/that one Bishopp / and not many shulde be appoynted to euerye one cytie / howe more is it off necessitie for order sake that one litle flocke shulde be content with one.

7. Item/who is ignorant off this/that for the moste parte wher not one but rather two muste haue the especiall cure and charge) there commonly thinges be moste negligentlye done and not so muche regarded and cared for as otherwise they woulde be.

The answer off the churche/touchinge this 7.
Article. to the reasons off the dissenting brethern.

To § 1. We se not by the scriptures/that anie authoritie is geuen to anie one aboue others/but rather to the contrary.

CXXXVII.

As concerninge olde wryters, we knowe that Ierome expresly declarethe that in the beginninge the churche was ruled equally by manie. But after when schismes began to springe the chiefe authoritie was geuen to one for authorities sake, and by mannes ordinaunce rather then by deuine authoritie, wherfore we cōclude that as for schismes the firste order of many was left ād one chiefe apointed. So nowe for the auoidinge of tyrānie a worse euell in the churche then schismes, whiche, as apeareth by the Bishop of Rome is grownded vppon one, we thinke it good to returne to the firste order off two or moo equall ministers accordinge to the institution off the Apostelles as Saint Ierome teacheth. And that those lerned men who do moste earnestly maintaine the gouernment off one, confesse that vntill the tyme off Dionysius, who was after Christe 300. yeres and more, the Regimente was equally committed to manye. And as for the newe, there be examples off the beste churche to the contrary. And Maister Caluin in the 8. Chap. off his Institutions the 41. and 51. diuisions declarethe expresly that there were from the beginninge more Ministers off the worde and that it is but off mannes ordinaunce that one was afterwarde made chiefe.

That is alleadged off the reformed churches in Germany the multitude ought to serue no more for one, then the best reformed churches, for two ministers off the worde.

As concerninge Nicene councell it is before answered, and in that they decreed there shulde be but one, it consequently folowithe that before the saide decree there were many.

And iff those godly fathers were nowe lyuinge and did se how Antechriste is established vppon one, they woulde more gladly returne to the firste order off many equall for the auoidinge off that moste horrible mischieff. As they then did for the auoidinge off Schismes appointe euery citie one.

To the 4.
S. A.
Hutt.
Vvhitesd
Nowell
Mulline.
VVatts
Crowley
Boesley
Pedder
Parry
VVilson
Sorby.
Bedell.
Fauconer
Railton
Crawley
Ashley
Sutton
Rawlings
Best and diuers others.

To the 5.

To the 6.

S ij Neglis

Negligence is no more in two then one, habilitie off welldoinge thinges is more in two then in one. And siknesse beinge so riffe in this citye / it is as muche as 2 can well doo/ and one maie be sicke. And one maie willfully and suddenly leaue his flocke

To the 7. Yea, but though he did so then he will not doo so nowe I warrant yow.

Wherfore/two be necessary/ells/in the suddaine sicknes off one onelie Minister / when manie other be sike also/ dewe visitation off the sike is not well seene to and preachinge omitted/as it hathe chaunced in oure churche/yea/and although we haue many. And therfore reason tellethe vs that it is expedient to haue two rather then one.

Horne/ec. Vpon the 8. Artic.

Item/where it is prouided that the Ministers shall by themselues or their deputies discharge the sermons and other their dueties when necessarie cases shall so requyre: we saye it is superfluous. for a necessarie cause nedethe not to be prouided for by lawe: besides that the alowinge off deputies by lawe made for that purpose openethe a windowe off negligence to the ministers in the executinge off their office.

Whitthead/ec.

A lawe dothe well prouide that suche maye be in a redynes whiche shall serue in necessitie/ It is prouided in manye cities/by a lawe that in dreade off fier euerie man haue a bucket off water at his dore/ whiche is a thinge necessarie. And vniuersally the multitude off good lawes be grownded vppon causes necessarye. Wherfore/we think that position / that necessarie causes nede not to be prouided for by a lawe/ought to be taken for no lawe: and where it is alleadged that it openethe a windowe off negligence to the Ministers/it is not so/ for the appointemente off those deputies apperteinethe more to the Seniors them to the Ministers by oure discipline.

Horne ec. Artic. 10.

Item/

CXXXIX.

Item/ in the Article of Catechisme/ we think it so superfluous and tedious to haue x. Catechismes in one after noone And also think that Maister Caluins Catechisme ought to be vsed no otherwise with vs then it is in Caluins churche that alloweth and vseth the same.

Whithead xc.

The first Catechisme is onely ordred for the children and is but an examination and apposinge off them. The other is not onely for children but for all the congregation/xc.

Now/ for so muche as the reasons and answers are verye long and yet some off them repeated/ in Maister Hornes obiections to the discipline. whiche he offred vpp to the Magistrate/ I will here passe them ouer and come to the saied obiections/ and the answers off the church to the same.

Horne and the rest off his side to the Magistrate.

WE come to that nowe (right honorable S.) whiche we were charged to doo by yonr commaundment and appointement: that for as much as for the apeasinge and finall puttinge awaie off the contention betweene vs and oure brethern/ we shulde shewe why we dissente from them/ and cannot proceade in the same passage and waye that they doo: We shall so open vnto yow oure defence and cause euen as we desier to be iustified bothe in oure cõsciences and before god. Howbeit/ we are verye sory that your H. hathe lymited vs so shorte tyme/ so as in a cause whiche (for the waightines ãd difficultie off it) ought to be debated vppon with more leasure/ and verie manye thinges to be wayed to and fro/ we muste off force in a manner holde oure peace and say nothing.

But oure truste is that your H. will heareafter/ remedy this displeasure/ in grauntinge vs longer tyme that we maye more amplie hereafter confirme oure cause/ whiche we are

S iij forced

CXLI.

forced to set foorthe naked and withowte anie defence at all whiche we will moste gladly doo and desier that we maie freely be permitted to doo. This is the thinge that we often sought for when we consulted amonge oure brethern for the correctinge and amendinge off oure discipline/ that/ as longe as the matter and cause was in consultation / we might so longe polishe and finish be more at large that was alleadged/ to adde vnto all oure sentencee/ before the sentences brought in/ and to strike owte and take awaie from them yf ought semed worthie to be taken awaie / albeit anythinge were put in / as firme and established by oure subscription : Whiche thinge we nowe eftsonnes desier moste earnestly at your H. Handes. that for as muche as nothinge is yet concludedand determined by your H. there be no such preiudice obiected vnto oure cause/ but that we mayeconfirme all oure allegations with firme and avalable argumentes.

And in deede/ seinge we muste nowe intreate in order off those thinges whiche we reprehende and condemne in oure bretherns made Discipline: This we first reprehend vniuersally/ that any other alteration or innouation off thinges shuld be in oure affaiers then suche as serue onely to the correctinge and amendinge off that Discipline whiche be the byn heretofore receaued and vsed in oure churche. Wherin/ we will seeme also somewhat to satisfie oure bretherns curious mindes. This we saie/ bicause there is almoste nothinge that we think is to be innouated with suche poste haste and in dede/ there are many and waightie causes whiche do altogether pull vs backe from theis innouations/ and byd vs stick still to oure olde discipline / and not for the pleasure off some men / and contrary also to your commaundement (geuen for the amendinge and not for the makinge off any newe Discipline) to contemne and caste away that whiche so many haue alowed.

Whithead and the rest off that side answere in this wise.

We

We had purposed (right honorable ad righteous Magistrates) as we also signified vnto your honours) to haue made no answere at all vnto their vnbrotherly reproches off
Maister Horne and Maister Chambers (for they are the onely Authors theroff) in as muche as they be vnworthy to be
answered vnto / seinge they haue no sure growndes / but bare
assertions onely / whiche are as easilie denied as affirmed.
And besides that Maister Horne saide openly in the hearinge off all his complyces / before Maister Bartue D. Cox and
D. Sandes / arbytres appointed by your authoritie / that he
was not desyrous that we shulde answere / wherin indede
he was noraltogether a foole. For he knewe well ynough
howe fond geare he had written / and would beare awaie this
bragg the while / not as though we woulde not / but coulde
not answere so light accusations. Whiche petit bragg (Wherin he so muche deliteth) we woulde haue byn content to haue spared him / had not your authoritie (who thought it meete
for vs in anie wise to make answere) come betweene: And to
case Maister Horne and Maister Chambers shall reade some thinges here in oure answere that they woulde not / let
them remember that they haue driuen vs to it / in that they
haue blustred owte in wrytinge so vnworthie matters
(and that so falsely) off suche a multitude off their banished
countrie men. For they (forgeittinge all humanitie and
Good manner) / obiecte before the Magistrate (and that
often) prouertie to a great manye off oures nowe in exile as a
most highe reproche. What then? Are they banished and poore willingly or par force? Were they not and might they not
(yff they set more by goodes then godlynesse) be richer? And
whens haue they this pouertie whiche ye Maister Horne and
maister Chābers caste so tauntingly in their teeth? And when
ce haue ye this plentye wherby ye looke so high againste your
brethern? Surely yow ought to haue aduised your self / seinge ye carry the common purse / before ye had so rashly and so
vndiscreetly published their wordes vnto the right honorable
Magistrate / with the reproche off your self and off your countrie

untrie men. In dede we woulde haue suffred theis (as comon reproches) to be buried in perpetuall silence iff it semed not otherwise meete to the right honorable magistrate, (whose authoritie we obeyinge as yt becomethe vs) shall answere particulerly vnto all the particuler chapters off your assertions.

To the preface.

Where Maister Horne and Maister Chambers desire licence to saie and vnsaie, to put too and take fro, to subscribe and reuoke, to doo and vndoo all, as they think good themselues, they seeme to require their owne right: for they desier no other then that they haue byn vsed hitherto to doo, as it is moste euidently knowen almost to all the whole congregation, notwithstāding this (albeit) it is againste S. Paules rule, who denieth it to be his propertie to saie yea and nay, neither haue we anye more merueil, that the same Maister Horne and Maister Chambers think the olde Discipline is to be reteined still as a thinge that bothe hathe permitted them free libertie to doo yet hitherto what they woulde at their owne pleasure, and shewethe no waye howe to amende those matters that they haue don a misse a great while. And yet bicause we haue prouided by the anthoritie bothe off the magistrat and off the congregation that the like shall not happen hereafter, they accuse vs off innouation forsoothe. Where they make cauillation aboute discipline to be amended and not to be newe made, and accuse vs as though we haue done against the magistrates commaundement: We answere that all occasions off oure olde controuersies were taken awaye by the magistrates commaundement the laste off February: but the olde Discipline, as a thing not perfect nor indifferent has the byn the speciall cause off our controuersies in dede: Therfore we affirme that it was taken awaye by that commaundemente, and power geuen to the congregation to make another, as it is declared in the plaine wordes off the same commaundement:

maundement: Furthermore/for as muche as we haue kepte still the greateste parte off the olde discipline whiche semed indifferent as it apeareth euidently in the booke off oure discipline/let them call it (seinge it so pleaseth them) the amendinge off the olde discipline/in asmuche as to amende/is nothinge ells than to correcte that which is amisse/to put owte that is euell and to put in that is wantinge.

Therfore/whither they call it oure newe made discipline or the olde amended/we will not striue with them abowte that matter, seinge/we geue them leaue to speak at their pleasure. Onely we declare that we haue done nothinge against the magistrates commaundement in that behalff.

Obiection to the title off the Discipline.

IN the tytle and entrance vnto their Discipline we reproue this as plaine false in that they saye the booke off their discipline was collected by 15. men appointed do doo the same by the congregation and the authoritie off the Magistrate/and so exhibited afterwarde vnto oure congregation by the same 15. men. For it was bothe collected before the matter was committed vnto them and confirmed before hande by many mennes handes subscribed.

Touchinge the 42. Whiche approued this discipline and confirmed it by subscribinge/this we maie alleadge there are 24. off the whiche lyue off other mennes liberalitie and almes/ so as they maye seeme rather to followe other mennes wills/ and to be inclined to their pleasures: specially/seinge so large and ample promises aswell to liue at liberties as to haue their slender liuinge releued/haue byn made to this intent.

Maister Borne and Maister Chambers denie the booke off discipline to be collected by the 15. men/bycause they beinge appointed off the 15. haue labored by all means that nothinge shulde be donne for the settinge off the congregation at a quiet

Horne:

Yet olde blind father Lidford beinge an almes man, was forced by the B. off L. to subscribe to the booke off prayer, among others, more blynde then he. VVhithead.

CXLIIII.

quyet staye. And when they perceiued that they could not hinder it/they came not with the reste/the 2. laste daies accordinge to appointmēt so as by that meanes/some of the iuste nōber off 15. men shulde be wantinge. was not the booke therfore bothe Lawfully collected and lawfully exhibited to the congregation bycause 2. or 3. off the appointed men withdrew themselues againste right and equitie? What shulde be determined in anie affaires/yff the matter shuld tarie / till all togeather (not one except) shulde agree throughly in all pointes? Where they saie the booke was collected before this matter was committed to the 15. men is it a plaine slaunder. Maister Horne and Maister Chambers might be iustly ashamed to cast pouertie in oure bretherns teeth nowe in exile (and that before the Magistrate) and to lye so openly / that 14. off oure company that subscribed lyue off other mennes almes. And yff so manye poore men haue forsaken Maister purse bearer Chambers is it not a plaine matter that they haue byn euell intreated at Chambers hande before tyme? But where they gather that the poore men seeme to haue folowed other mennes myndes in subscribinge to the Discipline/rather then their owne: it is fondly gathered: in asmuche as on the contrary parte it is moste true that they whiche (were they poore men) folowid not Chambers when he ranne a Waye with the bagge/ regarded their conscience more then the lyuinge forsomuche as bothe they and all other might be certeinly assured that they shulde moste greuously offend not onely the purse bearer Chambers but allso two or there other off the richer sorte off oure congregation. But howe muche more iustly might we returne this accusatiō (which they falsely bend againste oures) vpon M. Horne and M. Chamb. and manye other off their nomber whiche haue folowed Chamb. in runninge awaye from the congregation / bycause he caried and shewed them a well stuffed powche / as it were a standard to followe. for neither Maister Chambers nor Maister Horne durst euer haue departed from the congregation as they haue done but vppon truste off the powche / which
the

the one hathe allwayes borne/ and the other hath byn euer an vnseparable waiter vppon/ where so euer it were caried: and and yet in the meane while / this gaye fellowe Borne/ from alofte contemneth so great a company off his countrie men/ as beggers and caitiues in comparison off himselff.

But in case there be so many amonge vs that liue off other mennes almes/ as Maister Borne and Maister Chambers do reason. And seinge Maister Chambers tooke vppon him especially at the intreaty off Maister Borne/ the charge off gathering godlye mens almes publickely in the name of the churche/ for the relieff the off poore off oure congregation as it is already knowen vnto many and shall hereafter by the whole matter seuerally setforth/ be moste euidently knowen to moo: what mercie and pitye is this off there towardes their brethern to leaue so many miserable people behinde them/ contrary to their promesse made to the congregation/ and to runne awaie not onely from the congregation/ but also owte off the cytye snappinge awaie the bagge with them (whiche conteinethe many mennes almes gathered for the poore in the name off the congregation/ and to leaue them all destitute. / and also to leaue certeine preachers appointed by them (whiche haue serued the churche a yere and moore/ and to whom they promised that they shulde lack nothing) in a great deale off dett to other men for their necessary bourde.

And where they playe such prankes/ they caste oure brethern in the teeth still with pouertie/ by the waie off reproche/ before the Magistrate. Let them go too therfore/ seinge their pleasure is suche and nomber their owne copanye and leaue owte their seruauntes/ their boyes/ and suche as depende vppon Chambers purse (for he hathe made it his owne/ and dedicated it to his owne propertie) and let them tell vs then/ howe many there be left on their parte/ yff they be not ashamed to tell howe manie they be: Where we did comforte our poore brethern to oure power whom Chambers running awaye

T ij with

with the bagge. Had made astonished / and woulde haue had them vtterly discouraged / they lay it to oure charge as euell done: what is there manifeste declaration els but that the poore of our congregation shuld be vtterly destitute not onely of relieff but also off all hope of reliefe whiche hathe euer bin the vttermoste comforte off suche as bein myserie.

In the Discipline it selff an obiection.

Horne. The next thinge nowe wherein we agree not / is / that whiche is spoken off the 2. newe Ministers. This they treat vppon in the 7. Article. This we defende / that the scripture doth leane and inclyne rather vnto one / than vnto 2. whiche one / as he muste not be aboue the reste by lordeshipp / so yet ought he to be aboue other in charge and in burthē / in as mache as he muste nedes geue a greater accoumpte / then the reste for the flock cōmitted vnto him and to his charge. Theis we are able to proue. Firste / by the circumstances off the places off scriptures considered / secondly / by the interpretacions off auncient fathers / and the best lerned men off oure tyme or latter daies. Thirdly / in the examples of the churches instituted by the Apostells / and most holy men after their tyme / foorthly / this newe order off 2. Ministers or moo / hathe bene (as all the wysest men haue alwaies reasoned) the seedes ād fountains of all dissentions and cōtentions. And like as for order sake and for conseruation off the churches in peace / oure elders thought / that one shulde necessarely be aboue the reste: so also in this oure remembrance / the greatest lerned men as Caluin / Brentius / and many other do think. Off theis maters the beste instituted and reformed churches in Germany can also be the beste witnesses. Theis / we professe that we bothe can and will more largely shewe as farther occasion shal hereafter serue / whiche we cannot doo nowe for that we be lymited to so short a time.

The answere.

Whitehead. As concerninge the two Ministers off the worde. We
Affirme

affirme that it is lawfull by the worde off God to haue either 2. or moo.

 Where theis men saye the scriptures do leane rather to one that is to affirme onely/ and to proue nothinge/ where as Paule almoste in all his Epistles writeth allwaies as vnto moo off equall authoritie in euerie churche and not as vnto os ne principall. Where they alleadge the ancient Doctors/ Ierome whiche is the moste diligent in Historie matters/reporteth moste plainly that in the beginninge there were many/ and afterwarde for the auoidinge of dissentions/the chieff authoritie was committed vnto one as the chieff. But yet saithe he/ that was donne rather by the statute off men then by the authoritie off God. Where they speake so muche off the mischiffe off contention in the churche/ we confesse it is a great euell/ But/ that tyranny is a more pestiferous destruction to the churche/ and that tyranny crept into the churche by one/ the Bishopp off Rome/ maye teache vs at large. Therfore/ for as muche as bothe waies/ either by one or by moo/ euells maie happen/ we thought good to beware more diligently of the greater euell. Where they bringe in Caluin for one/ we maruell with what face they can do, that seinge it is owte off all dowte/ that he vpon one daie and in one houre instituted two Ministers off equall authoritie in all thinges in the Englishe congregation whiche is at Geneua. And also seinge that in the 8. chapter and 41. and 52. diuisions off his Christian Institution/ he declareth openly that there were from the beginninge moo ministers off the worde off equall authoritie in the churche off Christe. Where they alleage the examples off the churches off Germiany we also want not examples off the dutche churche at Emden wherin their be 3. Ministers off the worde off equall authoritie. And off the frenche churche off this Citie/ and off the Englishe churche off Geneua/ yea and Caluin himselff is counted superior to his felowes not by authoritie off office/ but in respect off his lerninge and merites. Therfore in asmuche as it is also permitted vnto vs by the magistrates apppnintement/ to. Huse one or moa: let them

leaue

leaue their wranglinge for a thinge indifferent/ as though it were for lyffe and lande. Where they professe that they will make large proffe off this matter at leysure/ let them professe their gaye glorious promyses so longe as they will/ so they knowe the longer they labor in this matter/ so muche lesse shall they bothe shewe and bringe to passe

The obiection to the 8. Article.

Horne. In the 8. Article Ministers committ and assigne the burthen and cure (wherwith they are charged) vnto others with ouer muche facilitie: We demaund also this/ whiche appeareth not plainly inough in their Discipline/ to whom perteineth it to allowe their allegations and excuses/ when they will leaue their charges vnto others.

The answere.

VVhitehead. What inhumanitie is it/ not to be content/ that the ministers off the worde (vpon waightie causes/ as sicknes or vrgent busines off importance) shuld be eased off their burthens? as though they that fynde faulte at this nowe/ permitted not the same to themselues before/ rough againste other/ and ouer fauorable to themselues.

And where they demaunde vnto whom it perteinethe to allowe their lawfull causes/ we wonder/ that they/ nother redde ioyntly in the same place the name off Seniors/ to whom the matter is committed/ nor remember that generall pointe in the 36. article/ that the gouernement off the whole churche is committed to the ministers and Seniors.

The obiection to the 13. Article

Horne. We allowe the translatinge off bookes. But that so open a lawe shulde be made for that matter/ that is the thinge we fynde fault withe. For it bothe conteineth that whiche is a pestilent matter to pure congregation/ by meanes off danger off
such

such as are wont, to traueile as strangers vpp hither vnto vs owt of Englande/ as also it maie be reprehended in that it seemeth to smell and tend openly to the priuate commoditie off some men.

The answere.

Where it is signified that certeine bookes godly and VVhithead fitt either to instructe / or comforte oure countrie men in this calamitie off oures and off oure countre / shuld be translated in to our tonge then the whiche there can be nothinge more profitable or necessarie/ they saie it is a pestilente matter forsoothe/ bicause it is so openly mentioned: as though by speaking nothinge/ it might be perswaded that we do nothinge here but slepe for wher they add towching the priuate commoditie off some in so common a profit / we cannot gesse what that meanethe in as muche as all men that haue in theis miserable daies/ yet hitherto caused bookes tobe set foorthe in oure tonge haue rather lost then wonne by them.

The objection to the 16. Article.

In the 16. Article the custodie off the treasure off the churche perteineth not necessarily to the Deacons by the worde off God. And at this daye many reformed churches do not observe it and moreouer it semethe more profitable vnto oure congregation to haue it otherwise. Fowrthly the moste parte off the auntientest churches keepe a plaine other custome. Horne

The answere.

Iff they be able to shewe so plaine a place in all the whole Scripture for anie other that ought to haue the custodie off the treasure off the churche as is in the 6. off the Actes off the Apostells/ for the Deacones/ we yelde vnto them. Yea/ and Caluin shall yelde also (whose name they oftentimes wonderous confidently and falsely alleadge) who/ in the 8. Chapter off the Institution off a Christen man in the 11. diuision / thinketh plainly as we doo / aswell concer- VVhithead

nings

ninge the custodie/ as the distribution off all churche mony and vtterethe the same in plaine wordes. In the primatiue churche/ saith he/ the Deacons receaued (euen as it was vnder the apostells) faithfull peoples dayly oblations and the yerely renewees off the churche/ to thentent they shuld bestowe them vppon true vses. We desier them nowe to shewe vs more p'ainly / vnto what other men that charge dothe rather belonge then to the deacons/&c. But they saye manie reformed churches obserue not this/ad that it will be more profitable for oure congregatiō to haue it otherwise: And that the moste parte of the auncietest churches keepe still an other custome. This (as we sayde before) is onely to affirme/ and proue nothinge. But thus they doo almoste allwaies. But where they speake off the auntientest churches / we beleue / they meane the popish churches/ but would not for shame vtter it: or elles let them shewe vs what auncient churches those be/ yet this we maye not ouerpasse how that they affirme that it will be profitable for oure churche to haue it otherwise: that is / that one/ as it is nowe/ haue the custodie alone/know alone/ and distribute the churche mony alone and make accoumpt alone/ and to himselff alone. But we are ready to proue either to the magistrate/or to the worlde (in case the Magistrate so permit it) bothe by testimonies/reasons/and matters in dede/ that this is not onely not profitable/ but also it hathe and is vtterly pernitious/ and to the plaine vndooinge off oure churche.

The obiection to the 17. Article.

Rome. We fynde faulte/ that the election off the Deacons is not free ynough. For the riche men muste be allwaies taken. Also in that they ought to depend vppon the will and councell off the elders/ where nowe a great parte off the elders bothe liue and depende vpon the Deacons purce. There mouth therfore semeth to be stopped/ so as they dare neuer reproue and euer sore correcte the Deacons when they offende.

CLI.

The answere.

There was neuer man that was in his right witt which denied it to be moste profitable for the churche, to haue suche men chosen to be Deacons, as the least suspition can be had in. Where Horne and Chambers affirme that a great parte off the Elders liue and depend vpon the Deacons purce, it is a plaine slaunderous reporte.

But admit there be one or two amonge them off the poorer sorte that shail perhapps haue nede now and then off some relieff off the churche monie. Do not yow (Horne and Chambers) knowe that they haue byn richer in tymes paste, and excepte they preferred Religion to riches) maye be richer when they will? And nowe as they are become willingly banished men, so are they willinglye poore men for the same Religions sake that ye will seeme to professe? Wherfore then had ye rather enuiously to reprehend pouertie in suche a one then gentlie to comend so great a vertue, but that ye are driuen hereto by griefe of your stomakes through malice. What? Dothe Paule require welthe in Elders (as ye doo) or vertue? Go too, and shewe vs owte off Paule that this your purce welthe, is so necessary in an elder? We dare affirme that suche a one shulde haue byn off more authoritie with Paule as also with all men that be godly, and more worthie to be an elder by reason off his pouertie, for the whiche he is so contemned at your hande. But poore elders dare not (ye muste vnderstande) reproue offendinge Deacons: Do not yow Horne and Chambers knowe that in the primatiue churche, Bishopps them selues, had their appointed liuinge owte off the treasure off the churche, whiche was in the Deacons handes: and yet the Deacons (in case they did amisse) were neuer the lesse sharply corrected off them? And yet theis men that requier such ruffling riche elders, woulde haue Deacons off the poorer sorte. But by what example, and by what reason? why cannot ye beinge Christians be content in exile aswell with poore Elders as with poore Deacons? we remember that one off yow saied openly in our hearinge, and in the hearing of manie other that

VVhitechd

yow

yow coulde not with your conscience be vnder such ministers and such Seniors as oure church hathe nowe chosen. If ye can finde no other faulte in them then willfull pouertie, the congregation also can not repent them yet off the ministers and Seniors whom they haue chosen: and as for this pure conscience off yours we passe not for it. But we think, yff well hebe to respected in anie that is in Ecclesiasticall Ministery it is to be be respected chieffly in Deacons, that they medle with the churche monie with owte sinistre suspition. In dede abowte 4. monethes paste / ye had Deacons / surely honest men we saie not nay / but yet suche as for their slender abilitie ye made such vnderlinges, that ye brought not onelie the honest Good men but also the ministerie off Deacons (to the great iniurie off the apostells ordinaunce) into very muche contempte. And in case we haue thought Good to be ware (by all meanes) off that euill, / ye ought not to haue byn greued at it, but rather to haue reioised in the churches behalff. But herein there is one great sinne / that this is not done by yow/ but rather against your mindes seinge ye think nothinge to be right, nor anie thinge to stande in force vnlesseit proceede off yow.

The Obiection against the 18. Article.

Horne.
Yff Caluin be so in your iudgemente I hope yow will allowe his 2. letters before.

The ministers shall be priuie howe muche monie ther is, but not howe it is bestowed. This is agaiste the custome of the aunctientest and beste instituted churches, and contrary to the Iudgemente and mynde off the greatest lerned men that be in theis daies as Caluin and others / whiche as they permit the distribution vnto the Deacons, euen so, will they haue it donne at the arbitrement and apoointment off the Elders.

The answere.

Whitehead.

The Ministers (saie they) shall be priuie howe muche monie

monie there is/ but not how it is bestowed. Where find yow in oure booke theis wordes: (but not how it is bestowed?) And yet when he hath added it/ off his owne/ lorde/ howe he triumpheth here off the custome off the moste auncientest churches/ off the mindes off the greatest lerned men/ namely Maister Caluin/ &c. In this matter the man truly semethe not to haue wanted space and tyme wheroff he had to muche to write so fonde vanities/ but that he lacked his eye sight and some what ells besides.

The obiection against the 19. Article.

Albeit they would couer the matter/ yet by makinge off lawes/ they make al openly knowen: for they disclose thus muche/ that we sende owte oure gatherers to bringe other mens nies liberalitie vnto vs: whiche thinge shall bringe great daunger to many in as muche as the enemyes off oure religion will easilie coniecture from whom this so great libiralitie cometh.

Horne

The answere.

VVhitehead

There is a great fore sight in theis men that they can reprehende that thinge in vs whiche they themselues haue done nowe alreadie theis 3. yeres but it is wel knowē that they send owte their gatherers/ no more then it is/ that we be at Franckford. And then he addeth that the ennemies maye easilie coniecture from whom this so great liberalitie commethe. We wonder what he meaneth or howe muche it is that he calleth so great. Dothe Chambers at vnwarres meane the greatnesse off his purce: for as for vs we haue yet hitherto sent owte no bodie to gather/ muche lesse haue we receiued as nie thinge by anye gatherer.

The obiection against the 21. Article.

We wote not what they meane by the scoole, but howe so

Horne

CLIIII.

so euer the matter is/it shall annoye vs verie muche,/yff they builde vp so many thinges with so solemne a profession, and shall bringe oure aduersaries into such a suspirion, that we receiue muche more off other men then commeth to oure handes in dede. And this shall comme off it that verie many shall for oure sakes be moste straitly handled and examined.

The answere.

Whitehead What yff 2 or 3 Papistes liste to lie/ that we receiue many thousands, shall this breed great daunger to vs and others, and shal many be moste straitly handled and examined therfore? They maye faine daungers owte off euerie thinge iff they will. But he thinketh it woulde not be knowen that there are studentes, lectures, and Disputations, yff we had spoken nothinge off the scoole in oure discipline. For it was not knowen that there was a colledge off studentes at Zurick before. It is a world to se howe circumspecte theis men be in wordes/when they are minded to speak any thinge against this oure foolishe symplicitie. For what madnesse is it, to think that those thinges whiche be euery daie open before mennes eyes are the more knowen, by one sentence wrytten in a booke whiche verie fewe shall looke in.

The obiection to the 22. 23. and 24. Article.

Rome. The shamefastnes off manie, is vnshamefaste ynough, and to be often diligently examined. And we thinke it necessarie that nothinge be donne in this behalff withowte consent off the elders, who as they beste knowe the state off euerie man so they can and ought to make an exhortation at the distributing apte and fit for euery mannes disposition.

The answere.

Whitehead The shamefastnes off some is almoste so farre attempted

ted off some shameles men that their harte is clene caste downe. For theis discreete disposers off other mennes almes / haue by passing to muche on monye vtterly caste awaye men / yea / bothe together the monie and men. And yet in the meane while / theis that withowte all shame / reason of shamfastnes forsooth / whom rather then those that haue any sparke off honeste shamefastnes left / woulde go vnto / they had rather almoste die / yea / theis gentle and shamfaste disposers haue with their odious behauiour driuen many men off notable good wittes and towardnesse / some to the printinge howse / some to be seruinge men / and to runne into England againe / with the perill bothe off bodie and soule. But off this case off euell handlinge / we shall commence matter againste theis men (yff god will) and the magistrate geue vs leaue / to thentent that goodmen maye be the more ware hensfoorthe that they committ not their liberall almes so easilie to anie one mannes fidelitie hereafter.

The obiection against the 26. Article.

The lawe ordeined for those that trauell by the waie shall *Horne* call vnto vs all suche as be the moste idle persons and the veriest vnthriftes / and also Papistes whiche will faine themselues to be Religious that they may be holpen as we haue lerned by experience.

The answere.

The trauelour off oure nation hauinge neede by the waye to be holpen on his iourney (yff the treasure off the churche *VVhithead* will beare it) please not theis men. They saie / they haue lerned by experience that idle persons and vnthriftes and also papistes are called hither by this meanes. By what experience / we beseche yow: before this lawe was made or sithens? yff they were called hither before this lawe was made / they were not called by occasion off this lawe. Let them ceasse therfore to

V iij impute

impute vnto a lawe/ that prouideth onely for those that be godly and needie/ those thinges that naugtie packes haue euer hitherto donne and will do still hereafter.

The obiection to the 27. Article.

Cearne.

It is not an almes/ but a compulsion. Besides this/ off theis that are founde to be the setters foorth off theis lawes their are not paste 17. or 18. Whiche haue competent ynough he to liue vpon and to sustaine themselues. And off them there woulde not onely fiue geue heretofore/ when collections were made/ and the summe off all their distributions came neuer to 13. Dallers/ they gaue so sparingly and so slenderly. And parhappes their is some what herein to keepe back and and fray awaie all such as be off the richer sorte from vs that they came not hither/ when they shall se so fewe riche dwell amonge so manie poore/ whiche neuertheles shalbe compelled to sustaine and beare verie great charges at sundrie contributions.

The answere.

VVhithead.

It is not a compulsion/ but an almes. For no man is constrained otherwise then his owne good will and habilitie is/ and that that is off good will/ is no compulsion. And there shall no man off the richer sorte (that is godlie) be fraide awaie from vs by this meane/ in as muche as suche as be godlie seke off there owne accorde/ whom they maye doo good vnto. And wher they obiecte vnto vs againe, the small nomber off oures/ whiche haue competent ynough to lyue vpon themselues/ theis shulde be some men off mightie habilitie that woulde haue the magistrate perswaded/ that other are but beggers in comparison off them. paraduenture Horne/ whiche is the deuiser here off/ is admitted vnder hande into the felowshipp off the purce with Chambers and thers off it commethe his so great swellinge/ such loftynesse and
contem

contempte off others: And where he addeth that there wer rebut fyue that gaue at the collections before tyme / and the summe off that they gaue / came scarse to 13. Dallers / it is a matter worthie to be knoremm. For abowte an halff yere paste and more when Horne and Chambers had geuen warninge openly for certeine thinges that they were offended at / we wote not what / that they woulde geue ouer their Ecclesiasticall ministeries / whiche is no noueltie for them to doo nowe / afterwarde they went abowte to gather euerie mannes almes to the intent they might seeme at their departure from their ministeries like good husbandes of other menes liberalitie to haue left somethinge vnto the churche. But seinge they gathered to this ende / and it was perfectly knowen to all men that their gatheringe was for this cause / certenly / we meruaile that there was so muche as one that woulde gaue anie thinge / or that the summe whiche they gaue / growed to so muche as 13. not Dalers but hallers or pheninges. But Chambers and Horne were not so euell knowen at that tyme: nowe yff they lyst to assaie / they shall proceiue / that there is not one / that will put them in truste with so muche as a myte. And yet sins they departed from the congregation / there hathe bin more geuen (by the grace off god) vnto the poore / then Horne and Chambers haue geuen off their owne / all the daies off their liffe.

The obiection against the 29. Article.

Horne:

This lawe hathe these discomodities: that firste / it discloseth the thinge ouermuche / that those whiche were wont to be liberall vnto vs / are moste desirous to keepe close / secondly / it is preinditiall to priuate men whiche haue felte manie mennes priuate beneficence. Thirdly it nippeth and thwiteth awaie agreat deale off that liberalitie / whiche might come to vs / in that we so appointe a strange collectour / and vnknowē to the geuers. Fourthelie it dothe wonderous suspiciously importe the infamie off certeine that haue vsed their labours. Fiftlie / it shall strike a feare and a terror vnto the geuer

when

ste vnderstande) maie not be in so great authoritie with all men/ nor be such buggarddes to the poore yff they maye not beare the bagge alone. O greuous and intollerable euilles that will growe off theis suspitions. Jn dede they make an ende off all this place withe plaine tragicall termes: this geare (saith he) shall cause vndooinge and a moste pestilent plage vnto the congregation.

We wonder that he cried not owte also: o heauen/ o eare the/ o neptunes seas/ but where they feare them selues so muche off suspitions/ we beleue/ they maie be owte off paraduenture in a while. For all men will within a shorte time (as farre as we see) geue ouer to suspect what manner off men Horne and Chabers be. Finally what faulte so euer they finde with vs in all this adoo touchinge the messager to be sente/ they themselues haue vtterly forced vs by extream tie and violence to attempte it. For seinge Chambers won d geue nothinge being present/ but vnto certeine off his owne/ and is noa we runne awaie with the purce/ we are vtterlie constrained to take this waie/ that oure poore perishe not for famine.

The obiection against the 30. Article.

Horne. This is amisse/ that the Deacons are bownden to visite the poore onely/ to knowe iff they neede: seinge it is chiefly required that they maye exhorte/ that they maie comforte/ that they maie relieue such consciences as be sick and burthened with synnes. A man maie aske them where it apeareth by plaine wordes off the scriptures/ that it is the Deacons office to receiue and keepe the treasures off the churche/ and that they alone ought to execcute and accomplishe this office.

The Answere.

VVhitehead Let the Deacons visit all sicke folke vniuersallie yff they will and exhorte them and comforte them/ we forbid the not. Onely we shewe that they are bownden by reason off their offics office peculiary to haue charge off the poore. Where they saie it is chiefly required that deacons shuld exhorte and comforte the sicke consciences off them that are diseased: Iff they saie they be bownde to doo that by reason off their office/let them proue it/that they doo not onely saie all thinges. But yff they respecte Christian pitie towardes their brethern / neither doo we exempte from the Deacons / that which is the common dewtie off all Christians. But for as muche as they haue but shened the Deacons before/with vnnecessarie charges as concerninge the office off Deacons/by reason wheroff they fraied manie from that right godlie office off Deacons / we haue thought good to declare what thinges they be whiche properly appertaine to the Deaconshipp / and what be the common dewties off all Christians. And leaste theis men might iustlie complaine as touchinge the lake off exhortinge and comforting the sicke/that matter is sufficientlie prouided for by the ministers off the worde vnto whom that charge dos the chiefly appertaine and by other lerned men also. And to that question that they harpe vpon againe/ it is throughly answered in the 4. Artickle In that they require plaine wordes off scripture off vs we cannot meruaile ynoughe / seinge they neither proue or shewe anie thinge/ either by plaine wordes or obscure wordes: but as thoughe we were scollers and they scoolemasters off Pithagoras rule / they onely saie and affirme all thinges and confirme nothinge. But they promesse they will doo it at leasure and god before. And that is ynoughe we trowe.

The objection against the 38. Article.

The time is ill appointed, it were a great deale better after the marte/ for the auoidinge off rumor and blowinge off dissentions whiche maie arise as it is nowe in example. Horne.

The answere.

The time is appointed well ynough. For theis dissentions are not to be imputed to times / but to men. And we truste VVhithead

E ij

CLXII.

so farforth we shall by the grace off God have henseforthe goodmen that shall quyetlie governe the churche in the true feare off god and love to their brethern.

The obiection against the 44. Article.

The 44. Article speaketh manifestly against the edicte off the Senate. For there it is specified by their clere and manifeste wordes. Furthermore the Senate off this honorable citie hath decreed, that iff there arise anie dissention or contentions amonge the strangers, concerninge Religion or their Discipline, they be sett at one with all diligence by the ministers and Seniors specially for this cause, leaste those whiche professe themselues to be banished fro owte of their countrie for true Religions sake, vtter an evell token what their minde is by reason off such controuersies and debates. And in case the matter cannot be apeased before the ministers and elders let them knowe that the Senate off this citie will take order therein, who as reason is, will looke moste sharply vppon the Authors off suche trouble.

The answere.

It is not against the meeninge off the edicte, as it was declared by the Magistrates themselues in oure churche before all the congregation the laste off February, by the mouthe off Maister Valeran pollane, and the saide Magistrate, (sainge the sentence pronounced by the saide Maister Valeran and written owte by vs, allowed it, accordinge wherunto, the decree is altogether set foorth.

The obiection against the 46. Article.

This lawe doeth not sufficiently forsee and provide for the quietnes off the congregation, vnles in this greater parte suche pastor and seniors be indewed, whose authoritie men

ought

CLXIII.

ought not to bringe into such cōtempte that we woulde so easlie reiecte them. The multitude is off their owne disposition, ouermuche licentious and grudginge at euerie superior power and this lawe is also againste the edicte off the Senate.

The answere.

Iff the ministers and Elders wilbe present no man waxeth them: yf they will not, who wil force them againste their willes? It is impertinent that he saith, they be easilie reiecte, whiche will not come when they be desired, or when they be present departe vppon their owne will. Where he saithe, that this decree is also contrarie to the edicte off the Senate, it is not ynough, excepte he proue it.

Whitehead.

The obiection against the 49. Article.

The subscribinge is ouer hardly and constrainedly done specially in so often alteration and innouation off lawes as they speake off.

Horne.

The answere.

The subscribinge is not ouer hadly nor constrainedly done, but so muche the lesse hardly and cōstainedly, in that there is an easie waye shewed to redresse yf anye thinge be done amisse: Where theis men would haue their decrees to be reputed for holie sacred cānons whiche maie not be moued. And as for this subscribinge, whiche they say is so cōstrained and harde, besides that it is prouided for by the edicte off the Senate, it is required also in their oulde discipline and institution.

Whitehead.

The obiection against the 54. Article.

The authoritie off the pastor and Seniors is all wiped awaie. For euerie thinge is referred to the confused multitude of the congregation.

Horne.

The

CLXIIII.
The answere.

VVhithead. Excepte the matter be vsed as we haue prouided in the Discipline, bothe the authoritie and libertie off the congregation is wyped awaie, and a meere tyranny established. Where he saith all thinges is referred to the confused multitude, it is manifestlie false. For it is allwaies added by such as the congregation shall appointe theretio: as it is also in the 54. article added, in plaine wordes.

The obiection against the 57. Article.

Horne. This Lawe is also contrarie to edicts off the Senate.

The answere.

VVhithead. This shulde not be saide but shewed.

The obiection against the 58. Article.

Horne. The assemblie off 4. 6. 8. or 10. is troublouslye done and withowte order, and will styrre vpp newe tumultes daily in the congregation. Such lawes as this condemne the authoritie and counsaile off the Elders.

The answere.

VVhithead. Horne and Chambers condemne the assemblie off 4. 6. 8. or 10. men for peace makinge: Where they haue almost euerie daie theis 2. monethes gathered corner creepinge assemblies to disturbe the peace of the church.

The obiection against the 59. Article.

Horne. The 59. article is manifestly repugnant against the 56. Article.

The

CLXV.
The answere.

The 59. is not repugnant against the 56. article for there Whitheed
is intreated off ciuill controuersies and here off others.

The obiection against the 63. Article.

This lawe also is against the edicte off the Senate.   Horne

The answere.

It is not against the meaninge off the edicte, as it is de- Whitheed
clared in the answere to the 15. Article. For it was declared by
the right honorable and godly Magistrates openly in oure
churche, that they thought nothinge lesse then to impeche the
lawfull authoritie off the congregation. And except the congregation whiche geueth authoritie to ministers be superior
to the ministers, they are not nowe ministers, but lordes off
the congregation, as to adde no further.

The obiection to the 68. article.

In this place we desier that oure olde discipline maie be Horne
looked vpon, that we maie se whither it be, to be so lightly caste awaie, seinge it proceded off so lerned men, and shall with
a meane amendinge be farr perfecter then this newe Discipline.

The answere.

Where they desier that the olde Discipline maie be loo- Whitheed
ked vppon, we answere, the more they shall looke vpon it, the
more euedently shall the naughtynes and imperfection off it
appeare, And it shall also more plainely appeare howe muche
the congregation hathe bin beholdinge to them that haue reteined such an vnperfit discipline so longe in the churche, onely, by
cause

CLXVI.

cause it permitteth all to the pastor. Where they saie that the Discipline proceded off so lerned men / yet / the same that wrote it / (were they neuer so well lerned) confesse themselues both that it was gathered in haste/ and geuen to the congregation as imperfit/onely for a tyme. Where they speak off the amending off that Discipline/ we marueill that it neuer came into their minde before.

The obiection against the 72. Article.

Horne. That concerninge testamentes in this daungerous worl de is a pernitious Lawe.

The answere.

Whithead. We cannot tell what serpente the lawe concerninge Testamentes hathe lurkinge vnder the herbe. They saye it is a pernitious lawe/ and they onely saye so / But we saie it is verie wholsome / and profitable against the fraude off falsaries and to the succours of the fatherles and widdowes.

The obiection the 73. Article.

Horne. Quietnes is not sufficiently prouided for by this meanes/ in asmuche as it is commaunded (as it were) that euerie one shuld looke and study for an innouation.

The answere.

Whithead. Quietnes/ is prouided for sufficiently/ in as muche as the matter muste passe quietlye and peaceablie / and also by writinge mennes consciences/ are also necessarely prouided for/ that in case any thinge be founde in the Ecclesiasticall ordinaunces vngodly or disagreinge / or ells vnprofitable for the church it maie be chaunged straight waies/ so as mennes pleasures be not holden for holy/ sacred/ and vnmouable as the papistes would.

The

CLXVII.

The obiectours conclusion.

In all this adoo/ we saie this for a conclusion/ that there Horne
be thre thinges / whiche they onely seeke/ the innouation off
ministers/ a purse and treasure/ I wote not what/ and the pur
ginge off their owne offences before committed

Nowe haue we alleadged as muche as we handsome
ly coulde bringe/ consideringe the tyme. We woulde also haue
alleadged verie many other thinges / so as it shulde plainly
appeare/ that oure brethern haue in ordeininge their Discipli
ne respected neither so great waightie reasons / nor so great
commodities off oure congregation But haue in the meane
while geuen that/ that shall be offensiue and slanderous to all
good men/ and to oure aduersaries and goddes enemies the
papistes high reioycinge and pleasure. The booke off the olde
discipline with a verie litle and small correction and amending
would cause manie more plentifull fruites off Christian har
tes to be brought foorth/ and would settle a great deale more
constant and more durable quietnes amonge vs.

The answere to the conclusion.

In all this adoo/ Maister Horne and Maister Chamb vvhithead
ers go abowte nothinge ells but to disquiete the cōgregation/
that Horne might rule the roste ouer all: Chambers beare the
bagge alone/ and they 2. together exercise a moste vnworthie
lordshipp ouer the poore/ and by them all other/ and that they
might haue no certeine discipline/ but that their pleasures mi
ght be holden for lawes/ and that nothinge shulde be thou
ght right or stād in force but what they doo/ yet hithertoo/ and
the same they go abowte nowe. And it semethe they haue vt
terly determined either to establishe a tyrannie/ or to leaue no
common wea'th at a'l in the congregation. Where Horne and
Chambers make rehersall here off the purginge off offences
comitted by vs/ they ought iustly to haue byn ashamed to mā
ke mention off offences seinge they haue neuer left for theis
3. or 4. Monethes to lade themselues with wicked doinges

R And

And as for occasion of offence, and slander geuen to good and godly men and to oure aduersaries and goddes enemies the papistes high reioicinge and pleasure/they accuse vs theroff so falsely/as they themselues haue geuen the occasion in dede.

For they coulde neuer abyde to haue any thinge amended nor themselues to be admonished off any thinge/ or to be comoned withall in anie wise. But for the moste light/ yea/ no causes in dede/they forsoke their ministerie straight waies/the pastor forsoke the flocke/ the Treasorer the poore and bothe forsoke the churche and moued others by their example to do the same.

Neither was it ynough for them to geue ouer their owne functions but they must drawe other preachers and readers with them also/to the intent the congregation shulde by this meanes be destitute off Goddes worde/and vtterly scattered as though it colde not possiblie stande withowte them. And when they had forsaken their owne churche/ they haunted/ partly the french churche and partly/ the dewtche churches and so raised rumors abroade and spred oure dissentions/firste/though this citie and then thorough other cities off Germany. And last off all/when they wolde not come to the churche in the marte time/ but by the Magistrates commaundement/ neither coulde they then be quiet they spreed the like rumours almoste throughowt all Europe.

Then I hope, it may be now spred againe withowt offence, allthinges wel waied.

And when they haue plaied theis prancks themselues/ they charge vs with their owne faultes and go abowte te laie the infamie vppon vs whiche they themselues haue stirred vp. Iff yow shall crie owte that olde matters are reherfed by this meanes/ yow ought to haue abstained from prouokinge vs herevnto: neither to haue mentioned offences committed/olde subscriptions/ ne yet to haue called vs backe thus to the olde discipline the fountaine off all contentions.

The names subscribed to the obiections
with a postscripte.

Robart Horne   Richard Chambers   Anthonie Mahewe
Edwarde Isaac   Christopher Brichbeck Richard Dauids
                                       Cutberd

Cutbert Warcope. Iohn Binkes. Nicholas earll.
Robart Harrington. Iohn Escot. Iohn Machet.

Horne

The reste off oure consentinge brethern we coulde not call together vnto this subscribinge / by reason off shortnes of time / whose names shall be put afterward hauinge your S. licencee therto.

The answere to the postscripte.

VVhithead

Where they complaine off shortnes of time in the ende as they did in the beginninge / and that they could not by reason therof cal their cōsentinge brethern togetherto the subscribinge: What meaneth that? For where they haue set to the names off them whiche dwell most farre a sunder and haue left owte almost none but the names off their owne seruants whom they haue allwaies at a becke / yet they could not call the rest off their brethern together forsoothe / to the intent they might by this shift make a shewe to suche as knowe not the matter / off some multitude off men off some estimation whiche are leste owte. And they desier also as in a matter off waight that they maye set too the names off the others afterwardes. And as here in the ende / they vaunte a certeine shewe of some great multitude that will subscribe: Euen so / in the beginninge and in many other places of their booke they make a great bragge as though they would exhibite some notable matter to the magistrate / so they maie haue time ynough geuen them to bethink themselues. But maister Horne and maister Chambers shall with theis their mightie and great promisses bothe off subscriptions declarations and confirmations bringe to passe as good as nothinge. But yet this they are desirous to bringe to passe in the meane time / that whiles theis gaye glorious promises off thers be loked for / they may a longe time hinder the peace and quietnes off the church whiche their onely desier is to haue disquieted. And iff it be possible that thei maie recouer a moste intollerable lordeshipp ouer the congregatiō: or in case they cannot obtaine the chief state in the cōgregatiō / that they may leaue the churche in

the

worste/or in no state at all/but that they maye rende it and all to scatter it. Theis be the deuises off Horne and Chambers. Theis be ther fetches/ right honorable and most righteous Magistrates. And yet we haue no distruste but almightie god for his mercies sake towardes oure most afflicted churche/ and that your authoritie for your equities sake and singuler beneuolence towardes vs/ will withstande the same.

And for as muche as we haue proued that one off theis thinges whiche they haue reprehended in oure discipline / be other againste gods worde/ or againste good reason: and for as muche also as we are ready to proue/ that all thinges conteined in oure Discipline / are taken owte either off Goodes worde or off the edicte off the Senate and Magistrate/ either owte off their owne olde discipline which they stick so fast vnto/ either ells off the iudgement off good reason/ we humblie beseche the right honorable and righteous magistrates that they will vouchsaffe to confirme it with their authoritie.

Where as bothe partes gaue consent that certeine others/ very worshippfull/ shuld also deale in this controuersie betweene them/ to appease (yff it might be) the same I haue here folowinge placed the order whiche they tooke for their quietnes.

To the ministerie and bodie off the congregation off the Englishe Churche off Franckford.

For as muche as at the request off all oure brethern and countrie men off this churche off Franckford/ we haue vndertake to endeauoure oure selues to make an ende of this sorowfull controuersie whiche so grieuously/ so longe tyme hath vexed this congregation/ slaundered Religion/ and infamed the name off all Englishemen we thought we coulde neither satisfie the duetie off Christian charitie/ nor the office off louinge countrie men/ iff we did omitt any thinge/ whiche/ by anie
probable

probable coniecture might seeme to bringe to effecte oure honest entreprise in this behalfe, wherupon we haue thought good to offer vnto yow oure brethern on bothe parties such a forme off agremente touchinge certeine pointes off your discipline as had semed vnto vs vppon conference betwene certeine chosen persons, on bothe sides before vs most conuenient, so to satisfie all men, that euery man might willingly and cheerfully submitt him selff vnto the the obedience therof. Desiringe yow all as ye hope to haue fauour at goddes handes in the bloude off Iesus Christe, so to applie your fauorable mindes eche to other that all striff and contention set aparte, yow maie ioine together in a blessed Christian and happie societie, peace and concorde, and the thinge whervnto we wishe bothe the parties shuld agree is as folowithe.

The forme off reconciliation.

Firste, where as in this whole treatie off reconciliation and alteration of discipline, some thinges might happē to seeme to tēde to the condēnation of some partie or parson: we do all frelie pronounce and testifie eche parte off other, that neither off vs do condemne either partie, or anie person as those whiche haue don anie thinge contrary to gods word, or probalitie off reason in this matter off discipline, but frindly and louingly euerie man dothe imbrace all men omittinge all rehersall and disputation off thinges paste with common and hartie praier vnto god, that from hens forthe we maie remaine, and liue together in brotherly loue to the glorie off god and comforte off vs all.

Concerninge the article for exercise off lerninge, that there be no mention made off the same in the booke off discipline but that for so muche as lerned men remaine in the congregation, that the ministerie shall for the furtheraunce off lerninge, labor to put in vre such exercise off lerninge as the lerned can performe and the abilitie off the churche beare.

Concerninge the receiuinge and distributinge off the treasure.

asure off the churche. The receauinge and distributinge therof dothe apperteine to the Deacons, yet nor so that they doo it withowt the knowledge and consent off the Ministers and Seniors: concerninge the kepinge off the saide treasure, it maie verie well apperteine to the Deacons, yet is it not off such necessitie but that the reste off the ministerie maie otherwise set order for the custodie theroff, as tyme and occasion shall serue.

3. Concerninge the Article off contribution, when the treasure off the churche faileth, it perteineth to the ministers and Deacons to tranell by the waie off exhortation with the riche to helpe in that nede withowte anie further compulsion.

4. Concerninge the Article off sendinge off common letters for the relieff off the congregation: That there be no mention made off anye parte theroff in the booke off discipline but that the ministerie with all possible secrecie vse such pollicies and meanes as maie beste serue to the relieff and mainteinance off the congregation.

5. Concerninge the Article off makinge off lawes, that they be made by the ministerie and bodie off the congregation beinge called together for that purpose. And iff the ministerie, or anie off them refuse to be present beinge by the bodie off the congregation required therunto, whithowte iuste cause by them or him alleaged, that then, after a dewe time geuen for the hearinge off the cause, yff they bringe not in good reason and iuste cause off suche refusall: Then to be depriued by the same from their or his ministerie and newe to be chosen.

6. Concerninge the article off the election off Ministers That a scrutente, be had euerie yere at the tyme off election for the examination off the Ministers off the worde, wherin shalbe by the appointmente off the congregation six or eight graue and wise men whiche shall heare what faults be alleadged against the same Minister, And yff the faults be waightie and worthie off open correction, to signifie the same to the congregation that the offenders or offender maie be corrected or depriued accordingly. Yff the offences be lesser

ser then that they ought to be publishesd / then the saide ministers or minister offendinge / to be monished off his faulte accordinge to the discretion off the Scrutiners.

Concerninge the Article off Testamentes. That no man by order in this congregation shall be forced to Register his Testamente / but that their be eight or 10. graue wise / substantiall and honeste men chosen by the congregation owte off whiche nomber the Testator shall haue his choise / or yff he omit the thinge / his executours shall haue the choise to take 2. off the saied 8. or 10. besides suche as are made wittnesses / whom the executers withe in a monethe after the death off the Testator shall make priuie to the Testamente / and that the same two / beinge required therunto / shall faithfully declare vnto euery partie comprehended in the will / so muche off the will as shall particulerly appertaine to euery off them / and shall keepe secrete all the reste off the will or Testament as they shall proteste before God and the congregation vppon there consciences / at the time off their election.

And nowe in case it shall seeme good vnto all your wissedomes as well off the Ministerie and bodie off the congregation off the one part as off the dissentinge brethern off the other part That we shall by oure mediation proceede anye further accordinge vnto this forme off reconciliation / whiche is here described: We doo hartely require yow / that signifinge your mindes vnto vs with as conueniente spede as ye maie / ye will also appoint owte on either parte / 2. Discreet and sober persons / louers off peace and concorde / whiche by conference with other two off vs / whom we shall appointe / may drawe theis Articles afore written into such a forme as they maie be conueniently anexed to the reste off your Discipline. The 19. September 1557.

Your lovinge brethern and countrie:

Thomas

CLXXIIII.

Thomas VVrothe.   Henry Knollys.   Edwin Sandes.
Frances Knollys   Iohn Browne   Thomas Eaton.
Roger Parker.   Fran. willforde   Ricard Springham.
Iohn Abell.   Iohn Turner.

The answere off the churche to this offre, or the effect off the same.

We cannot allowe this waie off reconciliation offred to oure churche by oure countrie men for as muche as we shulde condemne oure selues as euell doers, and oure doinges vngodly and vnreasonable, but we are assured we haue not done in oure discipline anie thinge contrary to goddes worde and good reason. The last off Septemb.

Dauid VVhithead. Henry Parry.   VVilliam Rawlinges
Iohn Hales.   Richard Beesley   Robart Beste
Thomas Sorby   Robart Crowley   Richart Luddington.
Iohn Pedder   Thomas wattes   Edmond Haries.
Thomas Ashley   Richard Rogers.

The copie off the letters off request sentfoorth for relieff off the poore by Maister Suiton 25. Iulij 1557.

To all them that beare an vnfayned Reuerence and zeele vnto the eternall Testament off Iesus Christe, ioyned withe the charitable and syncere bowells off mercie towardes the poore. Grace, Mercie and Peace from God the father by the same oure Lorde Iesus Christe his sonne the common and onely Sauiour off the worlde.

It is not like that the brute of the cõtrouersie, which hathe nowe at the ende off six monethes continued in this Englishe the churche at Franckford/is vnknowē to strangers: it is more like that so manie beinge priuie therto / it is caried and spread to farre abroad: and moste like by the fruites springinge theroff / that it hath byn vntruly reported by the willfull authors and stubburne mainteiners off it / not onely to the infamie/ reproche/ and discredit off the bodie off this churche and to the intent to stopp all reliefe from the poore members off the same/ but also/ that their vncharitable and leude behauiours shulde not come to light. For it is well knowen that diuerse charitable men (albeit their persons and names be neither knowen nor desired to be knowen) were / before the beginninge off this controuersie verie liberall in sendinge their charitie to the vse off this whole congregation vniuersally / and some were beneficiall to sundrie members off the same particulerlie / whiche sithe that time to oure knowledge they haue left vndone vtterlie. We the Ministers off the churche/ hopinge that theis men the authors and mainteners off this controuersie would in time haue knowen their faults and made satisfaction to the churche as it becomethe christen men to doo/ did not onelie with pacience suffer their slaunderous talke and vnquiet demenour / but also beare with their vniuste dealinge/ and as much as in vs laye studied to couer their faultie doinges. Neuertheles/ seinge no likelyhood off their amendment/ but moste manifeste proffes off their malice/ this poore congregation/ rather dailie encreasinge then in anie parte abatinge/ and thereby the pouertie theroff continually augmentinge/ we thought it oure bownden dewtie in conscience/ no longer to hide the matter/ but thus off necessitie constrained/ to disclose it / so as seinge they will not be as they ought to be/ they maie at leaste be knowen as they be. And thus we doo not for anie malice that we beare to anye mannes person (as god the sercher off all hartes knoweth) but that the truth beinge knowen/ such good people as through vntrue reporte / haue byn perswaded to withdrawe their good mindes and fauor from this poore congregation might vnderstande that withowte iuste cause they haue so longe done it/

ne it/and hereafter be the more willinge to renewe their charitie in the releiuinge off this poore churche off Christe. And to come to the matter/ye shall vnderstand that after maister Horne late pastor/and the Seniors that were ioyned in the ministerie with him had by a writinge subscribed with their owne handes/openly before the congregation surrendred and geuen ouer their offices/reteininge neuertheles the writinge off their surrender in their owne handes/ and yet beinge desired by the congregation not to leaue their ministeries / but still to exercise the same: they in no wise woulde doo it / wherby the churche was diuers daies destitute off the preachinge off goddes worde. Wheruppon/the more part off the congregation/mindinge to haue the churche kept in good order and to redresse those thinges that were a great occasion off the former contention/so that after there might be a perpetuall quietnes and concorde amonge vs/ went earnestly abowte the same. But it hapened contrarie to oure expectation / the former grudges continuinge/ and newe busines daily increasinge/which at lenght came to the Magistrates eare/contrary to oure mindes and determination. For when we thought that it shulde withowte anie further brute/ amongest oure selues haue bin pacified and ended as we would to god it had bin. Wheruppon the godly magistrates lamentinge muche oure dissention/ad desiringe oure quietnes came into oure churche and there / firste made vs to promesse one to an other / that from thens foorth no mention shulde be made off anie former grudge or contention betweene vs but that all thinges paste shuld be clene forgotten. Afterwarde/for the better continuance off loue amonge vs and good order in the churche/ with the consent off Maister Horne the pastor and the Seniors discharged him and them off their offices and willed the churche to chuse newe ministers and to make a newe discipline (for by reason off the vnperfectues off the olde Discipline a great parte off the former controuersie was) as iff there had bin neuer anie churche here before. Wheruppon the Church diuers times assemblinge/at lenght/the moste parte of

the

the churche thought moste reasonable that amonge other an order shulde be in this churche like as it was in the primative churche and is nowe in all well reformed churches / that the treasure shulde be in the custodie off all the Deacons and not off anie one man alone. Maister Horne with certeine off the Seniors and a fewe others woulde in no wise agree vnto it / but to their vttermoste resiste it / which gaue vs occasion off farther iuste suspition / that the treasure off the churche in time paste had not bin Christianly vsed.

And whereas also we had deuised an other order / that for so muche as the magistrate dothe permit vs to vse the customes and manners off makinge off willes that be vsed in Englande / that for the more suretie off oure frindes that were here or ells where / yff we were disposed by oure willes to geue vnto them anie off that litle substance that god hath lefte vs / (yff we shulde die here) owre willes shulde be seene and exemplyfied by the Seniors / ād so to be owte of all daunger off countrefaitinge at anie time: Horne / and Chambers onelie vppon fonde will withowte any iuste consideration / or good reason cauilled againste the same order / onely affirminge it to be pernitious. Theis thinges we finde manifestly at lenght / not to proceede off anie good minde or purpose but off contentious frowardnes growned vppon selff loue and gaine that vnder a colour of the churche they might gather good mennes deuotions / and neuer distribute anie penny thereoff or at the leaste / to none (had they neuer so great nede) vnles they woulde / either faune / and hange on them / or ells sustaine vncharitable tauntes and reproches at their handes.

For where Chambers aboue 13. monethes paste had off maister Whithead then Pastor and the Seniors then a letter to receaue of one special mā 10. powndes and besides / through Horns procurement / a generall proxie to Chambers / and his deputie / to gather the deuotion off good men for the relieff off this poore congregation / whiche by their owne proceedings here before the Magistrates (their owne hands wrytinge testifinge the saine) and otherwise by oure knowledge we are certeine/ they did put in practise/ and receiued muche therby/ yet Chambers vpon the accoumpt here left behinde him/ neither confesseth that he receyued the saide 10. powndes nor yet anie other summe / neither hathe he distributed (duringe all the tyme he was in office yet to this daie) in this congregation/ to anie one person (sauing to 3. scollers that came with him) one penny/ that he did not receiue here in this congregation and citie.

And yet/ at his departure hence/ he lefte 2. off the saide scollers (vnto whom neuerthelesse he promised sufficient prouision and findinge/ and neuer warned them to the contrary) in dette for their boorde and for other necessaries almost 10. guilderns whiche this poore congregation was forced to paie. Finallie/ where good Mistres Wilkinson off blessed memorie/ put Horne and Chambers in truste with the deuisinge and makinge of hir will/ whereby she gaue to this and other poore congregations of the poore banished Englishe men a Christian liberall relief: Albeit they haue caused some off the saied congregations to be paide of the same bequeste/ yet his thertoo wolde they not make this poore congregation priuie to the summe bequethed vnto it/ muche lesse paie it/ nor yet (accordinge to the order of oure churches discipline aforesaide) let the will be seene/ so as the frindles younge ientlewoman hir daughter shuld not be defrauded off hir right nor hir mothers will altered to hir losse. Furthermore/ Maister Chambers vnderstandinge that we were minded (accordinge to oure dewties) to requyre an accoumpte of him/ for the vse off his proxie/ getteth him suddainly hence (accompanied with Maister Horne) earely in a morninge/ withowte the consent or leaue takinge off the congregation or the Ministerie theroff/ and contrarie to his one openly made promesse/ that he would not departe/ till he had answered all that any man coulde charge him with.

And at his goinge awaie/ he left behinde him an accoumpt/ which by cuttinge owte the leaues/ and newe written/ semethe not to be nowe at the last as it was at the firste/ albeit

CLXXIX.

beit it was neuer so perfect as Christian fidelitie woulde haue required it to be. And moreouer/ albeit we haue twise writtē vnto him charitably exhortinge ād requiringe him to come hither/ and discharge himselff of those thinges that shall be saide vnto him in the behalff off this congregation/ and to their entent he shuld restore vnto it the proxie he receiued/ and no longer by himselff or his deputie exercise it in the name off this poore churche/ as we are informed he dothe: he neither commeth nor yet maketh answere to oure letters/ wherby we cannot but think that he meaneth not onely crafte and subtiltie (much vnworthie the integritie and fidelitie that he pretendeth) but also/ to hinder/ and as muche as in him lieth/ to vndoo this poore congregation/ not onely off that he hath already receiued and caried awaie/ (as he hath heretofore dealt with the companie off poore studentes at Zurick) but also/ through vntrew reportes off all good mennes deuotions and liberalitie that hereafter woulde ells be bestowed, Their reportes (whiche amonge many other vntruthes to hinder this poore congregation they slanderously brute abroad) are chiefly theis: firste/ that the poore off this churche be so well prouided for/ that the worste hathe after the rate of 2. shillinges by the weeke. Secōdly/ that some of the poore here/ be so stowte that they disdaine to aske relieff in their nede/ so that oure poore seeme either not to nede or not to be worthie off helpe. And thirdly/ that men here seeke to knowe the names off the geuers to this congregation to their great perill and vtter vndooinge/ whiche reportes be all vtterly vntrue/ but the truthe is that for lack/ many poore men haue byn driuen bothe to depart hence/ to seeke their liuinge in other places and some forced to go for relieff into England. Theis specialities (besides muche more that we haue thought good and very necessarie/ that good godly men shulde knowe/ bothe that they shuld not conceaue anie euell opinion off this congregation by false reporte/ and also/ that mindinge to relieff the poore and miserably afflicted membres off Christe their brethern in this churche/ they shulde when god shall moue them to departe with

Z iij   ante

anie thinge to that vse/ so deliuer it/as it maie sauffly come/ and iustly be distributed/where they would haue it bestowed. And therfore we/(considering the state off oure fellowe exiles liuinge here with vs in nede and pouertie/ and fedde by the onely good prouidence off god) desier all Christian men for the loue off oure sauiour Jesus Christe to consider/ howe pleasant a sacrifice howe sweete a sauor the relieuinge off the poore for his sake is before the face off oure heauenly father. A good mannes liffe/ is almoste nothinge ells then a continuall exercise off mercie. All the daie longe he hathe mercy and pittie/ saith the prophet Dauid.

Geue almes off thy goodes (saith the holie man Tobiah) and turne neuer thy face from the poore : and so shall it come to passe/ that the face off the lorde shall not be turned awaie from the. Be mercifull after they power yff thow haste muche/ geue plenteouslie: yf thou haste litle / do thy diligence gladlye to geue of that litle/ for so gatherest thow thy selff a good rewarde in the daie off necessitie. for almes deliuereth from deathe and suffreth not the soule to come in darknes. A great comforte is almes before the high God/ vnto all them that doo it.

Blessed is he that consideth the poore (saith the Prophet Dauid (the lorde shall deliuer him in the tyme off trouble/ ꝛc. The good man (saith Dauid) hath distributed abroad and geuen to the poore/ his righteousnes remaineth for euer: his horne shalbe exalted with honor/ he that geueth to the poore shall not lack/ saith the Wyse man in the prouerbes. As water/ quencheth burninge fire/ so doithe mercie reconcile synnes: whiche god shall rewarde and not forget/ and the doer shall fynde a staie to keepe him vpp when he falleth/ saithe Jesus the sonne off Sirach. Break vnto the Hungrie thy bread saith the Prophet Esaie and bringe the poore fatherles into they howse/ when thow seeste the naked/ couer him/ and hide not they face from thine owne fleshe. Then shall thy light break foorthe/ as the morninge/ and thy helthe flourishe right shortly/ thy righteousnes shall go before thee/ and
the

CLXXXI.

the glorie of the lorde shal embrace thee. Thẽ yf thow callest, the lorde shall answere thee: yf thou criest, he shall saye, here I am. Laie ye not vp treasures in earthe, where the rust and the moth maie destroy it, and theues maie digge it owte and steale it, saithe Christe, but laie vpp your treasures in heauen.

Geue almes off that ye haue and behold, (saithe Christe) all is cleane vnto yow. What ye geue to one off theis litle ones (saithe he) ye geue it vnto me. And also he saith, blessed are the mercifull for they shall finde mercie. when the ydolatrus kinge Nabucadnezer shuld be conuerted vnto god what saied the Prophet Daniell vnto him: redeeme they synnes with almes, and thy wikednesse with mercie on the poore, so perhappes god will pardon they sinnes. Think ye that god forgate abdias that preserued the hundreth Prophetes in caues and fedd them there? Paule and the other apostells diligently bothe with wordes and writinge did labor for the relieff of the pooore brethern that were at Ierusalem and ells where,

And we hope that god will open your hartes and mindes to consider oure state and by theis sayinges and examples moue yow to haue pitie on your poore brethern, whiche yff it shall please his mercie to graunte yow cheerfully to doo, it is not to be dowted, but albeit he suffer yow to slyde and fall for a time, yet will he heaue yow vp (when it shalbe his good pleasure) and preserue yow, so as at the lenght ye maie be partakers off the ioyfull kingdome off god whiche oure sauior Iesu Christ hathe purchased for his electe with the price off his blood. The holy spirite off god be allwayes with yow amen.

This controuersie which yow haue now harde from the 23. off January hitherto. I finde written by the handes off such as are bothe lerned and off credit, but yet, I muste nedes say, by those that were parties in this broyle. And for so much as Maister Chambers in this controuersie is very sore charged amonge the reste: who yet, was thought off manie wise and godly men, to be verye godly, vpright, and honest, as so no dowte he tooke his leaue of this lyffe: I haue therfore here thought good to place a letter whiche is yet off his owne des hande tobe seene/ wrytinge the same in his owne defence touchinge theis matters so as the reader wayinge bothe the one and the other/maie vse his iudgemente with discretiom.

The copie off the letter.

To the worship.Maister John Hales/M. Thomas Crawley. Maister John Willford/ and to Maister Whitthead/Thomas Sorsby/ William Maister and John olde at Franckford.

Immanuell.

I wishe vnto yow the peace off god with my commendations. The tenor of your demaunde hathe caused me to differr answeringe to your letters vntill this time not off purpos/to geue no answere/but that I then vppon the suddain wanted sure knowledge in that thinge wherby yow chiefly charge me. At my comminge from Zurick to frankford I was intreated by certaine men to continewe my traueiles/in gatheringe the Almes and liberalities off godly men/ to relieue therwith such poore dispersed Englishe brethern/As I shuld think moste meete to be relieued euen as before time I had done. This requeste put in writinge/subscribed by certeine/ was deliuered vnto me/not as letters testimoniall off authoritie/whiche as I neded not/or I required them not/neither yet that I shuld by force off them gather for the church off Franckford onely/ or specially/ whiche I purposed not/ but that I might be the rather moued to doo as before I had donne. And they then required (whiche was after promesse made to further my doinges with all faithfull secrecie/in suche sortes as I shulde from time to time deuise an require) to bestowe

we suche summes off monie as shulde hereafter come to my handes to suche vses and purposes as I thought good. Therfore/as by force off those letters I gathered not: So the gatheringe for Franckford churche hathe not byn nor is in my handes / nor off any other at my appointmente as ye do write.

Wherfore as I might/ so I did /and that by the aduise off manie honeste/graue/and godly men/ departe from thense withowte making that accoumpte/ to whiche I am not bownde/ nor leauinge for the relieff off the poore / off whom such haue had their portion in this blessinge for the time as I thought meete to be relieued. Vnto the Studentes whom I neuer placed there / I haue performed what so euer I promised. The accoumpt off receiptes / paimentes and remaines which ye require/ I intende not to make vnto yow. But I shall be ready at all times and in all places to make a iuste accoumpte off my whole dealinges in this behalff vnto them whiche haue authoritie to demaunde it off me. In the meane tyme/ as I shall by gods helpe truly do my indeauour/to relieue the poore as I shal haue wherwithe and finde them meete to receiue it: So shall I keepe the names and summes secret as I am bownde/till by them whiche haue iuste authoritie to louse me I be otherwise appointed.

Thus I committ yow to the grace off allmightie god from Strasbrough this 20. off June/ Anno. 1557. Richarde Chambers.

After I had written this answere to your firste letters reteining them in my handes vntill I might haue a conuenient Caxior: I receaued your Seconde letters the principall matters therin are answered before. To the rest that be any thinge materiall/ thus I saie. As touching the delaye off mine answere yow call contempte more vncharitable then truly as vnto godly wise men is well knowen. As my departure was not/ so my returne to Franckfurt alaie not be at your appoints

Aa

CLXXXIIIJ.

pointement. Your generall accusations off mis behauiors and contemptes in the whiche yow saie I am faultie, I admitt not. Iff yow can iustly charge me with particulers, I shall make answere to the contentation off all godly mindes.

Where the discipline off Christe is vsed in iuste causes, it is to be regarded: but your vnorderly abusinge off it, and againste me that am not off your churche, I esteeme not. Iff yow vse ciuill proffes againste me, I shalbe as ready to answere the cause as yow to entre the sute. As for your displayinge off me to our dispersed brethern to my vndeserued dispraise: in this matter cannot be such but that I shall easilie purge my self. As god knowethe who with his holy spirite mollifie your hartes and geue yow the vnfained true sight off your selues amen. From Strasbrough the 30. off June 1555.
Richard Chambers.
Deliuered the 20. off July to M. John Hales by John Escot.

Nowe, Whiles theis sharpe and greuous contentions grewe more and more at Franckf. (as ye haue harde) manye thinges happened in other places whiche maie in this place be shortly touched, to the glory off god (I hope) and also, to the great comforte off the godlie, who maie by the same, beholde moste euidently the maruelous prouidence off God towarde his poore afflicted and dispersed churche.

After that M. Bartue and the dutches of Suff. were safely arriued at Wezell in Westphalia, the brute theroff was the cause that moo Englishe people in shorte time resorted thither. It pleased god also, that M. Couerdale (after that he had bin withe the kinge of Denmark) shuld come to the same Towne, who preached there no longe time, till he was sent for by woulgange duke off bypont, to take the pastorall charge off Hargzaber, one off his Townes off Germany: at whose comminge to the duke, he made it knowe, bothe to him selff and to other noble mē abowte him off M. B. and the dutches beinge in the lowe countries. They vnderstādinge, the daunger that might come vnto them in those partes, as also calling to remēbrance, what great curteisie strangers had founde in Engelande

M. couerdale sent by the duke of bipont.

CLXXXV.

lande at the dutches handes: made offre that iff they were forced to remoue or otherwise if it pleased them/they shuld haue the Castle of Winchaim by Bedleberge within the liberties of Otto Henricus the Palsgraue and a godly Prince/ who most gladly (as well appeared) gaue consent to the same. M. Bartue and the Dutches acceptinge this offre/lefte Wezell and came vp to the saide Castle/ad there cōtinued/till leauinge Germany they traueled towardes the lande off Pole. The congregation that was at Wezell wantinge amonge them/partly the comforte whiche many off them had/by M. B. and my L. beinge there/and partly also other reasonable cōsiderations mouinge them; they left Wezel and folowed after. But passinge by Francfi, and perceaninge the contention to be amōge them so boilinge hott/that it ran ouer on bothe sides/and yet no fier quenched; many had small pleasure to tarie there/but went to Basil and other places/ whiles M. Leauer made sute to the lordes of Berna for a churche with in their dominions/whose letters he obtained with great fauour to all their subiects for the frindly entertainement off the Englishe nation. Theis letters obtained/M. Leauer/M. Boyes/M. Wilforde/ M. Pownall and T. Vpchaier/ came to Geneua to haue the aduice off that churche what was best to be done touching the erection off a new churche. They of Geneua/gaue god thanks for that it had pleased him so to incline the hartes off the lordes off Berna towardes them and gaue incouragemēt that they shuld not let slyppe so good an occasion. M. I. Bodliegh (who was no small staie as well to that churche as to others) and W. Bethe traueiled with them. And passinge thorough manie partes of the L. of B. dominion in Sauoy and Switzerland/they founde suche fauour in all places where they came/ as verelie maie be to the great condemnation off all such Englishe men as vse the godly stranger (I meane those who come for religion) so vncourteously.

M. Leauer and the company at lenght chose Arrow for their restinge place/where the congregation liued together in godlie quietnesse amōge themselues with great fauour of the people amonge whom for a time they were planted.

The curtesie off the noble men off Germany to M. Bartue & the D. off Suff.

Englishe men placed at Arrow.

Aa ij Not

CLXXXVJ.

Horne and Chambers come to Geneua.

Not longe after this, Maister Horne and maister Chambers came by Arrowe to Geneua, seminge at that tyme to like verie well off those congregations, (as the churche of Franck. also then did as apearethe by their letters afore) in so muche as the said Maister Horne and Chambers, did distribute larglie to the necessitie of those churches. So that it appeared that the olde grudge whiche had bin betweene the churche off Franck. and Geneua had bin cleane forgotten.

It came to passe not many daies after, that the lorde began to shewe mercy vnto Englande in remouinge Queene Mary be deathe, and placinge the queens maiestie that nowe is (whom god longe preserue) in the seate, the newes whereof, as it was ioyfull to all suche as were in exile, So it appeared that the churche off Geneua was not behinde the reste, who, (after that they had geuen to god hartie thankes for his great goodnes) consulted amonge themselues and concluded, that (for so muche as there had byn iarres betwene them and other churches, abowt the Booke off common praier and ceremonies) it was now expedient and necessary not onely that vnfained reconciliation shulde be betwene them but also that they might so ioine together in matters off religion and Ceremonies, that no Papist or other enemie shuld take holde or aduantage by a farther dissention in their owne

Kethe sent into Germany and Heluetia.

countrie, whiche might arise in time to come, yff it were not in time foreseen and preuented. To this ende was William Kethe, one off the congregation chosen to do this message, to them off Arrowe, Basill, Strasbrough, Wormes, Franckford &c. And to them off Arrowe and Francford this letter was wrytten which folowith and subscribed by the ministers in the name off the whole congregation.

The Copie off the letter written the 15. off December.

The Father of mercies and god of all cōsolation confirme and increase yow in the loue off his sonne Jesus Christ, that beinge in the conduits off the lion off the tribe

CLXXXVII.

off Iuda/ ye maie be victorious/ against Sathan and Antechriste to the ouerthrowinge off Papistrie and errour/ and establishinge of Christes glorious kingdome.

After that we hearde (dearely beloued) of the ioiful tidings off Gods faueure and grace restored vnto vs by the preferment off the moste verteous and gratious Queene Elizabethe: We lyfted vp our hartes and voices to oure heauenly father, who hathe not onely by his dewe prouidence norished vs in oure banishement/preserued vs/ and as it were/ caried vs in his winges/ but also harde oure praiers graunted our requestes/ pitied oure countrie and restored his worde. So that the greatnes off this maruelous benefit ouercomethe oure Iudgements and thoughts howe to be able worthely to receaue it and to geue thankes for the same. And when we had withe great comforte wayed the matter/to the intēt that we might at the leaste shewe our selues miudefull off this most wonderfull and vndeserued grace/ we thought amonge other thinges: howe we might beste serue to godes glory in this worke and Vocation off fartheringe the gospell off our sauiour Iesus Christe. And bicause/ all impedimentes and cauillocions off aduersaries might be remoued/ it seemed good to haue your godly counsell and brotherly conference herein/ whiche we desier to lerne by this bearer our louinge brother Bethe/ that we might all ioyne hartes and handes together in this great worke/ wherin no dowte we shall finde many aduersaries and staies. Yet/ iff we (whose suffraunce and persecutions are certeine signes off oure sounde doctrine) holde faste together it is most certeine/ that the enemies shall haue lesse power/ offences shall sooner be taken awaie/ and religion best proceade and florishe.

For what can the papiste wishe more then that we shulde dissent one from an other/ and in steed off preachinge Iesus Christe and profitable doctrine/ to contende one againste an other/ either for superfluous Ceremonies or other like trifles frō the whiche god off his mercy hathe deliuered vs. There-

Aa iij fore

CLXXXVIII.

fore, deare brethern, we befeche yow (as we do we not but yf our godly iudgementes will think it fo befte) that what fo euer offence hathe byn heretofore either taken or geuen; it maie fo ceafe and be forgotten that hereafter god laie it not to oure charges yff thereby his bleſſed worde ſhulde be any thinge hindred. And as we for oure partes freely remitt all offences and moſt intirely imbrace yow oure deare brethern, So we befeche yow in the lorde that vnfainedly yow will do the like on your behalff wheroff albeit, we aſſure oure ſelues, as bothe by good experience we haue proued, and alſo haue receaued by your letters: yet, to cut off all occaſions from Papiſtes and other cauillores, we thought it beſte to renewe the ſame amitie, and to confirme it by theis oure letters. Moſte earneſtly deſiringe yow that we maie altogether teache and practiſe that true knowledge off Goddes worde, whiche we haue lerned in this oure baniſhment and by goddes merciſull prouidence, ſeene in the beſte reformed churches: That conſideringe oure negligence in times paſte and goddes puniſhemente for the ſame, we maie with zeele and diligence endeauour to recompence it, that god in all oure doinges maie be glorified, oure conſciences diſcharged and the members off Jeſus Chriſt releued and comforted. The whiche thinge the lorde god who hathe mercifully viſited and reſtored vs graunt and performe. To whom be all honour, praiſe, and glory for euer and euer.

Your lovinge frinds, and in the name of vvhole churche.

Chriſtopher Goodman	VVilliam VVilliams	Iohn Pullain
Miles Couerdale	Anthony Gilby	VVilliam Bevoyes
Iohn Knox	Frances VVithers	VVilliam VVhittingham
Iohn Bodliegh	VVilliam Fuller	

The Anſwere returned from Franck.
by W. Bethe.

The grace off god and the aſſiſtaunce off the holy goſte

lighe

CLXXXIX.

lghten and strenghten yow to the vnderstanding and constant reteining of his truthe, to the fartheraunce off his honor and glorie and to the edifinge and maintenance off his churche in Christe Iesu oure lorde.

Dearely beloued, as your letters were moste welcome vnto vs, bothe for that ye reioice at the preferment off our godly queene, and also that ye studie howe to promote the glorie off god: So are we right sory that they came not afore the departure off suche as ye seeke a charitable reconciliatiō with all. For where as ye require that all suche offences as haue byn gyuen and taken betwene yow and vs maie be forgotten hereafter: there be not here paste foure left / which were then present when ye dwelt here and not one off the lerned sorte sauinge M. Beesley. Yet, we dowte not, but as they promised in their former letters, to forget all displeasures afore conceaued, so they will performe the same and esteeme yow as their brethern. And for oure partes, as we haue had no cōtention with yow at all afore time: so we purpos net (as we trust there shall be no cause) to entre into contention with yow hereafter. For ceremonies to cōtende (where it shall lye neither in your hands or oures to appeint what they shall be but in suche mennes wisedomes as shall be appointed to the deuising off the same and whiche shall be receyued by cōmon consent off the parliament) it shalbe to small purpos. But we truste that bothe true religion shall be restored, and that we shall not be burthened with vnprofitable ceremonies. And therfore, as we purpos to submit oure selues to suche orders as shall bee established by authoritie, beinge not of them selues wicked / so we would wish yow willingly to do the same. For where as all the reformed churches differ amōge them selues in diuers ceremonies, and yet agree in the vnitie of doctrine: we se no inconuenience if we vse some ceremonies diuers from them / so that we agree in the chief points of oure religiō. notwithstandinge, if anie shalbe intruded, that shalbe offensiue, we, vpon iuste conference and deliberation vpon the same at oure meetinge with yow in Englande (whiche we truste by gods grace

will

will be shortly) wil brotherly ioine with yow to be sewters for the reformatiō and abolishinge of the same. In the meane seasō, let vs with one harte and minde cal to the almightie god that off his infinit mercie, he will finishe and establishe that worke that he hathe begon in oure countrie, and that we maie all louingly consent together in the earnest settinge foorthe off his truthe, that god maie be knowen and exalted, and his church perfectly builded vp throwgh Christe our lorde.
From Franckford this 3. off Ianuarie 1559.

Your louinge frinds in the name off the rest off the churche.

Iames Pilkington	Henry Knolls
Iohn Mullings	Frances Wilford
Henry Carowe	Alexander Nowell
Edmond Isaac	Richard Beesley
Iohn Browne	Iohn Graye
	Christopher Brickbate.

An Answer brought from the congregation off Arrow by W. Bethe.

The Father off mercies and God off all consolation confirme increase and continewe yow allwaie in the loue off his sonne Iesus Christe our lorde.

Praised be God through oure lorde Iesus Christe whiche pulled downe marie that did persecute, and hathe set vpp the godly lady Elizabeth Queene off Englande, to restore and maintaine there, the pure preachinge off his word. And for that it hathe pleased god to moue your good hartes, for the furtherance off the same, with godly zeele and charitable desier by your letters, to shewe vnto vs your aduise and purpos and also to require oures to be returned and sent vnto yow by
oure

oure brother Bethe: We doo with moste hartie thanks vn- fainedly afore god certifie yow/ that to your counsell and conference with vs/we do consent willingly concerninge y⸗ our most godly requeste/for that we acknowledge/ that the same shall be to the aduauncement off his glorie and quiet nes off his churche. Also/we desier yow that as ofte as we ma ie finde hereafter anie occasion to consulte and conferre by worde or writinge/that then bothe yow and we so take and seeke the same as maie be moste to our vnitie in mindes/ and diligence to do good in the lordes worke. And farthermore for the forgettinge and puttinge awaie all occasions off offences we do likewise consente vnto your good ensample and reque⸗ ste/And so finally efor the preachinge or professinge off since⸗ re doctrine so as we haue seene and lerned in the beste refor med churches we do gladly heare your aduise to be so agreab⸗ le to oure purpos that we beseche yow to praie with vs/that yow and all we together that be faithfull maie continewe/ proceade/and prosper in godly zeele/charitable concorde and earnest diligence to honor and serue god and to comforte and edifie his elect all times and in euery place and especially no⸗ we in England. O lord not vnto vs but vnto they name be ho nor and praise for euer. From Arrowe/this 16. off Jan. 1559.

Your louinge frinds off the mi- nistery in the in the name and by the consent of the whole church.

Thomas Leauer.   Richard Lauzhorne.
Robart Pownall.   Thomas Turpin.

Nowe when as W. Bethe was returned to Geneua with answer from the congregations and companies/that we re dispersed in sundry places off Germany and Heluetia/ the congregation (after that they had rendred their humble than kes to the magistrates for their great goodnes towards them prepared themselues to depart sauinge certeine whiche remai
Bb   ned

ned behinde the reste/to witt/to finishe the bible/And the psalmes bothe in meeter and prose / whiche were already begon/ at the charges off suche as were off most habilitie in that congregation. And with what successe those workes were finished/(especially the Bible) I must leaue it to the Judgementes off the godly lerned / who shulde best Judge off the same.

But yff that Bible be suche/as no enemie off god coulde iustly finde faulte with: then maie men maruell that suche a worke/(beinge so profitable) shulde finde so small fauor/ as not to be printed againe. Yff it be not faithfully translated/ then let it still finde as litle fauour as it dothe bicause off the inconueniences that a false translation bringes with it. The Ministers off Geneua in an Epistle whiche they wrote/before the newe Testament haue theis wordes.

There is nothinge more requisite to attaine the right and absolute knowledge off the doctrine off saluation/ wherby to resist all heresie and falshod / then to haue the texte off the Scriptures faithfully and truly translated/ the consideration wheroff moued them with one assent (as they saie in that Epistle to requeste, 2. off their brethern / to witt / Caluin and Beza/essonnes to peruse the same notwithstandinge their former trauells. Beza also in his Epistle to the prince off condy and nobles of France hathe these wordes. Seinge then all theis controuersies muste be discussed by Goddes worde/ I suppose that this thinge ought chiefly to be prouided for/ that seinge all canot haue the knowledge to vnderstand the worde off God in theis peculiar languages/the Hebrue and the greek (whiche were to be wished) that there shulde be some true and apte translation of the olde and newe testamēte made the whiche diuers haue already labored to bringe to passe/ but yet no man hathe hitherto sufficiently performed it. For the olde translation (whose so euer it is) although it ought not to be condemned/ yet is it founde bothe obscure vnperfect and superfluous and also false in many places/to speake nothinge off an infinite varietie off the copies. The whiche texte therfore

fore many lerned and godly men haue labored to amende, but not with like successe. And yet howe necessary a thinge this is, who so euer shall reade those moste lerned wryters off the gretians, and shall compare their interpretations (whiche are manie times farr from the purpos) with the Hebrue veritie, he shall confesse it with great sorowe.

And the same euill was not onely hurtefull amonge the Laiten writers, but also the ignorance off the greeke tonge wherwith many off them were troubled, whiles they did depend off the common translation, they oftimes seeke a knote in a rushe (accordinge to the olde prouerbe) and fell into moste fowle errors. This cause therfore hathe moued me to compare moste diligently the diuersitie off copies, and to waie the sentences and Judgementes off the moste parte off the lerned men specially off them that this age hathe brought foorthe, skillfull in the languages, who are moo in nomber dowteles and better lerned then the churche hath had sithens the time of the Apostles, and so ease them some what that desier a more pure interpretation.

And that it might be done with more profit I haue also added annotations, in the whiche I haue also compared together the diuersitie off interpetations and as muche as I coulde I haue labored to make plaine and euident the sence and meaninge off all the darke places, etc.

Thus farr Beza, by whose Judgement and the rest ye se, that to haue the holy Scriptures truly and faithfully translated is a matter off no small importaunce. Here might I touche a thinge parhapp worthe the hearinge yff hope were off redresse, whiche is, that yff the lerned were but one halff so earneste, zelous, and carefull, to se that the holy Scriptures in this Realme might be faithfully translated and trulye corrected, as they are many tymes abowte matters nothinge so necessarie: I woulde not dowte to saie that they shulde do vnto god an excellent peece off seruice.

For the moste parte off oure Englishe Bibles are so ill translated (as the lerned report) and so falsely printed (as the sim-

Bb ij ple

ple maie finde)that suche had nede to be verie well acquainted with scripture/as in many places shulde get owte the true meaninge and sence. And it is high time to looke vnto this/consideringe/that in moste partes off this Realme preachers ye haue none/nor anie that can or will preache (verie fewe excepted)sauinge certeine wanderers/amongest whom (and specially in some sheers) are such ruffenly rakehelles/and common coseners permitted and suffred/by whose preachinges/the worde off truthe is become odious/in the eies off the people. Seinge then(I saie)that in moste places/the ministery dothe stande and consiste of olde popishe preistes/tollerated readers and many newe made ministers/whose readinges are suche/that the people cannot be edified/especially/where one is tollerated to serue 2. or 3. churches ād turninge their backes to the people. I leaue to the consideration off suche(who haue to deale in this matter)what great ād intollerable mischeiues maie come more and more/(by suffringe suche corrupted Bibles in churches and ells where)to the poore simple flock off Christe. But nowe to drawe to an ende, ye se (brethern) by this brieff and shorte discours/that the grudge wherupon this dissention hangethe is paste the age off a childe/ and therfore maie (withowte offence I hope)be called an olde grudge/ whiche/ as it seemeth/ was neuer yet througly healed / as will more and more appeare / as this discourse shall be from time to time continued/ till it be brought euen to this present tyme/ which time verely/is so extreame as the like hathe rarely bin hard off. For it is come to passe/ that iff anie shulde but with a godly griefbewaile the imperfections that remaine and craue for redresse: yea/but suspected/or shulde but by malice off an Atheist/a Papist/or Epicure be presented: such are not onely reuiled and taunted/ skoffed at and termed by theis odious names off precisian/puritain/contentious/seditious/rebell/traitor and what not: but also yff he come once in presence off the Bishopps/ and subscribe not to what so euer they will/ then/(yf he haue liuinge)to be depriued/or whither he haue liuinge or not/be he lerned or vnlerned/be he man or woman/

hale

halt or blinde,/ to prison he muste/ withowte all redemption.
   I wil not saie that (in the meane time) suche as are turne coates and can chaunge with al seasons/ subscribinge to what so euer/ and can cap it can cope it an curry for aduantage/ that suche/ I saie/ how ignorant/ how vitious/ and vngodly so euer they be/ liue at their ease in all pleasure and in some place are thought to be moste meete men for the ministerie. But this I maie be bolde to affirme/ that/ (although in very dede I neither do nor dare condemne certeine godly persons/ who off infirmitie/ but yet with most sorowfull and heauy hartes (as hathe well appeared by their most lamentable protestations with plentie off teares to their congregations) haue yelded to more then expedient it were they shulde/ (prayinge the lorde to let them se it in time) yet/ it maie not onely be saide/ but proued too I truste/ that neither is subscribinge allwaies a sure note off good subiect nor yet the refusall dew proffes off a rebell.
   The greatest Traitors and rebells that godly Kinge Edwarde had in the weste partes/ were priests/ and suche as had subscribed to the booke or what so euer by lawe was then in force/ but for all their subscribings/ there was no skirmishe/ where some off those subscribers left nor their karkaises in the filde againste god and their prince. Plumtree and his fellowe priests off the northe/ I dowte not but they were conformable and applyable to all orders and neuer staggered at subscriptions. But for all that/ time tried their traiterous hartes.
   But in all the sturres whiche haue happened either sithens the Quenes maiestie came to the crowne or before I haue not hard off so muche as one (minister or other) that hath lifted vp his hande against hir maiestie or state/ whom it pleaseth the enuious and malicious man/ to terme precision/ and puritain in great despite and contempt. In dede/ this haue I founde oute and lerned/ that euen suche as muste be cōtente and patiently beare those odious names of puritane precisian/ traitor/ and rebell/ haue yet bin the men/ who moste

Bb iij   faith-

faithfully (in their callinge) haue serued the Queens maiestie and their country bothe with in the realme and with owte the realme in Garnison and in filde/ hazardinge their bodies against hargabuze and cannon/ when as those who nowe so furiously charge them both owte off pulpits and other places durst not or at leste woulde not in anie such seruice off the prince and counirie be seene. For proffe hereoff/ yff yow call to remembrance/ who hazardid his liffe with that olde/ Honorable Erle off Bedford when as he was sent to subdue the popishe rebells off the weste/ yow shall finde that none off the clergie were hastie to take that seruice in hande/ but onely olde father Couerdale. When moste likelode was off daunger betweene the Skots and vs/ the preacher to the souldiars was firste Maister Sampson/ and afterward Maister Greshopp when as the right honorable Erle off Bedford that nowe is, had there the charge. The Erle off Warwick at his beinge in Newhauen/ had in dede with him certeine Ministers for a time/ but after that the Cannon came and began to roare/ and the plage off pestilence so terriblie to rage/ then (I weene) not a Minister there left/ but Maister Bethe alone. And whē as meanes were made to haue mo Ministers ouer/ to aide the saied Bethe (who had so muche to doo/ what with preaching/ and visitinge the poore sick Souldiars which were in no small nombers) there coulde not be faunde (as that right noble Erle can vppon his honor testifie) so muche as one whiche coulde be brought to so muche comformitie/ as to subscribe to any suche seruice off the Queens Maiestie.

When S. Henry Sidney had to do with the Popishe rebells off Ireland. Maister Christop. Goodman shewed his faithfull diligence in that seruice. When the Erle off Warwick was sent to subdue the popish rebells in the northe partes/ the preachers off the Queens maiesties Army were Bethe/ Temes/ and Sandon who offred themselues in that seruice voluntarily with owte all constraynte. And thus it is euident/ that theis with a nomber moo who are now so ill thought off / as iff they were traitors and rebells / haue yet byn so farre off from bringe seditious / that they haue at all times aduentured their liues againste seditious persons and rebells / when as suche as nowe so hardly charge them bothe by worde and writinge / haue byn right hartely well content / to take their ease and reste at home.

 Consideringe then / how many waies we are vniustly burthened and brought into hatred withowte iuste cause / I supposed / that no godly man wolde be offended / yff by suche lawfull meanes as I might / I sought bothe to purge my selff and the rest off my brethern / from suche heinous and odious crimes as some would seeme to charge vs. And that coulde I not doo so well anie waie / as by the gatheringe together off this discourse / wherin the indifferent reader shall finde / that the religion whiche we holde and professe / is not onely the true ād sincere religiō of Christe / and the self same with all the reformed churches in Christendome / but also that whiche this Realme hathe establisshed / touchinge the true doctrine comonly taught therein. By this discours also / yt maie be seene / bothe when / where / how / and by whom this controuersie firste began / who cōtinued it / who was on the suffring side and who readieste to forget and forgeue / that godly peace and concord might be had. Nowe / iff anie shall seeme to be offended with this that I had don / I do moste humblie beseche them / to way well and expende with them selues / firste / whither I haue geuen them anie suche cause / yff it be for that I haue in this discours brought to light some thinge that might haue bin keept secret / (the contention beinge amonge brethern) to the ende the common enemie shulde not haue cause to triumphe : let this satisfie them. firste / that the wicked and common enemye cannot (for his harte) more tryumphe ouer the Godly then he dothe allready and that throughe owte this whole realme. Againe / the crueltie off Cain to Abell / off Ismaell to Isaac / off Esau to Iacob / off the Patriarkes to their brother Ioseph / the hot contention betweene Paule and Barnabas and Paule and Peter &c, all theis beinge knowne /

to the worlde hathe turned, notwithstanding to the great glo
rie off God/as my assured hope is that euen this will also in
the ende.

And therfore/ as the lorde off heauen knoweth that the
keepinge off theis thinges almoste by the space off theis tw=
entie yeres in secret/ might suffice to witnes with me that I
had nowe no great pleasure to vtter it/so I wote not howe it
commethe to passe that euen in the middest off great striuing/
and struglinge with my selff what to doo /I coulde not be by
anie meanes resolued/or se iuste cause/why I shuld any lon=
ger conceale it.

Yff anie shulde thinke that I haue not with indifferen=
cie/ penned the storie: I referre me (to satisfie suche) to the
iudgementes and consciences off those persons/ who were the
plaiers off this tragedie/ (off bothe partes many yet liuinge)
assuringe my selff that neither part shall be able iustlie to char
ge me/excepte it be for that in verie dede I haue sought rather
howe to couer manie thinges/ then to laie them wide open to
the worlde/as I nothinge dowte to proue iff I might be but
harde indifferently / in so muche as in this discours I haue
(as muche as I coulde) passed ouer the names off all where cre
dit might seeme to haue bin impaired therby (sauing onely off
suche as were off verie necessitie to be noted for the better vn=
derstanding off the historie.

To conclude: againste the offences whiche some maie ta=
ke at theis my trauelle/ I haue sett the greate profit that this
maie bringe to goddes churche and to the posteritie/ who bee
inge taught by other mennes harmes (yff they be happie)
will lerne to beware the hope wheroff had greater force to
pushe my pen forwarde to the finishinge off this worke/then
the displeasures off certaine (arisinge so far as I se off no gro
wnd) coulde be to withdrawe me from the same, besechinge
almightie god so strenghe me with his holie spirite/that what
troubles or trialls so euer shall by the lordes good prouiden=
ce happen to me hereby/ he will vouchsaffe to geue me a con=
sented minde quietly and with patience to beare it / before w=
hom

CXCIX.

hom I proteste/ that in wrytinge this discourse I haue had respecte to his glorie / the defence off his sacred truthe/ the cleeringe/ so farr as I might/ off so many excellent lerned men (on whose neckes this sturre is laied as authors off the same) and not that I haue willingly sought the hurte/ hinderance/ or discredit off anie man.

And this I/ praie that your loue maie abounde yet more and more in knowledge and in all Judgement that ye maye discerne thinges that differ one from another / that ye maie be pure and withowte offence vntill the daie off Christe Phi.

Keepe the true paterne off the wholsome wordes whiche thow haste harde of me in faithe and loue whiche is in Christe Jesu. 2. Tim. 1.

Study to shewe thy selff approued vnto god a workman that nedethe not to be ashamed deuidinge the worde off truthe aright. 2. Tim. 2.

The answere off the ministers off Geneua to certeine brethern off the churche off Englande concerninge some controuersie in the Ecclesiasticall policie.

Einge right earnestly and often required by certeine deare brethern off the churche off Englande that we woulde in their miserable state geue them some kinde off counsaile whereon theire consciences might be staied/ the Judgemente off many being therin diuers: we did longe differre the satisfinge off their requestes vppon waightie causes. And we assure the reader that euen nowe also we moste gladly woulde houlde oure peace/were it not a matter of conscience to rekcte the sute of the brethern so often enforced and with mostegreuous groninges renewed. Off whiche stifned silence off ours theis were the causes/firste/as on the one part we dowte not off the credit off the brethern/as thoughe they had not sincerely described the state off the cause vnto vs / so on the other side it is moste harde for to suspecte suche thinges / so clene besides all office off Bishopps muche lesse perswade oure selues the same by suche persoñages done.

And farther/what men are we that we shulde determine vppon suche causes. Also/iff it were lawfull for vs either by authoritie/or els by consent or requeste of either parties/to geue sentence here vppon/yet were yt a mater moste wrongefull either partie not harde or not present to determine. Laste off all feare mistrusted leaste so great a mischieff shuld by this oure counsell (howe simple so euer it is) rather become rawe thē skined: it beinge a sore of so desperate a nature/as that it semeth to be/that praiers and patience can onely saluethe same.

Seinge then/that by the sundrie requestes off the brethren/we are so hardly perswaded/that off force we ought to geue them some kinde off aduise: We do openly proteste/that we so geue to same herein as those that will not in anie wise preiudice the other partie/muche lesse chalinge to vs a iusticiers roume ouer anie. And all those men (into whose handes theis do come) we do in the lorde desier/that they be not herewith offended/but do perswade themselues that theis contentes are bothe simplie and faithfully written off vs as vppon a questioned cause graunted/that the consciences off the brethern whiche desier it/might some waie be better apeased/wohiche to set altogether at nought were a dede wholie voide off charitie.

Therfore/the cause standinge as we are informed/we professe plainely and in Good faithe that our Iudgementes ouer theis questions are thus.

It is demainded/whither we can approue this disorder in callinge off men to the function off the Ministery / whiche ts/that the multitude off those whiche sue for order shalbe enrolled in the ministerie bothe withowte the voices off elders and also no certeine cure appointed them but lightly examined off their liues and behauiour/to whom also/at the luste of the Bishoppe shall libertie be geuen afterwards to preache the worde off god for a time prescribed/ otherwise to reherse onely the churche seruice.

We answere/that suche callinges off Ministers/whither we answere them by the rule off Gods expresse worde or ells by force off Cannons that are beste tried and allowed are holden and estemed of vs/altogether vnlawfull/abeit we knowe that it is better to haue halfe a losse then no bread. But we beseche god with oure whole hartes that it also will please him to bestowe vppon the kingdome off England also the same (that is) a lawfull and ordinarie callinge off men to the ministerie of the worde and Sacramentes. For it beinge either kept owte or hindred/the benefit of the doctrine of truthe muste of force by and by vanishe awaie or ells be holde vp by some meanes that is strange/yea/ altogether ghostlie and supernaturall.

Furthermore/we do in Goddes moste holie name most humblie sue to the princes soueraigne maiestie/ that with the whole force off her minde/ she endeuour the correction off this paint wherin the whole grounde and state of the churche off England and therfore of the Realme also/bothe stand and persiste.

And thirdly we do with teares beseche bothe those high personages that are of hir maiesties honorable counsaile/and those which haue succeded in the place off the popishe Bishopps/(vndowtedly through the speciall mercie off the high and Good god) that they owte off the selff same place where ouerthrowe and distruction did yssue/ they shulde vtterly destroye that tyranye whiche hathe thus caste downe headlonge the verie Christian church and we craue of them in the dredfull name of god before whose redouted throne of iudgement we allsshall be arested that with al consideration and mindfullnes

of

of the yeres paste and conscience of their dewtie and charges they will not slack to vowe and betrothe their whole diligēce, aswell in orderinge the meanes that maie accōplishe this thinge as in perswadinge the Queens maiestie therto, and that they cease not at all this thinge beinge vnacheued, cheifly, seinge god hathe bestowed vppon them, the princely maiestie off so singuler a Mistris as from whose handes they cannot but hope for all princely and excellent thinges, vnlesse they liste in their owne case to faile themselues. But some wil aske, howe shall we doo in this pointe, vntill then: verely iff the case were oures we woulde not receiue this ministerie vppon theis conditions iff it were profered: a great deale lesse woulde we sue for it. Notwithstandinge, we exhorte theis men to whom god hathe by this waie made entrance to the enlarging off the glorie off his kingdome that in the feare off god they do couragiously abide therin, yet with the condition that it maie be lawfull for them holily and regilioufly to exercise all their whole ministerie. And therfore maie also proposunde, and vrge those thinges in their cures which doo allwaies apperteine to the aduauncement off the better estate therin. For otherwise, if they be forced of this libertie and so willed to winke at manifeste abuses, that they shuld also approue theis thinges whiche dowtlesse ought to be redressed: what thinge els can we perswade them then that they shu'de retire from this, to their priuate lyffe rather then withoute conscience to norishe that mischief whiche dothe off force drawe, whith it the whole wastinge and decaie of all the congregation? Yet we hope that the Queens highnesse and so many honorable and good men will in suche sorte plante their diligence that rather priuiledge off libertie maie be graunted to the consciences of so manie godlie and lerned brethern then that theis horrible euells shulde folowe: To wete, that the pastors off the flockes shulde be constrained either againste the soundnes off their consciences to do that whiche is euell (and so to be chained in other mennes sinnes, or ells to resigne their ministerie, for that third necessitie that will ensue this whiche is, that is/that againste the princes and Bishops willes they shoulde excercise their office) we do so muche the more tremble at/by cause of those reasons whiche off themselues are plaine enoughe/albeit we doo not vtter them.

It is also desired off vs to answere plainely and truly whither we do allowe the distinction ordeined in the wearinge off copes and garments aswell for the common vse/as for the ministerie.

We therfore do flattlie answere the cause standinge as we do vnderstande/that those men that are authors hereoff do deserue moste euell off the churche and shall answere at the dreadfull barre off Christe his Iudgement. For although that we thinke that that politique order whereby not citizins alone/but also the degrees off functions are marked and noted is not to be discommended wholie at all: yit we are off opinion that not euerie marke and note is straight way to be vsed. For put the case that the ministers were commaunded to weare the pied coate off a foole or the garmente off a vice in a plaie/were it not manifeste skorninge off the ministerie so to do? And those that vse theis other garments and aparell commaunded/do seeme verely to vs to trespasse somewhat worse then so/bicause that the lorde hath not onely reared and set vs this priestlike apparell as a toie to be laughe at euen off many off the Papistes themselues: But it is also certeine/that the same is poluted aud defiled with infinite superstition. But some men will pleade the antiquitie theroff. Surely they are olde/and yet the Apostolique symplicitie wherin the churche did florishe/is a great deale more auncient then this. Also/yff it please him to wade yet further to serche abowte theis matters/it shall be easie enoughe to shewe that theis thinges/whiche after that/did serue for the note and marke off the ministerie were first vsuall amonge the prople and common. And therfore whence commethe it/thinges beinge altered after so longe a season/that this forein and strange guise shuld be retrined.

Doithe it not come off a zeele bothe euell and vnprofitable?

Ee iij But

But some man will saie: Theis thinges for all that are thinges off the middle sorte and indifferent. We graunte in dede that they are such yff your will consider them simply and in their owne nature/and aparte from all circumstances: but who are they that will so waie and consider them. For theis men that are yet Papistes/what purpos so euer this ciuill lawe dothe pretend/are surely by theis meanes established deeper in this superstition whiche hathe so ouergrowen them. And these men that began so earnestlie to abhorre superstition/that they nowe did deteste monimētes and reliques theroff. Howe muche are they offended and woūded herein. As for those whiche are further/and better lerned/what frute reape they theroff. And farther is this difference and marke off the functions of suche importaunce/that therfore the consciences off so many shuld be troubled: especially seinge the reason and purpos therof newlie set a broche is but drawen euen from those that are themselues the manifeste sworne enemies to sounde doctrine? What meaneth it also/that off those also that are termed to be Ecclesiastically brought vpp and are in the ministerie not the smalleste parte/are saide to haue their papistrie in their brestes abowte with them? Is this the good houre wherin they shall better profit by restoringe off this attire? or shall they not rather vaunte their crestes as in hope to haue poperie restored againe? If anie shall obiecte the circumsinge off Timothy and other like examples: we right earnestly praie him to consider what Paule woulde haue saide yf any man shulde haue made this lawe/that euery man that is in the ministerie off the gospell shalbe constrained to weare the garmentes off the Pharisies/or that they in the apparell off prophane priestes shulde preach the gospell and administer the Sacramentes/and not onely circumcise their children/ nowithstandinge that vnder some couler of reason/this ciuill cōmaundement might setfoorthe the same. yea to what ende are theis thinges brought in, for howe so euer they might at the first be tollerated till that by litle ād litle they might be takē awaie/yet beinge ones remoued owte off the churches/we se not withe what commoditie

moditie they can be restored to their possession againe. Therfore we do eftsonnes repeate that we before said/that we can not allowe this deuise nor yet hope for any good to insue theroff. Notwithstandinge/we will gladlie geue ouer this opinion yff we shall lerne better reason therfore. What then (will the brethern saie on whom theis thinges are so throwen (iudge yow what we ought to do herein? we answere/that there nedethe in this answere a distinction. For the case off the ministers and the case of the people are not allone herein. Furthermore: Manie thinges maie/yea/and ought to be borne and tollerated whiche are notwithstandinge not iustly commaunded. firste therfore/we answere/that albeit theis thinges (as we iudge) are not rightly restored to their possessiõ in the congregations/yet/seinge that they are not off those kinde of thinges whiche are of their owne nature impious and vngodly/they seeme to vs not to be off suche waight that the shepardes shulde rather geue ouer their functions then receiue the apparell/or that the flock shuld refuse the publick foode of the soule rather then to receiue the same from the shepardes/ that is apareled herein: onely/that as well the sheaphardes as their flockes maie not sinne againste there consciences (so that the puritie off doctrine it selff remaine vntouched) we do perswade the ministers/after they haue bothe before the queens highnesse and also before the Bishoppe set their consiences at libertie by modeste protestation (as dothe appertaine to suche Christians as seeke not sedition and tumulte) and yet graue accordinge to the importaunce of the cause/that they do in dede openly in their parishe/still beate vpon those thinges/ that maye serue to the vtter takinge aware off the stumblinge blocke. And that as God shall geue occasion they will wholie geue them selues bothe wiselie and meekely to correct all those abuses/but yet to beare those thinges whiche they cannot streight waie change/rather then forsakinge their congregation they shulde geue occasion to Sathan/ that seketh nothinge els to stirre vpp greater and more perilous mischiefs then theis. As for the people (the doctrine remaininge vnhurte) we

do eys

to exhorte them, that for all theis thinges they will diligent tly heare the same, to vse the Sacramentes Religiously, and so longe to grone to God with earnest amendment off liffe vntill they obtaine off them that which dothe appertaine to the full redresse and amendment off the churche.

But againe yff that the Ministers be commaunded not onelie to tollerate theis thinges, but also that they shall withe their subscriptions allowe them as lawfull, or ells by their stillnes foster them: what can we ells perswade them to doo but that hauing witnessed their innocencie and in the feare off the lorde tried all meanes, they shulde geue ouer their functions to open wronge. But oure hartes betide vs off Englande muche better thinges then theis extremities.

It is demaunded off vs what we do Iudge off the trolling and descantinge off the Psalmes, crossinge off those babes that shalbe baptized, and off the demaundes in baptisme, also off the rownd vnleauened waffercake and knelinge in the lordes supper.

We answere, that kinde off singinge semethe to be the corruption off the pure ancient churche seruice and glorifinge of God therin. And as for crossinge off babes, whatsoeuer practise there hathe byn theroff in time of olde, yet is it moste certeine that it is truly in theis dais throughe so late greenesse off the superstition so moste abhominable, as that we iudge those men to haue done assuredly well that haue once driuen this rite owte off the congregatiõ wherof also we se not what the profit is. And we do wre not but the demaũds in baptisme haue creapt into the churche vpon this occasion, because that through the negligẽce of the bishops the same forme of baptizinge of childrẽ was reteined which, at the first rearing of the primatiue churche, was to be vsed at the baptizinge off those that beinge off yeres did entre the profession off Christe. This thinge also we maie perceiue by manie the like, yet in vse in the popishe baptisme. Wherfore euen as the creame and charme vsed in baptisme are by gods lawe abolished, although they were ancient, so wishe we also theis demaundinges, beinge

not

not onely vaine but folishe shuld be also passed ouer albeit that S. Augustine himselff dothe seeme in an Epistle off his to sustein it by certeine deuised construction.

The bread whither it ought to be made with leuen or withowte we thinke it not greatly to be striuen for/althoughe we Judge it more fit and consonant withe Christes institution to haue the bread at the commmunion/whiche is vsed at the common table:for why did the lorde vse vnleuened bread/bicause that inthat houre wherin he thought good to institute his holie supper/not one man in all Jewrie vsed anie other. Therfore/it behoueth vs to restore the Jewishe feaste off vnleuened bread or ells must it be graunted that is better to vse the common and accustomed bread off all tables accordinge to the example off Christe / notwithstandinge that the bread that he then tooke was vnleuened: For off the practise off the primatiue churche whiche the Greek churche dothe yet in this behalff reteine we ouer passe to write off.

Furthermore Knelinge at the verie receypt off the sacramente hathe in it a shewe off Godly and Christian reuerence and might therfore in times paste be vsed with profit/yet for all that bicause owte off this fountaine the detestable vse off bread worship did folowe/and dothe yet in theis daies stick in many mindes/it semethe to vs that it was iustlie abolished owte frō the congregations. Therfore/we do besethe the most Good and great God that it woulde please him to giue bothe the Queens maiesties highnesse and also the Bishopps such aduise as shall be moste nedefull for the perfect doinge awaie off theis corruptions/ and that at once. In the meane time/bicause theis thinges/ also are not suche as are in their owne nature Idolatrous we do Judge that they ought so to be dealte with/as we haue aduised in the thinges goinge next before.

It is demaunded off vs whether we allowe that baptisme whiche is administred by midwiues.

We answere that not onely we dissalowe the baptisme as the rest off thinges before spoken off/but that we do iudge ge it also intollerable. For it is a thinge that hathe risen aswell of ignorance of the verie vse of baptisme, as the publique ministerie of the churche. We Iudge therfore that the ministers are bownde sharply to rebuke this abuse, muche lesse ought they to holde this false baptisme, for good and firme. The reason why, the lerned on oure side haue often declared. And we are also readie when it shalbe nedefull to declare.

It is also reported vnto vs that the kaies of bindinge and losinge are practised in certeine courtes of the Bishops, neither by the sentences and iudgements of elders, whiche office that churche hathe not yet receiued, nor accordinge to the worde of God: but the authoritie of certeine lawiers and other like, whiche is more, often times by the authoritie of some one man, and that also for suche kinde of actions as are pure monie matters euen as the misuse of the same was in popery.

Wherto we answere that it semethe to vs almoste incredible that any such customes and examples (beinge most perverse) shulde be vsed in that kingdome, where as puritie and soundnes of doctrine is. For the right of excommunication and byndinge of the offender shalbe founde neuer to haue bin before the time of the Papistes in the power and hand of one sole persone, but did apperteine to all the whole eldershipp, frō whiche also the people themselues were not rashlie shut owte. Bicause this also the lawierlike hearinge of suites that appertaine to liuinges did fall to the Bishops charge altogether through abuse. For that place wherin the Apostle talketh of daies men vmpires at Corinth is to no purpose where as the magistrate is a Christian: nor did the Apostell euer thinke to burthen the Eldershipp with the hearing of suche meere ciuill causes. And it is most certeine, that the Bishopps of the elder age of the churche, haue had the determining of such controuersies not for anie authoritie that they had therin but through the importunitie of suters, and that as how solders vmpires and daies men Also notwithstandinge amonge those men where this were she

wed

ded vnto/ those did most wisely gouerne themselues whiche chose rather to folowe the example off Christ oure Sauiour/ who refused to be the vmpire in deuidinge off the patrimonie/ or els Iudge in the matter off adulterie/ when bothe the same were preferred vnto him.

Therfore/ yff in Englande anie thinge be done contrary to this/ surely we ought to thinke that by suche sentences and Iudgementes/ ther is not anie man before god any more bownde then by the popishe excommunications. And we wische that this torment howse off consciences and lothsome prophanation off the Ecclesiasticall and meere spirituall iurisdiction might by the authoritie off the Queens Maiestie owte off hande be abolished no otherwise then the marringe off the very doctrine it selff. And that Eldershippe and Deacons maie be restored and set vpp according to the worde off God and cannons off the pure churche/ whiche thinge/ yff it be not done/ verelie/ we are sore afraide that this onely thinge will be the begininge off manie calamities/ whiche we would god/ would turne awaie from vs. For it is moste certeine that the sonne off god will one daie from heauen roughly reuenge theis manifest abuses/ wherwith the consciences off oure brethern are troubled/ excepte spedely/ redresse be had therin.

In the meane whiles/ the thinges whiche are not well done by the one partie/ maie be well enoughe tollerated (as we thinke) by those men whiche beare the thinge whiche they can not change. Yet thus farre: as that they allowe not the thinge it selff for good/ but do onely redeeme their vniuste disquieting by patience. But yff so be that they shalbe forced/ not onely to tollerate this facion but also to approue this excommunication as lawfull and be constrained to aske vnlawfull absolution to assent to this manifest abuse/ we then exhorte them that they will rather suffer anie kinde off trouble then to do herin against their consciences. But to what ende is all this: For verilie/ we do promes oure selues muche better thinges then theis/ yea/ off all thinges the beste euen at this pinche/ especially off that Realme in whiche/ the

Dd ij restorin

restoringe off Christian Religion hathe byn sealed and confirmed with the bloud of so many excellent martirs also. Onely, we feare this, leaste that which hathe befallen so many countries shuld happen to Englande, to wit, leaste, bycause the due frutes off repentance are not brought foorthe, the angrie god shuld dooble oure darknesse, the light of his gospel beinge firste taken from vs. Off this content are oure dailie preachings in oure congregations, and verely, we thinke the same ought to be done off all Ministers off Gods worde especially in theis oure daies. That they chiefly set forwardes this principle off the gospell whiche dothe apperteine to earnest amendiment off lyffe. For this point achiued, vndowtedly the lorde shall geue bothe counsaile and zeale and all thinges els whiche do necessarely apperteine to the accompishement off the reparation off the churche, alreadye begone. And before all we doo require and with teares humbly craue that oure good and right worshipfull in the lorde the brethern off the Englishe churches, all bitternes off minde set aparte, whiche we surely feare, after what sorte it hathe on either side forced this euell, would patiently beare and suffer eche other, so longe as puritie off Christian doctrine it selff and soundnes off conscience dos the remaine: Willingly to obaye the Queene Maiestie who is full off compassion: And all other prelates. And fynally, that with all concorde of minds in the lorde, they manly set against Sathā, who sekethe all occasion of tumulte ād infinite calamities: yea, although they haue not like iudgement of all sorte off prealats at the firste. For this oure writinge, god is oure witnesse, dothe not tēde to this purpos, that either parte shuld vse it against other as that we shuld send it to yow as an apple of contention: Although we haue concerninge theis matters declared oure Judgements, euen symplie, as vppon a supposed case, (god is oure witnes) beinge ouercome withe the continuall sute off oure brethern. And we ioine oure dailie praiers to the groninges off all the godlye on that side the seas, that it maie please the moste mercifull god hauinge compassion on mannes frailtie, to directe the Queens highenes, and all the

nobles

nobles off the realme off Englande. Also euery prelate, and fynally, eche workman off this spirituall buildinge with his holy spirite moste effectuously, so as the worke off the lorde so often begonne and so often staied may luckely be set forwarde to the great quietnes and concorde off all men not onely the olde staines in the doctrine it self and Ecclesiasticall discipline also, beinge at lenght vtterly done owte, but also all monstrousnes of errors and whiche Satan newlie seketh to bringe into the churche againe driuen awaie. Whiche vouchesaffe to bringe to passe through his holy spirite, the moste kinde father in Iesus Christe, his verie sonne eternall and consubstantiall with him, in whiche persones, we professe one god, and not diuers, ought to be worshipped for euer. Amen. at Geneua the 24. October, 1547.

Your brethern in Christe to all your godlines moste assured.

Theodorus Beza, &c.
Remundus Caluetus
Nicolaus Coladonus
Io. Gaiagnæzius
Io. Tremlerus
Iohan Finaldus.
Ge. Fauergius.
Car. P.
Egid. Causcus.

Io. Parnilius.
Ruds Fauerius.
Vrb. Caluetus
Sim. Golerlius
Pet. Carpenterus.
Fransc. Portus.
Cor. Barlierdus
Hen. S.
Ablen. Dupleus.

CCXII.

A Copie off the letter sent to the Bishopps and Pastors off Englande, who haith renunced the Romaine Antechriste and professe the lorde Jesus in sinceritie.

The Superintendent Ministers, and commissionars off charges within the Realme off Skotland: To thair brethern the Bishopps and Pastors off England, who haith renunced the Romaine Antechriste, and do professe with them the lord Jesus in sinceritie, desire the parpetuall encrease off the holie spirite.

By worde and writ it is come to our knowlodge (reverend Pastors that divers off our deerest brethern) amongst whom are some off the beste lerned within that Realme, are deprivit from Ecclesiasticall function and forbidden to preach, and so by yow that they are staiet to promote the kingdome off Jesus Christe, bicaus their consciences will not suffer to take vppon them (at the commaundement off the authoritie) such garmentes as Idolatres in time off blindes haue vset in thair Idolatrie, whiche bruit cannot be but moste dolorous to our hartes, mindfull off that sentence off the Apostel, sainge, yff ye byt and deuoure one another, take head leaste ye be consumit one off an other. We purpose not at this present to entre into the grownd off that question whilke we heare off, aither parte to be agitate with greiter vehemencie then well liketh vs: to wit. Whidder that such apparell is to be coumpted amongs thinges that are simple indifferint or not, but in the bowells off lord Jesus we craue the Christian charitie maie so preuaile in yow, in yow we saie, the pastoris and leaders off the flock within that Realme.

That ye doe not to others that, which yow woulde not others

CXCIIII.

others shulde doo to yow. Ye cannot be ignorant how tender a thinge the conscience off man is. All that haue knowledge are not a like perswadet. Your consciences reclames not at wearinge off such garmentes/ but many thousants both godlie and lernet are otherwise perswadet whose consciences ar re continually stricken with theis sentences: what haith Christe Jesus to doe with behall? what feloshipp is thair betwixt darknes and licht ? yff surplese/ corner capp/ and tippet haue byn badges off ydolatres in the verie acte off their ydolatries what habt the preachers off Christian libertie and the open rebuker off all superstition to doe with the dregges off the romishe beast? Our brothern that off conscience refusse that vnprofitable apparell / doo neither damne yow nor molest yow that vse such vaine tryfles. yf ye shall do the like to tham / we dowte not but thairin ye sall pleese god and conforte the hartes of many whilke are wonded with extremitie/ which is vsed against those godly and our beloued brethern. Colou re off rethorik or manlie perswasion will we vse none/ but charitablie we desire yow to call that sentence off pitie to minde : feed the flock off God which which is committed to your charge caringe for them not by constranit but willingly not as though ye were lordes ouer goddis heritage/ but that ye maie be examples to ye flock. And farder also/ we desier yow to meditate that sentence off the Apostle/ saing: geue none offence / neither to the Jewes nor to the Grecians nor to the churche off God: In what condition off time ye and we bothe trauiell in the promoting off Christs kingdomm we suppose yow not to be ignorant. And therfore/ we are more bolde to exhorte yow to walke more circumspectlie/ then that for such vanities / the godly shulde be troubled. For all thinges that maie seeme lawfull/ edifie not. Yff the commaundement off authoritie vrge the conscience off yours and our brethern mo rethen they can beere: we vnfenedlye craue off yow/ that ye remember ther ye are callit the licht off the worlde and the earthe.

All ciuill authoritie hath not the licht off God allwaies
Dd iiij schinin

schininge before their eies in the statutes and commande-
ments/ but thair affections oftimes sauour to muche off the
earthe and off wordly wisedome.

And therfore/ we think that ye shuld baldlie oppone
your selff to all pouer that will or dare extoll the self not
onely against/ God but also against all suche as do burthen
the consciences off the faithfull farder then god hes burthe-
nit theim/by his owne worde. But here in/ we confesse oure
offence in that we haue entred farder in reasoninge then we
we purposet/ an promiset at the beginninge. And therfore/ we
shortly returne to our former humble supplication/ which is/
that our brethern who amonges yow refuse the Romishe rag-
ges/maie finde off yow the prelatis such fauours as our heid
and maister commandis euery one off his members to shee
we one to an other/whilke we lucke to resaue of your gentle-
nes/not onely for that ye feer to offend Goddes maiestie/ in
troubling off your brethern for such vane triffles. But also/
bicause ye will not refuse the humble requiestes off vs your
brethern and felowe preachers off Christ Jesus/ in whom/
albeit their appeere no great wordly pompe/ yet we suppose
yow will not so farr despise vs/ but that ye will esteeme vs to
be off the nomber off those that fight against that Romain
Antechriste/ and traueil that the kingdomme off Christ Jesus
vniuersally maie be mainteened and auanced. The daies are
euill. Iniquitie abownds. Christian charitie (alas) is waxin
colde. And therfore we ought the more diligently to watche.
For the howre is vncerteine when the lorde Jesus shall ap-
peere/before whom we your brethern and ye may geue an de-
coumpt off our administration.

And thus in conclusion/ we once againe craue fauor to
our brothern which graunted/ ye in the lorde shall commaunde vs in thinges off dooble more importance. The lorde Jesus
rewle your hartes in his true feare to the ende. And geue vnto
yow and vnto vs victorie ouer that coniured enemie off all
true Religion. To witt/ ouer that Romaine Antechriste/ whose wonded heid Sathan by all mannes laboris to cure againe/
but

but to destruction shall he and his mainteiners go/by the power off the lorde Jesus. To whose mightie power and protection we hartely committ yow.

    Subscribet by the handes off Superintendentes one parte off Ministers/ and scribet in oure generall assemblies and fourth session theroff. At Edenbroug the 28. daie off December 1566.

Your louinge brethern and fellow
preachers in Christ Iesus.

Io. Craig.	Io. Row
Iaco. Mailuil.	Da. Lyndesay
Rob. Pont.	Io. Erskin.
Guil. Gislisonus	Io. VViram.
Nic. Spittall.	Io. Spottiswoood.

Thus haue you heard in theis 2. letters/ the Judgementes off those excellent churches of the french and the Skottishe touchinge the thinges in controuersie. Nowe/ yff to theis I shuld adde all other whiche are off the same Judgement and of their opinion: the nomber off churches would be so many/ that the aduersaries shuld euidently se and perceaue what small cause they haue to charge vs thus with singularitie/ as though we were post alone/ and none to be off oure opinion. And it maie here also be noted/ that the moste auncientest fathers of this oure owne countrie/ as maister Couerdale/ maister O. Turner/ maister Whithead/ and many others some dead some yet liuinge from whose mouthes and pennes/ the vrgers of theis receiued first the light off the gospell (could neuer be brought to yelde or consent vnto such thinges as are now forced with so greate extremitie.

Finis.

Correction off thos faultes which might some what stay the reader the first nombre shewing the page/the second the line.

Page 2. line 18. enioned, reade enioyed. pag. 3. lin. 5. is, R. yt. pag. 10. li. 22. your, R. yow. pag. 25. li. 12. discent, R. dissent. pag. 27. li. 4. parie R. partie. pag. 38. lin. 24. ende, R. tende. pa. 44. li 9. cericine, R. certeine. pa. 47. li. 20. lette, R. letter. pa. 65. li. 17. subscription, R. superscription. pa. 72. l. 36. world, R. would. pa. 76. li. 10. stucke the pastor, R. stucke to the pastor. Li. 15. wison, R. wilson. pag. 82. lin. 19. were, R. where. pag. 86. li. 5. congregagation, R. congregation. pag. 97. lin. 30. dinner, R. dynner. pag. 123. lin. 7. the, R. then Pa. 132. lin. 22. incompent, R. incompetent. pa. 179. l. 23. td, R. to. pag. 194. lin. 8. cou-seners, R. couseners. pag. 200. lin. 22. to R. the.

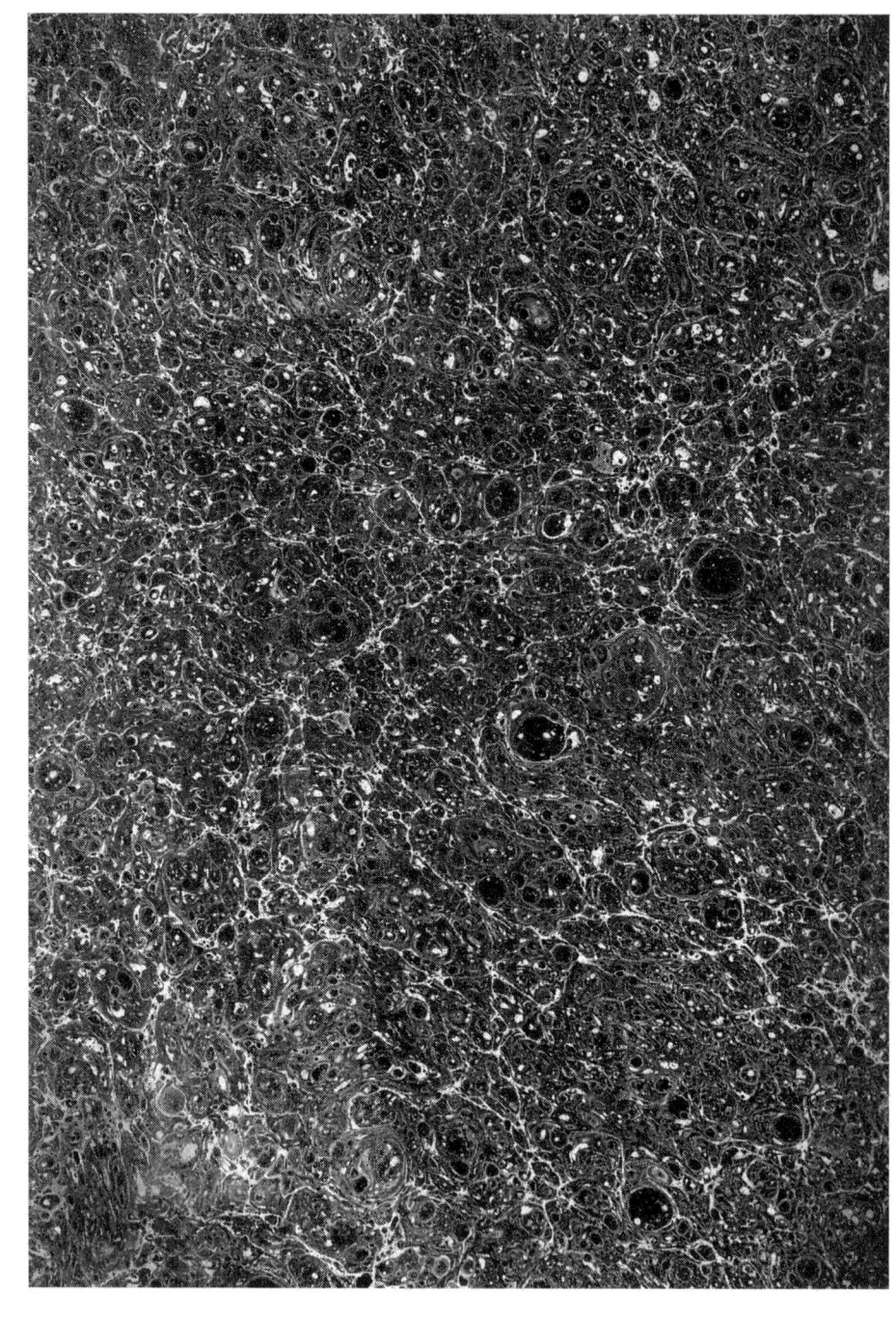

Dean WHITTINGHAM was, by his training, and by his ten years' [1550-1560] residence on the Continent, rather a Diplomat than a Scholar and a Divine. It was CALVIN himself that forced him into the Ministry in 1559; in order that he might take charge of the English Church at Geneva, when KNOX returned to Scotland.

Queen ELIZABETH rewarded WHITTINGHAM's splendid services at the Siege of Havre in 1562, partly as Chaplain to the English Forces there and also as a private soldier, by giving him the Deanery of Durham; without his having previously served as the Incumbent of any parish.

This personal friend of Lord BURLEGH was considered so skilful in affairs and so good a linguist that he was once thought of, to be made a Secretary of State.

In the Rebellion of the North in 1569, his military experience enabled him to secure Newcastle upon Tyne from the Rebels.

This many-sided man was also one of the chief Editors of the Geneva Version of the English 'Bible.'

Hearing, in France, that the Magistrates of Frankfort on the Main had been so good as to make their City a Refuge and an Asylum for the flying French and Flemish Protestants; WHITTINGHAM and other Englishmen came there in June 1554, and founded a Church: the Troubles of which form the main story of this book.

This 'Brief Discourse' introduces us to a famous company of Protestant Divines; CALVIN, KNOX, and a perfect galaxy of Archbishops, Bishops, Deans, and Writers, of the Church of England.

It likewise contains Accounts, by Eye Witnesses, of the English Protestant Exiles, in Queen MARY's reign, at Basle, Duisburg, Emden, Frankfort, Geneva, Strasburg, Wesel, Worms, and Zurich.

But, apart from this Historic Picture of the Exile, it also records the very beginning of the Rift between the English Conformists and Nonconformists; or the Origin of English Puritanism.

It likewise describes the formation, the continuance, and the destruction, of the first Nonconformist Church in English History.

www.ingramcontent.com/pod-product-compliance
Ingram Content Group UK Ltd.
Pitfield, Milton Keynes, MK11 3LW, UK
UKHW021349010925
7662UKWH00051B/1687